FORM AND IDEOLOGY IN CRIME FICTION

FORM AND IDEOLOGY IN CRIME FICTION

Stephen Knight

Indiana University Press
Bloomington

Printed and bound in Great Britain by
Redwood Burn Limited
Trowbridge & Esher

Library of Congress Cataloging in Publication Data

Knight, Stephen.
  Form and ideology in crime fiction.

  Bibliography: p.
  1. Detective and mystery stories, American—History
and criticism.   2.   Detective and mystery stories,
English—History and criticism.   3.   Crime in literature.
I.   Title.
PS374.D4K5   823′.0872′09   80–8335
ISBN 0–253–14383–7   1 2 3 4 5   84 83 82 81 80

For Margaret

Contents

Acknowledgements

I am grateful to the Librarian and staff of the University of Sydney's Fisher Library for their generous assistance, especially for giving me ready access to the library's Detective Fiction Collection. I would also like to thank the staff of the British Library and the London Library, Jan O'Reilly, who has typed the manuscript with skill and tolerance, and above all my wife, Margaret, whose editorial skills and support have contributed a great deal to this book.

The author and publishers wish to thank the following who have kindly given permission for the use of copyright material: John Farquharson Ltd, on behalf of Ed McBain, for the extracts from *Cop Hater*, published by Hamish Hamilton Ltd; Mrs Helga Greene, for the extracts from *Farewell, My Lovely* by Raymond Chandler, published by Hamish Hamilton Ltd; and John Murray (Publishers) Ltd, for the extracts from *The Complete Sherlock Holmes Short Stories* by Sir Arthur Conan Doyle.

S.K.

Introduction

Not much has been written about crime fiction, but treatments of the subject vary greatly. Some writers present with a connoisseur's relish material they see as no more than entertaining. Sutherland Scott and Richard Usborne are good examples. (See references at the end of this introduction and each chapter for details of critics mentioned.) Elsewhere crime fiction has been treated more seriously. Its development was traced some years ago by Régis Messac; Alma Murch has written more recently and more concisely on the topic. Julian Symons has described both the history of the genre and changing attitudes to it. Some critics have been less objective: starting with firm evaluative premises they condemn writers like Mickey Spillane and James Hadley Chase as gross and corrupting, but praise those with a polished style like Raymond Chandler or with intricate, quasi-intellectual content like Ellery Queen and Dorothy Sayers. George Orwell and Jacques Barzun have written in this way, and a whole series of 'culturally' attuned critics have supported the attitude—examples are to be found in collections of essays like Bernard Rosenberg and David Manning White's *Mass Culture*.

A less evaluative approach has tried to establish why crime fiction is so compelling. W. H. Auden and C. Day Lewis (writing as 'Nicholas Blake') see the form as a substitute for religious patterns of certainty; Ralph Harper, Gavin Lambert and several psycho-analysts find the basis of its patterns in the psychic anxieties of writers and readers. Another type of analysis has seen social attitudes and the pressures of the modern environment as the basic drive in the crime fiction: Colin Watson and Thomas Narcejac have, in different ways, related the stories to the collective patterns of modern experience. The articles on crime fiction found in *The Journal of Popular Culture* and John G. Cawelti's work in particular also take this broad social view, rather more objectively and seriously than Watson or Narcejac. My own approach develops from this position, in the context of recent work on the sociology of literature.

While not ignoring the specific situation of the writers discussed, and while trying to see some of the personal characteristics that their works develop, I will argue that major examples of crime fiction not only create an idea (or a hope, or a dream) about controlling crime, but both realise and validate a whole view of the world, one shared by the people who become the central audience to buy, read and find comfort in a particular variety of crime fiction.

I hope this book is not written in too heavily academic a manner (such a mode of discourse would ideologically assert that academic heaviness is the only appropriate way to view the world and crime fiction). But there are some general ideas, some definitions and some principles it seems necessary to set out here, by discussing the three main methodological features of this study. These are that it deals with selected central and popular examples of crime fiction in some detail and to a large degree in isolation; that it considers them in terms of their immanent social ideologies and that it finds these ideologies immanent in form as well as content.

There are several reasons for taking some central examples of crime fiction as the basis and giving them a detailed, largely isolated treatment. A close analysis is necessary to establish just what is the implicit meaning of a story, and so a selection of examples is inevitable or the book would be endless. And it is sound method to judge the centrality of examples by choosing books which have been bought or borrowed, enjoyed and so assented to by many people. The fact of success in itself is an important, even a compelling reason for choosing certain books to examine. Literary criticism has shied away from commercial success as a ground for treating a book seriously. Literary critical skills have not been used to study the interests and needs of mass society: they have been turned inwards in a fully ideological way to gratify and ratify the taste—and needs too—of the highly educated minority who validate their position by displaying a grasp of complicated cultural artefacts. In universities in particular it is striking that humanities departments study what interests them while other areas—medicine, engineering, economics, political science, anthropology, sociology—study the workings and the needs of society at large. A good literary critic should be able to say why a mass-seller works, and how it works. The dismissive certainties of most comments on popular culture do not satisfy those requirements.

Given that the texts studied here are popular examples of crime fiction, the reason for treating them in a somewhat isolated way is not only to provide space for close analysis; it is also to avoid the common fallacy of presenting a steady historical progress from work to work, and rather to concentrate on the nature and function of the texts themselves. This method helps to make criticism consider a work in terms of its social relations rather than only in terms of its relations with other works. Literary historicism very easily becomes a discussion of the world of literature alone: it talks of genres developing as if they grew autonomously, without social and historical causes. And the other temptation if you are writing, say, a history of crime fiction is to fit everything into a neat linear development to the present. This both privileges the writer's position in the present and injects an assumption that developments are neat and orderly, readily described by a tidy scholarly mind. These are dangerous, deluding ideas that can easily obscure the varying, overlapping forces embodied in a single work. A complete historical study of each text, that would detail such patterns, is not offered here, because the concern is to outline the ideological nature and function of crime fiction partly by detailed analysis, partly by contrasting different versions of the form; consequently, only some gestures in the direction of a full history can be made, but at least a spurious, simplistic history is avoided.

The second main feature of this study, implied in the preceding paragraphs, is to establish the social ideologies of the works discussed. This clearly moves away from the traditional mainstream of literary criticism, but the departure is already present in selecting popular literature as a topic. To treat such material in terms of its social function merely verifies the reasons for choosing such a topic.

Much work in recent years has discussed what is usually called 'the sociology of literature'. One aspect of the subject area is some distance away from this study. Best represented by Robert Escarpit's early work, it is interested in the social situation and relations of writers and readers—their class, age, attitudes and finances. Data from such research would give a great deal more confidence and precision to work in the other major wing of the sociology of literature, which tries to establish the social implications, the ideologies of texts themselves. This is what I have tried to do here. I have also offered some interpretation of audiences, based partly on the in-text evidence and partly on what external evidence is available, but I am well aware of the need of further specific social research to verify, and perhaps modify, some of the suggestions made here about audiences for different forms of crime fiction. It has seemed better to make a beginning, to offer analysis, than to remain silent about audiences as most literary criticism does, and so pretend that the book is an aesthetic object without any social relations.

Social function has been a recurrent theme in recent discussion of cultural products. A crucial notion has been that stories, myth, books, rituals are not so much an answer about the world, but a set of questions shaped to provide a consoling result for the anxieties of those who share in the cultural activity—the audience. Cultural productions appear to deal with real problems but are in fact both conceived and resolvable in terms of the ideology of the culture group dominant in the society. The work of French critics like Pierre Macherey and Roland Barthes has been crucial in comprehending how culture functions like this.

These are important perceptions, because they show the process that occurs while a story is being heard or read. The content of the text, its omissions and selections, is important. Plot itself is a way of ordering events; its outcome distributes triumph and defeat, praise and blame to the characters in a way that accords with the audience's belief in dominant cultural values—which themselves interlock with the social structure. So texts create and justify what has come to be called hegemony, the inseparable bundle of political, cultural and economic sanctions which maintain a particular social system to the advantage of certain members of the whole community. But plot alone, and content alone, are by no means the only—perhaps not even the major—element in the process of producing ideology in literature: form is crucial.

The third feature of my approach is to argue that ideology will be produced as much by the form as the content of the work. Literary critics like F. R. Leavis in Britain and the New Critics in America showed that the detailed language of a text was richly productive of meaning, and recent work in semiotics has both sophisticated their insights and given them social and political direction. Meaning has also been identified in a second aspect of form: Erich Auerbach's important book *Mimesis: The Representation of Reality in Western Literature* has shown how writers in different periods have used dissimilar ways of presenting material because of their different views of reality. Literary critics in general have avoided the system of knowledge—epistemology—and the concept of being— ontology— which the presentational form of the text implies, but I shall be discussing this feature of texts in some detail. The third formal aspect I will analyse is overall structure; it is well enough known that the shape and strategy of a whole work is permeated with meaning. Medievalists have discussed this topic at length, distinguishing Gothic from 'Modern' structures, sometimes identifying world-views implicit in the forms—D. W. Robertson Jr's work on Chaucer is a good example. Some critics of modern literature—notably Terry Eagleton in *Criticism and Ideology*—have similarly shown that 'organic' form in the novel responds to and ratifies the idea that the individual is the essential seat of knowledge and the real social unit.

Now what this means in terms of crime fiction, and what I will try to outline, is that each work discussed here has a special formal way of presenting the world to us. This basic idea is embedded in the textual language, the presentation of incidents, characters and motives, and also in the overall structure. The text may not be simple or single in its meaning: it may well contain a conflict of world-views, which realises perceived conflict in the world but which is artificially and consolingly resolved by the plotting and the structure of the novel. Such strains or 'fissures' in the text, as both Macherey and Barthes have in different ways shown, reveal the areas of central anxiety, the space where the ideology works at its hardest to assert that all is normal, change need not be feared.

Naturally enough, differences of form between writers are not trivial or arbitrary; they are essential elements in the meaningful innovations which the story offers to its audience, intimately connected with the differences in content between texts such as the setting, the crimes discussed, the nature of the detective. My emphasis on form here should not suggest that content is trivial: form is stressed because it is so little observed, even in recent and quite searching studies in the sociology of literature. The selection of content detail is also a primary and controlling way of establishing ideology, especially the setting, the crimes, the criminals, the character and methods of the detective. These will change significantly from text to text. A rural female amateur may identify a treacherous, in-family murderer. An urban police detective may track down professional burglars. The varieties are as manifold as the number of authors, audiences, anxieties.

So form and content together create the crucial realisation of a pleasing, comforting world-view. Form will always be treated here in terms of its major different elements, that is style, presentation, structure, but its discussion does not always precede that of content.

Whichever aspect of the creation seems initially more revealing will be taken first, and sometimes when the elements cannot be lucidly disentangled for discussion they will be taken partly together. And, to warn fully of complications, in some texts it will be found that the meaning depends on contradictions being enacted between form and content.

In the last chapters I will be dealing with modern crime fiction from our own period, and so will discuss, in the light of the earlier texts, how our own anxieties are realised but how ultimate realities are ideologically obscured by our crime fiction. This seems to me the proper purpose of literary criticism, to relate to our own period the patterns that have been discovered in the past. Much literary criticism is self-gratifying connoisseurship, fondling old texts as if they were objects in a museum, ignoring their dynamic social force and the history they speak. But we can and should read in the texts, as Robert Weimann has put it, their past significance and present meaning. In this way the techniques of the literary critic can be used to comprehend the forces at work in the world we all inhabit.

REFERENCES

W. H. Auden, 'The Guilty Vicarage', reprinted in *The Dyer's Hand*, Faber and Faber, London, 1948.

Erich Auerbach, *Mimesis: The Representation of Reality in Western Literature*, Princeton University Press, Princeton, 1953.

Jacques Barzun, introduction to *The Delights of Detection*, Criterion, New York, 1961.

——, introduction to *A Catalogue of Crime*, Harper & Row, New York, 1971.

'Nicholas Blake', Introduction to 2nd English edn of Howard Haycraft's *Murder for Pleasure*, Davies, London, 1942.

Roland Barthes, *Writing Degree Zero*, Cape, London, 1967.

——, *The Pleasure of the Text*, Cape, London, 1976.

——, *Elements of Semiology*, Cape, London, 1967.

——, *S/Z*, Cape, London, 1975.

John G. Cawelti, *Adventure, Mystery and Romance*, University of Chicago Press, Chicago, 1976.

Terry Eagleton, *Criticism and Ideology*, New Left Books, London, 1976.

Robert Escarpit, *Sociology of Literature*, 2nd edn, Frank Cass, London, 1971.

Ralph Harper, *The World of the Thriller*, Case Western Reserve University Press, Cleveland, 1969.

Gavin Lambert, *The Dangerous Edge*, Barrie and Jenkins, London, 1975.

Régis Messac, *Le 'Detective Novel' et l 'influence de la pensée scientifique*, Champion, Paris, 1929.

Pierre Macherey, *A Theory of Literary Production*, Routledge & Kegan Paul, London, 1978.

Alma Murch, *The Development of the Detective Novel*, rev. edn, Owen, London, 1968.

Thomas Narcejac, *Une machine à lire–le roman policier*, Denoel, Paris, 1975.

George Orwell, 'Raffles and Miss Blandish', reprinted in *Dickens, Dali and Others*, Harcourt Brace Jovanovich, New York, 1946.

G. Pederson-Krag, 'Detective Stories and the Primal Scene', *Psychoanalytic Quarterly*, XVIII (1949) 207–14.

D. W. Robertson Jr, *Preface to Chaucer*, Princeton University Press, Princeton, 1962.

Bernard Rosenberg and David Manning White, (eds), *Mass Culture: The Popular Arts in America*, Free Press, Glencoe, 1957.

Charles Rycroft, 'A Detective Story: Psychoanalytic Observations', *Psychoanalytic Quarterly*, XXVI (1957) 229–45.

Sutherland Scott, *Blood in their Ink: The March of the Modern Mystery Novel*, Paul, New York, 1953.

Julian Symons, *Bloody Murder*, rev. edn, Penguin, Harmondsworth, 1974 (*Mortal Consequences* in the USA.)

Richard Usborne, *Clubland Heroes*, Barrie & Jenkins, London, 1974.

Colin Watson, *Snobbery with Violence*, Eyre & Spottiswoode, London, 1971.

Robert Weimann, *Structure and Society in Literary History*, Lawrence & Wishart, London, 1977.

1 '. . . some men come up'— the Detective appears

At the centre of modern crime fiction stands an investigating agent—an amateur detective, a professional but private investigator, a single policemen, a police force acting together. Specially skilled people discover the cause of a crime, restore order and bring the criminal to account. This function has been so important in recent crime stories that two well-known analysts sought the history of the genre in detection from the past. Régis Messac goes back to the classics and the bible for his earlier examples in his enormous book *Le 'Detective Novel' et l'influence de la pensée scientifique*. Dorothy Sayers does the same in her first *Great Short Stories of Detection, Mystery and Horror*. Both writers take detective fiction to be the same as crime fiction. But before the detective appeared there were stories that suggested how crime could be controlled. Most would have been oral, and many of those that were written down were evanescent, in pamphlet form. Yet enough material has survived to establish the nature and ideology of crime fiction without detectives. *The Newgate Calendar* is a convenient source for such a study. This will make it possible to see clearly the patterns of meaning established through the persona of the detective. These begin to emerge in *The Adventures of Caleb Williams* and *Les Mémoires de Vidocq*, which will also be examined in this chapter. The full, confident deployment of the detective in recognisably modern ways takes place in the texts discussed in later chapters.

I The Newgate Calendar

Stories about criminals survive in reasonable numbers from the late sixteenth century. Robert Greene's 'cony-catching' pamphlets are good examples. In them smart criminals trick the innocent 'conies' (or 'bunnies' in a more modern version of the same metaphor) out of money and property, but come to an inevitably bad end. The narrative always has a moral framework: there is a striking resemblance to the sensational and sententious stories and confessions we still find in magazines and newspapers. The 'true confessions' of criminals in pamphlet form have survived from the seventeenth and eighteenth centuries, and this material was sometimes organised into books of memoirs like Richard Head's *The English Rogue*, or more obviously fictional accounts like Daniel Defoe's *Moll Flanders*. But to recognise that these narrative forms still exist can obscure the fact that this material was based on and re-created ideas about crime and society no longer current, as becomes clear in examining a very successful collection of crime stories, *The Newgate Calendar*.

There is no one book with this title. The first large collection of crime stories called *The Newgate Calendar* appeared in 1773. The title had been used before, but then a shrewd publisher saw a market for a reasonably expensive and well-produced set of volumes which brought together accounts of the crimes and punishments of major criminals. Some of the material came from official records, but much was gathered from contemporary accounts hurriedly published as the criminal was punished—usually by execution. By no means all of the criminals had been kept in Newgate, but the famous prison provided a useful catch-all title. The collection was reprinted, expanded and altered many times. Knapp and Baldwin's edition of 1809 was a particularly well-known and successful one, and versions kept appearing until the late nineteenth century; abridged editions still find a publisher from time to time.

A short moral preface offered the stories as dreadful warnings; an early version recommended the collection for the educational purposes of parents and also—presumably as a diversion—for those going on long voyages. The intended audience is clearly not the huge numbers of poorer people who bought pamphlets. In the 1830s James Catnach was printing up to a million copies of the confession of a particularly thrilling murder, and many people might read or listen to a single pamphlet. They could not afford access to the bound collection we can now study. But the difference of price and format does not disqualify *The Newgate Calendar* as a means of access to widely held ideas about crime and society. The collection's only new feature is its moralising preface, and the tone of this is invariably present at the end of separately published stories, however flimsy the pamphlets they appeared in. Although this is a collection, there is no special organised structure—indeed the accounts change their order from edition to edition. The meaning of form is to be a major topic in this book, but the difference in form between the widespread pamphlets and the collected *Newgate Calendar* has no special significance, and the collected version can be examined for evidence of a view of crime and society that was widely spread through different classes.

The details of setting and action, and particularly the way criminals are caught, are the best initial guides to the implicit meaning of *The Newgate Calendar* stories. With these in mind, it is both necessary and fairly easy to see how the form in which the stories are presented gives this material convincing life as a credible way of maintaining social order and personal security. A typical *Newgate Calendar* tale of crime and punishment will show the important and recurrent content details.

Matthew Clarke was born in 1697, the son of a 'poor honest farmer'. Unlike his family, Matthew was 'idle'—no fuller explanation is given for his dislike of work. To support himself he 'lurked' about the country, committing small crimes. The verb used suggests that already he is in hiding, a threatening outcast. He was unwilling to marry as his family wanted; his refusal to play his part in normal social activity is stressed as a publican sees him wandering at harvest-time, when everybody is engaged in productive labour. Matthew accepts the haymaking job that is pressed on him, not from any residual conscience or wish to earn honest money, but because 'employment might prevent his being suspected'. His motives rise solely from his antisocial state, which he will not abandon. A maid in the publican's inn is a former girl-friend; while kissing her in the kitchen he cuts her throat, then robs her and the house.

At once he is struck by the awful nature of his action and runs away. As he is on the road 'some men come up', see that he looks frightened and notice blood on his clothes. They take the 'terrified' man to a justice, and he confesses at once. Before long he is executed and hung in chains where the murder was committed. A brief moral points out how he harmed his fellows and gained nothing: the girl would have given him, for affection, more than he stole by murder. The concluding comments rise above this secular pragmatism to state that, apart from the honest profit involved, a life of integrity, virtue and piety lets us hope for the blessing of God.

These components are typical of *The Newgate Calendar* stories. The criminals are ordinary people who reject the roles society and their families offer them. Even when a hardened villain appears, the story gives a brief sketch of how he or she fell into that state. Sometimes the criminal is led astray by another renegade from a life of integrated industry. Those who commit crimes are not innately, incurably evil. They have turned aside from normal patterns, and fail to take their chances to resume a life of common morality. The setting of the stories also creates a basis of ordinary life. Farms, towns, shops, inns and roads in everyday Britain are the places where crimes appear: here are no foreign settings for fantastic horrors. In the same way the crimes are generally simple and direct ones. Robbery and murder in the act of robbery are most common, though murder as a crime of passion is fairly frequent. Forgery and rather small scale treason occur from time to time, but elaborate accounts of major treason and unusual crimes like piracy are normally associated with well-known figures like Lord Lovat and Captain Kidd. There are not many foreign criminals, and those who do appear are residents in Britain, have no specific alien villainy and are hard to distinguish from the native-born except by name.

The general effect of these content details is that crime is not seen as some foreign, exotic plague visited on the British public, but as a simple disease that can, by some aberration, grow from inside that society. The heart of the social body is the family. The criminal turns away from family ties and duties, and is finally so outrageous that the family stops trying to help or amend its straying sheep. The family mirrors not only the corporate peace, but the social order: static, hierarchical and male-dominated. Wife-murder is a capital offence, but husband-murder is punished by burning, and in some cases the story tells with relish that the executioner failed to throttle the woman before the flames took hold. This particular crime is called petty treason: attacking a husband is a little version of high treason, attacking the head of the national family.

The way in which the criminals are caught is a crucial feature in crime stories of all kinds, and here it confirms this sense of an organic model of society. There is no special agent of detection at all. The stories imply that just as society can sometimes suffer from disorderly elements, so it can deal with them by its own integral means.

Some of these evil-doers, mostly murderers, are transfixed by guilt in the process of their crime. More often the sense of guilt makes them act rashly afterwards, so drawing attention to themselves and to crucial evidence, such as bloodstains, or stolen property. The idea behind this is that the Christian conscience is suddenly awakened, the objective Christian pattern reasserts itself against the subjective criminal rejection of those values. The criminals go to their inevitable execution as penitents, making (by courtesy of the pamphleteers, no doubt) short prayers on the scaffold, warning others to learn by their fates. One of the main ideological features of these stories is the basic notion, and hope, that the all-pervasive, inescapable Christian reality provides a protection against crime.

The other, more common explanation of how criminals are caught asserts that society itself is so tightly knit that escape will not be possible. The murderer is seen in the act and caught at once, or seen, described by the witness and soon recognised. Sometimes the criminal's identity is obvious from the crime, and the fugitive is gathered in. Similarly a known robber is recognised from a physical description, by meeting an acquaintance, or having identifiable property on his person. A highwayman may be taken through some accident of recognition or given away by some friend or accomplice who has, in his turn, been a victim of conscience or pursuit. The striking thing is the imprecise, unspecific, scarcely explained or motivated way in which these things happen. Pure chance is very often the mechanism by which a criminal is recognised. The generality and arbitrariness extends to the people involved in the recognition and the arrest. They are imprecisely characterised, or not described at all. In Matthew Clarke's case 'some men' ride up to him, and that is a very common turn of phrase in *The Newgate Calendar*. If there has been a murder 'some gentlemen' will come along and take the criminal to a magistrate, or hurriedly raise the 'Hue and Cry', a formalised general hunt where everyone is on the look out for the proclaimed criminal.

The vague generality and unconcerned use of chance in the stories does to some extent arise because the capture is regarded as inevitable; the methods themselves are of little interest since the ideology insists that they must succeed. But there is more to it; the events, given in appropriately unindividualised terms, imply that the very community the criminal shunned can muster its forces and throw up the hostile body. Because of the 'bloody code' in force at the time, identification almost always leads to death—the only alternative is nearly as absolute an exclusion from society, transportation. A few stories tell how criminals have tried to rejoin society by returning illegally. They are given no second chance: execution is the mandatory penalty for this crime.

Throughout all this material runs a belief in the unity of society, and organic metaphors are very often used—'crimes injurious to their country', 'acts harmful to the body of the state'. Society, the stories imply, can deal with its own aberrances without mediation, without specialists. The watch will arrest an identified criminal and the courts will pass sentence, but no skilled agent is needed to detect the criminal. The processes of the law are in the background and its officers serve society only in established, invariable ways; they are not independent agents acting upon society. This whole 'organic' view emerges strikingly in the common feature whçre a criminal is executed or hung in chains near the scene of the crime. In many ways the stories are shaped to give a model of unmediated social control of crime.

It is easy enough to see that these two systems of detecting crime, personal guilt and social observation, could only develop in a deeply Christian world, with small social units where everybody is known, where hiding is hard and socialisation tends to be public. That had been the general situation in medieval England—though the notorious difficulty of finding and convicting medieval criminals suggests that the crime-control system implicit in *The Newgate Calendar* was never more than a brave hope. But in the period when the stories were printed, the implied social model was disappearing. Not everybody was devotedly Christian, many people lived in large and increasing conurbations, and there was a hardened and relatively successful criminal class, hostile to the 'normal' society, which had, in London at least, its own fortresses, later known as the 'rookeries' of central London. In fact *The Newgate Calendar* is not offering a real account of crime control: it is ideological in that it offers hope and comfort to people, and in that it is itself based on ideologies, the twin beliefs that we are all Christian at heart and that our society is integral and at root a single healthy body. This would be what is normally called a 'strain ideology', that is, an optimistic account selecting and ordering material to provide a consoling fable in the face of disturbing reality.

The constant patterns of detail and plot that have been described are one way of seeing such an ideology at work: anything that would contradict its validity is excluded. Pierre Macherey has recently argued, in the book translated into English as *Theory of Literary Production*, that the silences in a text are crucial to its ideological force. But he, like Roland Barthes, has also drawn attention to 'fissures' in the text. These are not so much large scale omissions of material, but moments where the text shows itself unable to gloss over tensions inherent in even the material that is presented. Both critics see these signs of strain as crucial to the overall force of the text; Macherey interprets them in a more consistently political way, while Barthes' reading, though aware of the social implications, is more directed towards semantic, even aesthetic understanding of the effect. In *The Newgate Calendar* there are some examples of these fissures, specific moments where the strain ideology is most tenuously stretched to deal with contradictions that cannot be fully ignored.

The case of Mary Edmondson tells how one evening she called for help from the door of her aunt's house; 'some gentlemen' came from a nearby inn to find her aunt murdered and a cut on Mary's arm. One of the men, a Mr Holloway, makes careful inquiries. Mary says that burglars did the damage, but she is arrested and executed for the crime. Yet she never confesses, and insists to the very end that she is innocent. The story admits that only circumstantial proof is ever brought, and finally says: 'Nothing has ever yet transpired to overthrow the proofs of her guilt; and until that happens, we must look upon her as one who was willing to rush into eternity with a lie in her mouth.' The guilt system has failed, and the evidence from social observation is stretched very thin. The narrator finds material in the Christian principle to assuage his doubts, but there is clear lack of a system of close investigation to arrive at proof. As if to compensate for this lack, we are for once given the name of the 'gentleman' who satisfied himself of Mary's guilt, and we are assured that his inquiries were minute—but they are not described at all.

This 'crack' in the text shows the weakness of Christian guilt as a defence against crime; the account of the murder of Mrs King in 1761 reveals, as a complement, the inadequacy of the notion that society is fully and defensively integrated. Again the contradiction is explained away from inside the ideological system. Mrs King was murdered by Theodore Gardelle, her Dutch lodger. He hid her body in pieces all round the house, and said she had gone away. A fortnight later a servant came across some of her, and the lodger confessed readily enough. The problem is that nobody knew she was dead. The narrator resolves this challenge to the notionally organic society by excluding Mrs King, without any evidence other than the problem, from respectable society. She must herself have been a shady isolate: 'But who is there, of honest reputation, however poor, that could be missing a day, without becoming the subject of many important enquiries? without occasioning such fears, that no rest could have been had till the truth was discovered, and the injury revenged?'

One other contradiction is passed over in silence—and often still is by our modern ideology. These stories frequently claim that the laws of England fall on all who cause harm to the corporate social body, whatever their station in life. But we actually find that the nobility elude the severity of the law, unless they are traitors and so faithless to their own real class. A Mr Balfour kills the man his former sweetheart chose to marry. He escapes overseas, becomes penitent, is eventually pardoned and inherits the family title. Lord Balfour has the chance to become a reconstructed member of society, not given to those ordinary criminals who cannot arrange or afford escape overseas, and so die. In another story Lord Baltimore shows no sign of repentance at all. He has a girl kidnapped, tortures and rapes her, and then manages to get off by legal trickery. Here, where the law is obviously a mediator because it can be manipulated, the unusual feature of a detailed court scene occurs. The plotting recognises reality, but this does not impinge on the ideology, as the next story follows on with no sign of the law's fragility or its mediation to maintain class hierarchy. What was for the bulk of the people a strain ideology, revealed clearly in these contradictory instances, was, of course, an 'interest' ideology for the propertied classes who benefited from the deeply conservative social structure and from the corresponding ideology that is dramatised in these stories, as in so much of the culture of the period.

The patterns of meaning that can be seen in the preceding description of the content of *The Newgate Calendar* are brought to life within a specific theory of knowledge and view of the world by the form of the stories: the form validates, makes real and convincing, the ideology present in the selected material. To a modern eye the formal pattern seems very simple, but analysis shows it to have quite far-reaching implications. To start with the prose style, the bulk of each story is told in a straightforward narrative prose, easy for unskilled readers to follow—particularly when it is read aloud. Its syntax and vocabulary do not need to be scrutinised closely before surrendering their meaning. The suggestion in the prose is that we look straight at our world and know it. But for all its simplicity, this is by no means a value-free narrative. It frequently uses words that directly involve values: 'this miserable wretch', 'this damnable villain', 'with fiendish cruelty'. It is, then, a world the reader can observe, but he continually judges his observations by assumed and shared moral values. These standards are called up by key terms, which do not need demonstration and definition in each new story. Towards the end of each account the prose style changes, and confirms these shared values in a final Christian exhortation, suitably shaped in its own form. The more elaborate and slightly archaic tones of the preacher and the Authorised Version are the medium of the conclusion, setting the secular lessons we have learned in the light of eternity with a less demotic, less world-oriented prose style.

There is a formal element that comes between the detailed verbal selection and the large overall structure of a story. I shall call this 'presentation'. It is the aspect most studied by Erich Auerbach in his book *Mimesis*, and this is basically what he means by 'mimesis' itself, the detailed presentation of reality in the scene. In *The Newgate Calendar* the presentation is in part very specific. Geography, tools of trade and of crime, names and ages of criminals and victims are all given in crisp factual detail. This does not extend to a clear view of the individual and the causes of action. Like the shared moral values that guide our feelings about the events, the motivation tends to be general—fear, greed, lust are the explanations often given. Sometimes—as in the case of Matthew Clarke—we do have a more detailed individualistic account of causes. But even this greater precision of motive does not explain the basic attitude, only the specific development of the generally described states of mind. We know why Matthew accepted the job of haymaking, but not in any detail why he was 'idle'. And this restricted type of detailed motive is only found in the cases of criminals: it reflects the fact that the criminal has turned away from the general collective values into individualistic action, and so now specific motivation may be relevant, as the great generalised truths of collective society have been abandoned. The same process occurs in medieval romance: the audience knows the hero only in general ethical terms, but knows the detailed physical appearance of his enemy, because this ogre has abandoned the world of ethics. So even when the text offers a specific motivation of an act this does not actually change the generalising nature of the narrative's presentation of character.

In the same way, the narrative does not articulate the plot details in a subjectively perceived, or a rational, detailed way. Major events are explained by general objective evaluations, stating whether these acts are sinful or morally right. If the plot needs to bridge a gap in events, sheer coincidence is convincing enough. This is not clumsy or crude: the random events of chance fit comfortably into a world-view which does not aspire to explain the intricacies of behaviour, but assumes that events occur beyond human control. Indeed, chance has positive aspects, for the plots show it to be one of the weapons of normalcy, one of the ways in which the global society restores its healthy order, controls individualistic disturbances without any specific and subjective comprehension of them. The general, shared value-judgements and uncomprehended ordering of human events both cohere and derive in a divine, not a human realm of thought and order.

In accordance with this world-view the narrator is not omniscient. The all-knowing hero-narrator, so important to the nineteenth-century novel, was already a feature of eighteenth-century fiction, and this revealed the growing force of bourgeois individualism. In *The Newgate Calendar* the narrator can do no more than watch, listen, record reports and apply 'normal', shared evaluative reactions. This gives the impression of an unmediated, direct form of narration which responds to the underlying idea that society needs no special mediation to restore itself. The narrator is himself a member of the social body, not the specially gifted subjective voice that the rational novel was to lean on for its account of human action, and for the structural unity that replicated the creative and resolving power of a single mind.

The presentation found in *The Newgate Calendar* has its structural corollary in the episodic nature of the stories. Many of them are no more than one narrative event; the longer ones have a structure which does not move steadily through each sequence by cause and effect to a climax, but rather is a series of episodes, the last of which gives the capture and punishment of the criminal. The stories relate to each other by mere juxtaposition and by having the same underlying principles—*The Newgate Calendar* is no more than the sum of its parts: stories can be easily added or removed, their order can be changed and the whole is not in any real way different. This sort of structure has been fully discussed in the context of medieval literature, and it clearly responds to a particular view of the world. The system of values in an episodic story is outside the text, assumed by the society and readily applied: the artist does not need to give a detailed justification of the value system. Nor does he need to create within the text an aesthetic effect of single unity, an enclosed system of development and pattern: the sense of coherence and integrity, like the sense of values, is generalised through the culture, and neither needs to be recreated in the work of art. Episodic structure, medievalists have said, is vertical: it looks up to objective heavenly verities for its truth; these are also the base of the organisation, with no need to create subjective artistic models of human order. The ideology of a Christian world, socially integrated, is behind the apparent 'bittiness' of *The Newgate Calendar* stories as a collection and behind the 'bittiness' of the longer stories in themselves. This structure and the readiness to rely on chance, on generalised human action and on shared values are all formal aspects of that same faith—or hope, or delusion—that society is one here in the world and has its resolution and ultimate guidance in heaven. The popularity and the effectiveness of the stories lie to a large extent in this successful formal realisation of the implicit beliefs revealed in the selection and direction of the content.

The image that *The Newgate Calendar* presents, a world of integrated Christian society, was still credible through the nineteenth century, though the real world was increasingly unlike the one assumed and implied in these stories, and though other versions of society and the control of crime were being dramatised in fiction. Any thorough cultural analysis reveals how patterns overlap in many confusing ways; there is rarely a simple linear progress to be found and one society can sustain quite contradictory views of the world at one time, many of them quite outdated. Even while the calendar was in its early editions, professional thief-catchers, such as the Bow Street Runners, were at work. They were not a salaried force, though, often little more than paid informers—and they made little impact in crime fiction. Dickens uses two Runners in *Oliver Twist*, but they play no crucial part in the plot or the implicit meaning of the novel. In fact its final sequences are fully in tune with the ideology of *The Newgate Calendar*, and show finely how a great artist's imagination can bring into dramatic clarity the essence of ideas elsewhere found in fragmentary and muffled form. As Sikes is pursued by the people of London the Hue and Cry of the whole city is seen as a great river. This organic symbol of London itself realises integrated, objective and remorseless nuances of society's imagined power against crime. And Sikes is also tormented by conscience. In the grand climax, as he is about to lower himself on a rope to safety he screams 'The Eyes': Nancy's dying eyes haunt his conscience. He slips, the rope catches around his throat, and Sikes hangs himself. This public, autonomously generated execution is a vivid and precise symbolic statement of the ideas about society and crime behind *The Newgate Calendar* stories.

Oliver Twist has been called a Newgate Novel; many of them appeared through the nineteenth century. The name indicates the force of *The Newgate Calendar* tradition; the collection of stories was a widely accepted representation of a particular world-view and its attitude to crime. The title of the collection itself reveals a good deal, and so do the names carried by similar publications. *The Malefactor's Bloody Register* is the sub-title of the 1773 edition, and other titles and sub-titles include *Chronicles of Crime*, *The Tyburn Chronicle*, *Chronology of Crime*, *The Criminal Recorder*, *Annals of Crime*. Each title refers to a system of classifying events or objects. That in itself is interesting enough—in keeping with the view that crime was an aberration, the vocabulary of social organisation embraces it, crime is not an evil world elsewhere, but is just the other side of our orderly, classified world. The calendar is a Newgate one, the annals are those of perverted deeds. But the titles do not only imply crime is a negative aspect of an integrated whole; the classifying involved in the titles responds to the understanding of the world basic to the Calendar's ideology. The words used all refer to unsorted collections of data: lists, registers, chronicles, annals do not analyse and conceptualise their material, but merely record the objective phenomena of life. A conceptual, standing-off—and therefore subjective and ultimately alienated—intelligence is not represented in the titles. They reflect the limits and the ideology of the stories: the world implied is one where people have names and locations, and so can be categorised, but where order lies in the continuing process of social life, and the only synthesis needed lies in the assumed Christian values. Human intelligence is limited to repeating and applying that system: it is in literary terms episodic, that is clerical rather than analytic.

This clerical activity in itself was part of a developing world that made the organic model of the Calendar increasingly unrealistic; reading, publishing, selling books were all aspects of the wider bourgeois and capitalist forces that the ideology of the Calendar works to conceal. In crime fiction an increasing number of writers and readers would need new models though which to contemplate the nature of society, the criminal threat in particular. The detective was to be a central part of those new patterns, but he did not spring into life as we know him overnight; some surprising and revealing versions of crime prevention preceded the figure who has come to dominate our own crime fiction.

II *The Adventures of Caleb Williams*

William Godwin's novel, published in 1794, deals with a crime, but appears to have little else in common with *The Newgate Calendar*, though the author knew it well. Caleb Williams is a single, intelligent detecting hero. His story has much of the unified structure of a novel, with a conceptual, probing and subjective presentation. This may suggest the modern detective novel came into being at once. But Godwin's novel is less than, and more than, the modern detective novel: it is both a preliminary to and a comment on the crime novel as we know it. Godwin does not believe in the absolute value of the individual hero's intelligence as a bulwark against crime. His search for a different central value shows that subjectivism, rationalism and individualism did not immediately appear in crime fiction as imagined guardians of life and property. As Steven Lukes shows in his book *Individualism*, both before and after the French Revolution many thinkers, including radicals like Godwin, did not see the individual consciousness as a viable basis for a successful social structure. A specific set of pro-individualist attitudes and a world-view supporting the power of such a figure was necessary before the hero-detectives we know could be presented with confidence and fictional success.

Godwin's novel indicates that the comforting and old-fashioned fables of *The Newgate Calendar* would not satisfy a questioning intellectual of the period. But the internal contradictions and overall sense of gloom in his novel make it clear no ready alternative fictional system of crime control, no compelling new ideological comfort was available. The unexamined 'organic society' theories implicit to *The Newgate Calendar* are inadequate to keep society ordered properly, in Godwin's eyes, but he is by no means satisfied that a subjective questing intellect will do either. Later writers were content with such an individualist authority against crime. Godwin's sense of the weakness of the solitary thoughtful enquirer as a basis for general hope is one that crime fiction has only recently come to share, as the last chapter of this book will show.

The plot of the novel alone exposes the basis of Godwin's theme. Caleb Williams, an intelligent lower class youth, is befriended and educated by Mr Falkland, a local squire. Caleb becomes his secretary: he is not only indebted to Falkland but a part of his household. Falkland is essentially a good man, very conscious of his honour and the outward respect he must maintain for his own peace of mind and authority. His qualities lead him to disapprove strongly of Tyrrel, a neighbour whose bullying and cruel nature degrades the rank and ignores the responsibility of a squire. In a climactic argument Tyrrel, who is sharp-tongued as well as physically brutal, disgraces and beats Falkland in public. Falkland murders him in secret immediately afterwards—though the novel does not reveal this at once. Falkland has ignored the advice of John Clare, a poet who represents the absolute value of the novel; he warns Falkland to control his temper and use his authority in charities that amount to a programme of slow reform.

The facts about the murder are established by Caleb; an uncontrollable curiosity makes him study Falkland and reveal his crime. Once Falkland realises Caleb knows what has happened, he persecutes him. Caleb is pursued across Britain, imprisoned and, largely because of Falkland's prestige, steadily discredited and humiliated. After a long series of painful experiences, in prison, among outlaws and in hiding, Caleb confronts Falkland, who is now physically and mentally a much reduced man: guilt and the fear of exposure have both worked upon him. In the original ending of the novel Caleb fails again: Falkland once more outfaces him, and he ends his story as a raving madman with little time to live. A few days later a less emotionally involved Godwin wrote a less stark ending that finds room for some positive feeling. Here the confrontation kills Falkland, but Caleb realises he too is at fault: he feels that the debts he owed Falkland should have made him speak openly about the matter long ago, when Falkland's better self would have led him to acknowledge the crime and make amends.

Godwin's view is finally stated through Caleb: while much is wrong with the existing patterns of society, the flaw is structural and cannot be put right by one-to-one conflicts between men. The individual attack on Falkland which Caleb pursues has isolated and destroyed them both; obsessive subjective inquiry is a misuse of Caleb's personal and intellectual strength. Godwin presents the recommendations for a better society that he had given in theoretical form in his recently finished book *An Enquiry Concerning*

Political Justice. A small, mutually honest and affectionate society is
the model he believes will work. It is essentially a system where the
individual is subsumed, supported and protected; but unlike that of
The Newgate Calendar it is not a static, conservative system that is
assumed to work of its own inertia. Godwin's emphasis on love and
truth-telling reveals his early years as a nonconformist minister but,
more importantly it emphasises his conviction that a successful
society demands constant mutual effort.

Godwin's belief that only a new corporate society can heal the
injuries created by the existing corporate one indicates that for him
individualism had not become a valid view of the world: his
rejection of a one-to-one conflict shows, by contrast, how deeply
individualist, how fully subjective in basis, are the later crime stories
which rely so heavily on single conflicts to realise a fictional idea of
crime control. Yet Godwin is not only interesting for this negative
revelation of the ideological base of later crime fiction. The forces
that shaped the bourgeois and Romantic faith in individualism
were already at work, and operated against Godwin's conscious
will. The book's title is an obvious example. Originally it was *Things
As They Are: The Adventures of Caleb Williams*; but the personal
subjective sub-title appealed much more than the general objective
main title, and by the 1831 edition Godwin himself sanctioned a
reversal of order. The external attitudes that induced this change
are present within the novel. Godwin's first ending was a deeply felt,
subjectively presented account of the destruction of an individual. It
was only cooler reflection that enabled him to change this emphasis
and bring the novel finally back to the theoretical, super-personal
argument implied by the original title. This rewriting did not only
go against Godwin's feelings as he finished his story; as he worked
backwards to bring his narrative to that climactic point (a
technique crime fiction was to make its own) his basic collective
ideas came inevitably into conflict with the implicit individualism
embedded in the structure of the novel form itself.

To speak generally, the shape of a novel has certain implications.
The idea that someone has written all this down and that others will
read it carefully in itself indicates that writing and reading are
worthwhile ways of spending time. They are not merely techniques
involved in social and economic activity, but are ends in themselves.
The idea that someone has invented a story, that it has a named
author and a named individual hero or heroine all add the
implications of individualism to the intellectualism the form itself

ratifies. The whole asserts that one person can create, in the context of a single character, experiences and thoughts that we will find useful—whether for entertainment or instruction. The value of individualised experience is strengthened particularly when, like *Caleb Williams*, the novel is told in the first person. Many critics have argued the novel responds to a bourgeois social formation that has time, education, money; one product of fully divided labour is conceptualised analysis alienated into books, outside normal activity, and there is a corollary emphasis on the subjective value of the individual.

The climax of the novel form is in the work of Austen, Eliot and James: the subtly developed, perfectly controlled response of one pair of authorial eyes and ears fictionally creates the myth, so important for our period, that a single individual, if clever and patient enough, can unravel the world of experience. The system of knowledge (an epistemology)—watching, listening and thinking— reveals subjective, humanly controlled motives for events, and so validates an idea of being (an ontology), in which the individual can believe that he or she is truly 'real', and can exist alone. The self is known against society, not in it. The structure of the plot—carefully linked, leading up to a climax of action which is also a crucial revelation of the gathered meaning of the novel—provides the model of order, aesthetic and moral, which the individualist consciousness feels it can derive from the raw material of experience. This structure is opposite to the effect and the implicit meaning of the episodic pattern discussed in the case of *The Newgate Calendar*, where the belief in an organic society, divinely controlled, is the gathering point, and no overt artistic or moral organisation is therefore required in art.

To some degree then, *Caleb Williams* responds to the individualistic and artistic pressure of the novel form. Caleb is intelligent and to a degree perceptive and analytic; writing his own story is a last effort to communicate and establish his own good intentions and explain his errors. To that extent a subjective world-view is present. But, more revealingly, there are some telling fissures, moments of contradiction, where Godwin's collectivist intention works against the meaningful control of the rational, organically structured novel. At the beginning of Volume II, Caleb says: 'I do not pretend to warrant the authenticity of any part of these memoirs except so much as fall under my own knowledge', and this theme is recapitulated at the beginning of the third chapter of the same volume: 'It will also most probably happen, while I am thus employed in collecting together the scattered ingredients of my history, that I shall upon some occasions annex to appearances an explanation, which I was far from possessing at the time, and was only suggested to me through the medium of subsequent events.'

The omniscience of the narrator (which can even include a first person narrator) is a crucial part of the illusion by which the classic novel asserts the world is comprehensible to a gifted single intelligence. Caleb does want to move from 'appearances' to 'an explanation', but he recognises his limitations and the sheer difficulty of making the world explicable through one brain. Elsewhere Godwin makes it clear how Caleb actively errs in his intentions and his explanations. His confidence will rise, then sag as new events contradict him. His attempted escape from prison is a good example, and a convenient contrast with the many successful escapes of later detectives. Caleb's misjudgements and blunders are communicated through his detailed presentation and mishaps as well as by the overarching design of the novel.

If Caleb is shown to be unreliable, there remains the author; Godwin's own voice, like that of Henry James, could still realise through the uncertain characters the power of an individual authorial intelligence. But even at this level, uncertainty shows through. The two endings are a crucial piece of evidence of course, but there are so many changes of feeling in the novel, so many prevarications about the value of people and the nature of events that Godwin does not have, and is not seeking a single authoritative version. A particularly sharp example of this breach of individualistic control comes in the curious sequence where Tyrrel is briefly seen as a man who might be redeemable; truth lies in social interaction, not in single summaries.

In its large structure *Caleb Williams* is continuous and has a meaningful climax like the classic nineteenth-century novel, but the material is not totally subdued to rational development and orderly control. Caleb's experiences are often lengthy and random; they do not give the sense of a controlled, climactic development, that crucial pattern by which the 'organic' novel expresses its mastery of events (as Terry Eagleton argues in *Criticism and Ideology*). In *Caleb Williams* there is a general sense of Caleb's increasing delusion and his multiplying errors, but the incidents could be reordered to a certain extent without destroying this impression.

The novel also finds room for themes outside the persona's consciousness and development. Godwin includes material on the disgusting and damaging state of prisons at the time; there are passages arguing that the revolutionary views held by the outlaws are not a proper response to contemporary injustice. These sequences, like Caleb's errant adventures, pull against the organic structure of the fully individualist novel; they press home formally Godwin's distrust of the single intelligence and so enact the idea that some form of collective security is necessary.

The use of coincidence in the story has a similar anti-individualist effect. Coincidence is, of course, the bugbear of the rational novel, because a world-view that holds human beings can, and so should, control their actions in a comprehensible way, must reject sheer accident as a cause of events. Literary critics, dependent for their organised livelihood on the rational explanation of rational novels, have come down very heavily against coincidence. *The Newgate Calendar* used sheer chance as one of the functions by which divine order confounds the aberrant; Godwin employs several chance meetings, especially between Caleb and Falkland. In a rationalist context this is bad plotting, but the effect (and, in my view, the cause) is to suggest that human beings do not control everything about them. At best they respond to their often random experience, and by mutual support this is made easier.

Caleb's own prose style is another formal feature which hints at his limitations. He is often wordy and ineffective. He says of himself early on: 'I delighted to read of feats of activity, and was particularly interested by tales in which corporeal ingenuity or strength are the means resorted to for supplying resources and conquering difficulties. I inured myself to mechanical pursuits, and devoted much of my time to an endeavour after mechanical invention.' The intellectual, stilted frailty of the style seems clear enough to a modern reader, especially in its contrast with its content. However, it might be dangerous to assume that Godwin has consciously created a voice which implies Caleb is too involved in cerebration for his own—and others'—good. Godwin's own style in *An Enquiry Concerning Political Justice* is often ponderous, and Angus Wilson has suggested it is a natural eighteenth-century voice. This may be so; but Caleb's prose certainly does not bespeak a consciously confident control of the world, as does Jane Austen's voice. Godwin may well have had at least some sense of dramatising Caleb's persona in language: even at his most philosophical he is rarely as pompous and self-indulgently wordy as Caleb at his most introspective.

The central thematic analysis of the novel, like its formal patterns, basically rejects an individualistic view of the world. Although the story tells of a single crime, Godwin's analysis of its origin is socio-political as well as moral, and so, in its own conceptual way, his work has a social base as broad as the one intuited through *The Newgate Calendar* descriptions. Of course, conceptualisation is in itself a form of alienation from real processes of living. But Godwin was acute enough to see the failure of contemporary society in structural and ideological terms, not saying in merely idealistic and moral terms that certain people were 'evil'. His analysis remains an impressive one, and is more historically and politically important, because more far-reaching, than the elements of historical allegory suggested by Gary Kelly in his recent book on the Jacobin novel.

Anthropologists and sociologists since Godwin wrote have distinguished between two value-systems, often called shame-oriented and guilt-oriented. In a shame-oriented society values are public and shared, and anyone who acts contrary to them is disgraced, losing status in society as a result. Honour is crucial to the individual; acts, clothes, bearing and speeches all reflect a knowledge of what honour requires for its continued possession—and its corollary display. Shame is greatly feared since it is an exclusion from the valued, and ultimately mutually protective group. The Celtic notion that a poet may satirise a man to death arises from this system. In a guilt-oriented society, on the other hand, the individual creates his or her own ideas of rectitude, and misbehaviour is felt personally as guilt even if it is not publicly criticised or even recognised as wrong. Morality is private, and public displays of virtue and honour are seen as hollow shams.

We are now in general thought to be guilt-oriented, though there are strong strains of shame-orientation running through our culture—but to recognise them would contradict the prevailing individualist ideology. The fascinating thing about *Caleb Williams* is that Godwin clearly grasped the socially functional importance of the honour–shame system. He sees Falkland's obsession with honour as his major fault, the direct cause of his crime, and Caleb articulates this judgement. Honour is in the novel the living structure of what in the *Enquiry* Godwin called 'government'. By this he did not mean just the Westminster-based organisation of the country but the system that ratified authority at all levels, the set of instrumental values which governed private as well as public life.

Although Caleb can identify and criticise this system through the sharp intelligence Godwin gives him, neither he nor the novel espouses a system based on guilt. Caleb finally sees his great disaster as having lost his reputation, that central totem of the shame-oriented society. He is writing the story 'with the idea of vindicating my character'—'character' here is used in the old sense of a testimonial, a public knowledge of a person's value. And Godwin himself offers in the revised ending a new version of a corporate society where Christian affection has replaced honour as a central mechanism of value and mutual support. But as the novel has not been able to dramatise this process in action, and as the chosen novel form requires an internal demonstration of the values finally espoused, Godwin's offered system is hardly convincing. The effective weight of the novel lies in the attack on the existing system and the telling exposition of the isolated state of the intellectual individual. Indeed, just as later writers have theorised the account Godwin gives of Falkland's system of values, so Caleb's own career has since been shown to be an archetypal one for the alienated intellectual. Godwin's imagination works very accurately as he shows Caleb, at last free from prison, disguising himself as various types of contemporary outcast—a beggar, an Irishman, a wandering rustic and finally a Jew. When Caleb looks for work he takes up jobs that later sociologists would describe as classically those of alienated skilled workers—freelance writer, jobbing watch-mender, teacher. And finally, the best touch of all, Caleb becomes an etymologist, a man who works in the world of isolated words themselves.

When Godwin rejects the authoritarian ideology of the honour-based society he does not adopt the ideology that was largely to replace it, but offers instead a corporate substitute. His world-view remains a collective, Christian one, though one arrived at by the rational mechanisms that were to destroy such a world-view—and such a world. In the *Enquiry* he recommends education for all, believing that all would then see the need to be mutually loving and supportive. He does not conceive that education and intellectualism could become of themselves a profession and a life-style, and a theoretical defence against the disorders of ordinary existence—and (in fiction at least) against threats to life and property. In his amateur detective Godwin makes essential weaknesses out of just those qualities which would dominate the armouries of the great fictional detectives—curiosity, subjectivism, individualism, arrogance, lonely endurance. After a crucial change of viewpoint in the context of Romantic theory and the full development of bourgeois ideology, that lonely questing figure would become a hero, an absolute value. When author and audience could believe in the subjective individual as a basis of real experience and could see collectivity as a threat, when rationalism was more than a tool of inquiry and had become a way of dominating the whole world, when professionalism, specialisation and rigorous inquiry replaced the values of affection and mutual understanding as means of controlling deviance, then the figure that Godwin presents as misguided and destructive would emerge as a culture-hero bringing comfort and a sense of security to millions of individuals.

III The *Memoirs of Vidocq*

The 'autobiography' of Eugène François Vidocq presents the first professional detective in literature, and so has considerable historical importance. But if the misleading positivist simplicities of literary history are set aside and the text examined for its own ideological function, the *Memoirs of Vidocq*, like *Caleb Williams* and unlike *The Newgate Calendar*, has a curiously ambiguous effect. To a degree the *Memoirs* are surprisingly realistic, yet they are also exaggerated and melodramatic. These two strands partly derive from two levels of authorship, Vidocq's own experiences and the imagination of his rewriters and translators. The literary professionals who remodelled Vidocq's experiences directed them towards a shape like that of the novel and a world-view like that of later crime fiction. But Vidocq himself had a world-view and an idea of its suitable literary realisation; both were more like *The Newgate Calendar* than the ideology and literary form that are emergent in the *Memoirs*. Vidocq was a criminal who turned police informer with such success that in 1811 he became a full-time inquiry agent in the newly formed Sûreté, the plain-clothes detective arm of the recently founded national police. When he retired in 1827 he arranged for the publication of his memoirs; two volumes appeared in 1828, another two in 1829. After a lengthy account of how he worked his way through the prison system into the police force, the *Memoirs* tell a series of fairly brief encounters with criminals. Typically, Vidocq is given a particularly difficult case, to catch and bring proof against some hardened criminal and, usually, his accomplices. He gains information or infiltrates the gang with disguise, patience and cunning as his major methods. He displays courage and swift judgement when his lowlier police colleagues come to make the arrest. The crimes are usually robbery with violence and the action is mostly set in the seamy quarters of Paris, though sometimes Vidocq will pursue his man to a country inn or a provincial town. The criminals are seen as a hostile and powerful enemy, not as aberrant members of normal society; Vidocq is supremely skilful against them, frequently taking care to humiliate the most powerful and feared villains by showing how easily and completely he outwits them.

This makes Vidocq quite a hero, but he was apparently annoyed by aspects of his characterisation. According to his own preface to volume I of the memoirs, his publisher forced a rewriter on him, probably a literary hack called Emile Morice. Vidocq was disgusted with his handling of the material and had him sacked. The preface claims that from the last chapter of volume II the work is Vidocq's own. In fact, it is generally agreed that it stemmed from a new rewriter, L. F. L. L'Héritier. The obviously fictional elements, stock melodramatic situations and theatrical climaxes are more common in the last volumes than the first, and volume IV actually includes a short novel about Adèle d'Escars which L'Héritier had previously published. The stylish and formal nature of Vidocq's preface suggests that even this was part of the new rewriter's work.

Whoever wrote it, the preface disagrees with what had been done, and the complaints are revealing. The hero has been falsely represented. The 'teinturier', the 'dyer' of the material, has coarsened Vidocq's language and has in any case written badly—there is a 'multitude de locutions vicieueses, de tournures fatigantes, de phrases prolixes.' The charge that his character was not respectable enough sounds credible from a retired detective, though it has other implications to be considered later. The stylistic criticism may well reveal a new rewriter taking a professional pot-shot at his predecessor. As the complaints go on, they lead us into the wider meaning of the stories.

The character Vidocq wishes for is not only decently-spoken: he is also to be lively. The preface regrets the changes of 'les saillies, la vivacité et l'energie de mon caractère' into a figure 'tout-à-fait dépourvue de vie, de couleur et de rapidité'. This seems obscure, since the character, even in the first volume, is vigorous enough, but the preface gives an important clue when it criticises the plotting of the rewritten version. Vidocq complains that 'les faits étaient bien les mêmes, moins tout ce qu'il y avait de fortuit, d'involontaire, de spontane dans les vicissitudes d'une carrière orageuse, ne s'y presentait plus que comme une longue préméditation de mal'.

Vidocq feels his character is diminished because the action is too planned and too many rational links have been made between events; he is not able to show himself nimble enough, spontaneously reacting to sudden threats, bad turns of luck, troublesome surprises. What we might regard as a sophistication of plot, according to this preface both falsifies reality and reduces the heroic human character who faced and defeated the potentially baffling vicissitudes of life among criminals. Although a mediating, heroic detective agent is the means of restoring order, the view of reality the *Memoirs* present is essentially like that of *The Newgate Calendar*. The world is not analysable in unified conceptual terms, but given to sudden starts and threatening abnormalities. The hero gains status (and honour is important) by demonstrating his power to respond successfully to sudden disturbance and to restore order again. But he is not involved in a systematic explanation of events, a comprehended chain of cause and effect. The rewriter, on the other hand, has begun to create his own idea of reality, a world that can be explained, by pulling together the incidents into a more fully motivated and unified plot.

This process continued in the work of the second French rewriter. In the third and fourth volumes more and more of the chapters connect. An arrest in one chapter brings information that leads to another arrest in the next. These details all indicate that the form of the memoirs is moving away from episodic structure towards a unified organic narrative. The English translator confirmed this development strongly. The direct, racy effect of the original is slowed and given a more thoughtful, pausing, analytic tone, partly by the frequent use of an often balanced, judgement-implying syntax and partly by a more conceptual, analytic and polysyllabic vocabulary.

That tone itself meshes with the added passages that explain a sudden and amazing event in the original. In chapter XXVII Vidocq tries to trap Constantin Gueuvive and his men. He has become a member of the gang, active as look-out during a robbery. When the criminals are dividing the spoils Vidocq's colleagues, tipped off by him, arrive to make the arrests. But he does not want them to reveal who he is as there are more accomplices to gather in. In French, the police beat on the door and:

> Soudain, je me lève et me glisse sous un lit: les coups redoublent, on est forcé d'ouvrir.
>   Au même instant, un essaim d'inspecteurs envahit la chambre. (vol. II, p. 348)

This is driving, dramatic narrative. But the English is more interested in telling us how it was that Vidocq could hide:

> Amidst the confusion occasioned by these words, and the increased knocking at the gate, I contrived, unobserved, to crawl under a bed, where I had scarcely concealed myself when the door was burst open, and a swarm of inspectors and other officers of the police entered the room. (p. 200)

The lack of spontaneity that Vidocq's preface complained of is much more evident in the English, and the translation is plainly more conceptual and rationally connected.

These patterns have their large structural analogue in the fact that the editor of the 1859 English edition consciously streamlines the shape of the *Memoirs*. In his preface he says he has 'thought it needful to suppress all such matter as appeared to us to be foreign to the Work as an Autobiography, or in any way so to act as to interrupt the continuous thread of its history.' He leaves out stories he judges digressive, some of the longer dramatised conversations which are a feature of the French, and some informative but, to him, rambling discussions of Vidocq's world. He cannot, though, bear to exclude the moving humanitarian digression about Adèle d'Escars, and so prints it—a finely quasi-organic compromise—as an appendix. He feels the *Memoirs* need a continuous explanatory thread, the orderly developing structure that validates a subjective control of experience. In reworking Vidocq's material (which may have been in note form originally) first French then English literary intellectuals dramatised their own ideology through language, presentation and structure. The detective hero is still a rugged and unintellectual man, but his exploits are presented in terms that increasingly respond to the bourgeois individualism which permeates the classic novel.

In spite of these changes, much that relates to an earlier world-view, one that Vidocq himself would apparently support, has survived in the *Memoirs*. A series of literary conventions is used which tends towards heightening the excitement, conveying tension in a scene. The presence of excitement does not automatically mean rationalism is excluded, of course: the Romantic poets in England and Rousseau in France indicate emotion and rationalism were not yet seen to be at odds with each other in high culture, and John Clare in *Caleb Williams* represents that authority figure of Romanticism, the poet-philosopher. However, such a resolution of feeling and thought is not supported by Vidocq or the basic structure of the text. The preface asserts that vitality, wit and direct feeling are not consistent with an organised rational unity of plot, and in this particular text sensational feeling, exciting crises are at odds with organised thought. This spontaneous excitement arises from an old-established, integrated view of society. Where Godwin and his alienated hero invented a new corporate social model that might work well, Vidocq, uncerebral and unalienated, has a sense of being deeply involved in the flow of ordinary life. As I have argued, organic structure, conceptual analysis and ordering are absent from texts which see an integrated ongoing social process as reality—albeit one that now needs specialised heroes to defend it, and is not satisfied by the old pattern of heroes who exemplified widespread qualities. The exciting crises present a hero who can respond successfully to sudden unexpected threats in a world not considered to be fully comprehensible to humans but which can be hostile in random ways. This is a pattern familiar from myth and folklore: the quick-wittedness, courage and speed of reaction that Vidocq displays on behalf of his society relates him to heroes from the past, not to the rational detectives of our period.

A typical set of crises (with an obvious heritage in folklore and popular story) shows Vidocq in disguise. The villain boasts that if Vidocq were present, he would destroy him utterly. Vidocq answers, on one notable occasion, no, Vidocq is so clever that even if he were here you would give him a drink—and as he says this our hero holds out his glass for a refill. To jaded rational palates this may seem contrived: but the incident creates in finely melodramatic and spontaneous terms the cunning and élan of the character—so important, the preface insists, to the real Vidocq himself. The enemy is not only defeated but made to seem foolish beside the spirited, life-restoring hero. This itself relates to the shame-oriented consciousness, for to make a fool of the enemy is to deprive him of status and power. Although Vidocq is in disguise, the assertive power of his 'name' recreates the honour he attaches to it. This is just the triumph Vidocq means by his 'saillies'.

Spontaneous cunning does not prevent Vidocq from reflecting at times. But when he ponders a problem he does not methodically plan a way through it. He thinks about its difficulty, shrugs, and trusts in his 'bon génie' to resolve matters—and gets on with the action to find an answer as sudden and complete as the problem is random and difficult. Later detective fiction will place great stress on the methodology of the detective, and the translation, as has been shown above, does introduce some aspects of this. It also usually omits reference to Vidocq's 'bon génie': so irrational an explanation of success is discordant with the translator's notion of the meaning the events should dramatise. But in what we can establish of the original spirit of the memoirs the scientific method is not yet a viable or emotionally real approach: to detail the cerebral technique, to intellectualise would diminish the authentic 'caractère' of the hero.

Although Vidocq boasts of his 'génie' and has high moments of melodramatic cunning, the basis of his success is still realistic plodding police work. Indeed, this is where we find the central illusion of the Vidocq *Memoirs*. Hard work, information, bribery, undercover activity are the means to arrive at a climax, the moment where the hero's brilliance emerges. A figure of Herculean courage and endurance, of Odyssean cunning, is built on an infrastructure of solid French police activity. The audience is offered the convincing background and minutiae of action and the consoling resolutions that locate a specially gifted figure on their side. *The Newgate Calendar* provided the familiar English background and the illusion that social observation and Christian guilt would somehow identify the criminal. *Caleb Williams* gave the final illusion that if Caleb had encountered Falkland honestly and lovingly, all would have been amended. A central illusion, a way of shaping an optimistic ideology which is attractive and viable in terms of a culture group's expectations and beliefs is a major feature of popular, successful crime fiction. Vidocq's memoirs recognise real crime in a real setting, and resolve its pressure through the hero's agency; but even his special ability is socially integrated. Vidocq's talents are normal ones raised in power.

In one exemplary case, Vidocq is looking for a female hunchback who lives near a market and has yellow curtains. He ponders the problem, decides he can rely on his 'bon génie' and plods round Paris to discover more than a hundred and fifty possible locations. He then reasons that hunchbacked women tend to be gossips and tend to be keen cooks (they have no other ways of catching a husband), so he watches the food shops—with eventual success. The unalienated hero uses just the collective wisdom of the people he defends. In the same way his crucial feats are often only exaggerated versions of the ordinary—he arrests a man bravely, he hides under nothing more unusual than a bed, he can stand on watch for long hours. It is his speed of reaction, his instinct to do these rather ordinary things at the right time that gives him his special status.

Even in his moments of extreme success and melodrama, Vidocq is not an isolated hero as the later detectives are to be. He works for the police, he is in intimate contact with the people of Paris, protecting their money and avenging damage to them and their property. He is not really one of the crowd, of course: he is much better than the average policemen and is often in conflict with them because of that; and he is not an ordinary Parisian at all. But when he is on the job he disguises himself as one of them, becomes one of them, as it were. He is a hero who operates for and through the people, not a hero distinguished in manner and method by isolation and alienated intelligence. Vidocq fills a need in *The Newgate Calendar* pattern that occurs when the criminal is no longer seen as an aberrant member of society but as a member of a hostile class. Against hardened criminals, impervious to guilt and able to hide successfully, the special skills of Vidocq are necessary to make crime control convincing in story, just as they were in reality.

As a result of this need for an agent of detection, we frequently find Vidocq engaged in one-to-one conflicts with a criminal. In later crime fiction the personalisation of good in the detective and of evil in the villain is an important way of obscuring the social and historical basis of crime and conflict, in keeping with the individualist mystifications of bourgeois ideology. But this limited personalisation of conflict does not yet occur in Vidocq's memoirs, though there is a tendency in that direction. One restraining force is seeing criminals as an enemy class: they have areas, language and relationships that bind them as a common enemy. This class sense is based on moral, not social or economic criteria, and assumes there is no other classification of people other than good or evil. It does not, however, limit crime as dramatically and simplistically as the later presentation.

The other important pressure against an individualistic, one-to-one drama in the memoirs comes from their structure. Vidocq fights many battles against the members of the criminal class, but no single one is made central, asserted to be the climactic release of criminal pressure. So Vidocq acts like the knight of romance or the hero of folklore, repeating his victories in a reassuring series. His complaint that too much plot-linking damages his 'caractère' implicitly recognises it is in episodic action that the figure of the socially integrated agent gains its true force, has formal authority to dramatise its meaning. The episodic structure, as has already been argued in the case of *The Newgate Calender*, replicates a society that believes itself integral but not comprehensible in analytic terms. And where the constant change of places and characters in *The Newgate Calendar* created the idea that the crucial protective values were pervasive through society as a whole, here, where evil is seen as a hostile force, the agent needed to protect society must himself be the constant feature, the personification of the values of morality and quick-responding defence. Vidocq's irritation at the vulgarity of the language given him indicates his awareness of his special dignity as this defensive figure. He needs a language which will pass among the people, but still distinguish him from them, just because he is, by his work, among them all the time and disguised like one of them.

In simpler, intentional terms, Vidocq was no doubt anxious to put his own unrespectable criminal life behind him, but this past in itself also links his literary figure with the pattern of a hero who acts episodically to help his people. The criminal past of the detective or at least his intimate knowledge of criminal life is a common feature in detective stories, and the *Memoirs* show this strongly. Ian Ousby has discussed the phenomenon in some detail in *Bloodhounds of Heaven*. The absence of a lone enquirer in *The Newgate Calendar* excludes such possibilities, but an intimate knowledge of evil is a familiar pattern in heroic stories of the past—a journey to hell, temptation and partial sin are elements of the archetypal hero's life as Lord Raglan and Joseph Campbell have outlined it.

One basic explanation of the hero's criminal contacts is that as detectives still know (sometimes to their cost) successful crime-solving demands intimate contact with the underworld. Or, a little more elaborately, it may be that an audience both ignorant and fearful of crime and criminals needs to feel its hero is equipped with greater experience and knowledge to justify his success. Freudians like Charles Rycroft go further still, arguing that the detective represents the superego, the criminal the id. When the detective and the criminal are close or identical this represents our own internal struggles between selfish antisocial behaviour and the acceptance of social sanctions. In Vidocq all three forces may well operate: his knowledge is functional, it makes him credible, and the disguise feature in particular seems good support for the Freudian analysis. In this respect too, Vidocq is more integrated with society than later detectives: he really has been a criminal, where later detectives, while often retaining some criminal contact, were to be much more distanced from criminal reality, just as they were to be alienated from the society on whose behalf they were to operate.

In general, we can see the memoirs of Vidocq as a more up-to-date system of imaginary crime control than the one offered in *The Newgate Calendar*. In response to Vidocq's real experience against crime, the detective has emerged, and the contemporary view of the criminal threat found the figure consoling. But this detective is not a rational and conceptual operator, and is by no means an alienated figure, however far his 'teinturiers' and his translator wanted to move in that direction. The events, the setting and the character of Vidocq himself resisted that.

Godwin's approach, though not his conclusions, had shown the growing pressures that enshrined rational individualism, and Vidocq's rewriter and translator suggest how this world-view was to affect crime fiction. It is no surprise then, that the development of crime fiction in France followed their course rather than Vidocq's, stressing skill and individual authority in the figures who contained crime and finding suitable forms in organic literature rather than in episodic reality. The Leatherstocking novels of James Fenimore Cooper realised the figure of the lonely, skilful, determined hunter and Dumas' *Les Mohicans de Paris* is only the best known of many such stories. Here the pursuit is still physical, the special knowledge employed sense-available and natural, but in the figure of Prince Rodolphe in *Les Mystères de Paris* the weight of superior education, class and morality all fall on the erring criminal. In his part of *The Holy Family*, the first criticism written about crime fiction, Marx identifies Rodolphe as an archetype of bourgeois, authoritarian consciousness, which feels that a little reformist kindness will solve the criminal problem, and pays no attention to the real origins of crime.

Marx would, of course, be equally critical of the organic Christian society envisaged in *The Newgate Calendar* and the *Memoirs* view that criminals are a naturally evil class. But he sharply identifies Sue's implicit movement away from an objective sense of society in action towards a subjective dream of order created by values that in reality were—and are—quite inappropriate in the face of social conflict and its manifestation as crime. Dumas and Sue merely indicate some of the passing trends in crime fiction as moral and literary stereotypes filled out the figure of the detective. A new pattern was to grip the imagination of readers and writers of crime fiction for a long time, because it would use the power of romanticism and intellectualism to validate the alienated individual detective. This would create a confident new illusion to console the anxiety caused by crime, and would dramatise powerfully a world-view that is beginning to emerge in the last texts examined in this chapter. This development, the beginning of what we recognise clearly as detective fiction, was the work of Edgar Allan Poe.

REFERENCES

Texts
The Newgate Calendar or The Malefactors Bloody Register, from 1700 to the Present Time, J. Cooke, London, 1773.
Caleb Williams, OUP, London, 1970.
An Enquiry Concerning Political Justice, Pelican, London, 1976.
Mémoires de Vidocq, 4 vols. Tenon, Paris, 1828–9.
Memoirs of Vidocq, 4 vols, Whittaker, Treacher and Arnot, London, 1829.
Memoirs of Vidocq, Bohn, London, 1859.

Criticism
Erich Auerbach, *Mimesis: The Representation of Reality in Western Literature*, Princeton University Press, Princeton, 1953.
Roland Barthes, *The Pleasure of the Text*, Cape, London, 1976.
Joseph Campbell, *The Hero with a Thousand Faces*, Pantheon, New York, 1949.
Terry Eagleton, *Criticism and Ideology*, New Left Books, London, 1976.
Garry Kelly, *The English Jacobin Novel, 1780–1805*, Clarendon Press, Oxford, 1976.
Steven Lukes, *Individualism*, Blackwell, Oxford, 1973.
Pierre Macherey, *Theory of Literary Production*, Routledge & Kegan Paul, London, 1978.

Karl Marx and Friedrich Engels, *The Holy Family or Critique of Critical Critique*, Foreign Languages Publishing House, Moscow, 1956.

Régis Messac, *Le 'Detective Novel' et l'influence de la pensée scientifique*, Champion, Paris, 1929.

Ian Ousby, *Bloodhounds of Heaven: The Detective in English Fiction from Godwin to Doyle*, Harvard University Press, Cambridge, 1976.

Lord Raglan, *The Hero*, Watts, London, 1949.

Charles Rycroft, 'A Detective Story: Psychoanalytic Observations', *Psychoanalytic Quarterly*, XXVI (1957) 229–45.

Dorothy Sayers, *Great Short Stories of Detection, Mystery and Horror*, Gollancz, London, 1928.

Angus Wilson, 'The Novels of William Godwin,' *World Review*, June 1951, 37–40.

2 '. . . his rich ideality'— Edgar Allan Poe's Detective

Poe was the first to create the intelligent, infallible, isolated hero so important to crime fiction of the last hundred years. He wrote three stories featuring this detective, and each differs from the others. The three together imply that the isolated intellectual and imaginative life is a sufficient and successful response to the world and its problems. This crucial nineteenth and twentieth-century ideology is familiar to us now; Poe's genius was to shape a literary form that gave it persuasive life. A study of the three texts will show this was not easy or always successful, but a pattern emerged which was artistically meaningful enough to be repeated over and over, with relevant modifications, and satisfy an increasing reading public, assure them that disorder could be contained by activating values that leisured readers could all share.

I 'The Murders in the Rue Morgue'

The character and methods of the detective are crucial to the ideology of modern crime stories. Name alone proclaims the Chevalier C. Auguste Dupin a gentleman, but two features separate him from the anonymous authorities who conduct inquiries in *The Newgate Calendar* and the upper-class detectives of later English crime fiction. First he is French, living in a culture different from that of the language of the stories and second, developing further that initial alienation, he is cut off from his own class. He has only a small income and the life he chooses is intellectual: 'Books, indeed, were his only luxuries.' This sketch of a contentedly alienated intellectual is the theme of the first paragraph that describes Dupin, and it is of central importance in the whole configuration of meaning in the stories. The French setting owes something to Vidocq's memoirs, something to the enlightenment tradition: the international aspect of Dupin is a strength in cultured, outward-looking English-speaking circles and also suggests that the individual isolated in his own society may find moral support among other willing outcasts through the world.

The narrator meets Dupin in a library and recognises him as an attractive figure worth imitating and supporting. Dupin, for all his authority and modest income, is actually the narrator's protégé: as the representative of readers seeking consolation and comfort, the narrator not only describes but sustains the great detective. Poe does not at first place his hero in a cash-nexus with the society he protects, though this crucially bourgeois element will develop. They live together in 'a style which suited the rather fantastic gloom of our common tempers', in a deserted and crumbling house 'in a retired and desolate portion of the Faubourg St Germain'—then as now a token for French intellectual and artistic life. They lead a strikingly asocial life-style. Sometimes they roam the streets at night, but mostly they read—again at night, or with shades drawn in the day. They sustain themselves by 'that infinity of mental excitement which quiet observation can afford'. They are scholars, observers, with a taste for a Gothic setting. Arnold Hauser has shown how the bourgeois rejection of aristocratic classicism involved serious study and a highly developed sensual imagination. In essence and in setting these attitudes have distinct relations with the developing forces of bourgeois individualism.

Dupin is not merely an empirical observer. He has 'a peculiar analytic ability' and Poe takes pains to distinguish this from mere factual observation, what he elsewhere calls 'calculation'; the fuller 'analysis' stems from the hero's 'rich ideality'. The pattern is a secular version of Coleridge's distinction between 'understanding', which dealt with sense-available data, and 'reason'—'the source and substance of truths above sense'. Where Coleridge based 'reason' in Christian intuition, Poe rests his 'analysis' on the imaginative power, operating with intellect and feeling combined at full strength. Poe probably drew the term 'ideality' from the new pseudo-science of phrenology, where it meant 'the imaginative faculty' or 'the poetical faculty': it conveniently expresses both the mentalism and the basically idealistic unreality of the area where Poe's hero is specially gifted.

Where Dupin does 'analyse', his body expresses disengagement from ordinary living processes. His manner becomes 'frigid and abstract'—two telling adjectives for the alienated intellectual. His eyes become vacant and his voice, 'usually a rich tenor, rose into a treble which would have sounded petulantly but for the deliberateness and entire distinctness of the enunciation.' The hero in story has features which distinguish him from normal men, and this is often marked physically: the most splendid example is the Irish warrior Cuchulainn, whose terrible warp-spasm precedes his most awesome feats of arms. Poe has the imaginative instinct to centre his hero's distinctive change in his senses. They are heightened, denatured, even emasculated—passive perception is his area of heroism.

Dupin is distanced further by his special qualities, yet they provide, paradoxically, his link with normal social life. The stimulus that makes him so transcendent is the observation and comprehension of ordinary life. A darkened study is not the place where he enjoys his epiphanies: it is when he applies in actual observation all the skills and powers gathered in privacy that his heroic self emerges. The story does not admire the hero seated in his study, but applauds when problems are resolved outside the private chamber. There is much about the presentation of Dupin that recreates this double feature, this mixture of withdrawn intellectualism and skills applied in an available world.

His statements, for example, very often express a paradox, insisting on the essential simplicity of what appears incomprehensible. 'They have fallen into the gross but common error of confounding the unusual with the abstruse' he says of the police and their errors in the Rue Morgue. Dupin translates the mystifying into the lucid, a peculiarly attractive message for an audience valuing intellectualism yet fearful of and baffled by the complexities of real life. The opening sequence of the story leads to the famous argument that draughts is more complex than chess. This is the subtle-simple paradox in reverse: what seems ordinary may be deep and splendid. These paradoxes are a vital piece of Poe's rhetoric, by which he makes intellectualism serviceable in terms of ideology. He assures the audience that provided they find from somewhere an intellectual power—if only in wish-fulfilment and fictional form—the poor-seeming and bemusing world will become both rich and comprehensible.

If Dupin performs this jump from the abstruse to the usual in these pure arguments, it is all the more clearly seen in his actual detection. After the hero has been described, Poe sets out the classic 'thought-reading' episode. Dupin breaks in on the narrator's thoughts after a fifteen-minute silence with just the phrase the narrator has in mind. A prodigious feat, redolent of the super-natural as well as the theatrical. But Dupin then explains, and the mysterious becomes accessible; he did nothing superhuman and, most importantly, nothing actually poetical or very imaginative. The thought-reading depends on Dupin's knowledge of the narrator's recent experience and close observation of his gestures and movements. The 'rich ideality', in action, is little more than common-sense. No matter how limited the readers' experience and cerebral powers, they can follow, and feel they too could perform such wonders of problem-solving. It is a brilliant and crucial piece of illusory writing. The sequence is larded with expressions of amazement and an aura of mystery, but great powers are expoun-ded in terms we can ourselves match, richness is found in simple techniques—just as in the game of draughts.

At times Dupin's knowledge is more special, when he refers to Cuvier's description of the orang-outang or shows his familiarity with Maltese marine customs. But this too is no set of mystic insights: it is specific information, explained to us in the text. The basis of Dupin's detection is his assessment of physical data. The material known is real, sense-available, though its analysis is projected at an ideal and theoretical level. The epistemology is at once based on facts and developed through ideal categories. Dupin is both in and above the real world.

The modern detective novel has made so much play with specific physical clues that much in 'The Murders in the Rue Morgue' may now seem obvious. The mystery of the unidentifiable voice, the strange tuft of hair, the inhuman violence itself are all fairly easy to penetrate for readers long used to reified, object-dominated stories. Yet their force in Poe's time is new. There were no clues of this sort in the stories discussed in the previous chapter, and a crucial part of Dupin's force is the ability to see the significance of real objects and sense-data, move through them by Poe's sleight-of-hand, and operate theoretically, untramelled by everyday reality. It is both a triumph over and a release from the mundane puzzles of the physical environment.

Poe combines the twin nineteenth-century legends of the scientist and the artist. Dupin sorts and resolves the puzzles of data in the manner of Cuvier himself. One of the great excitements for the intelligentsia of the period was the growing sense that a sufficiently patient inquirer could explain the structure of puzzling phenom-ena. Another powerful theme, found mostly in art, was that the fully sensitive individual could pass through the limits of the physical environment to see and know at some higher level. Poe's masterly illusion is to make Dupin move from and through the scientific to the special authority of the visionary. But in this story at least, a 'poetic' passive knowledge of higher truths is not Dupin's ultimate being; as he goes out at night into the real world and unfolds tangible mysteries, so he can also be a man of action. At the end of this story he takes out his pistols in case his visitor is troublesome, and his inquiries in the Rue Morgue are detailed and much more accurate than those of the police. He perfects ordinary human observation, then sorts out the data with his illusory 'ideality', and finally applies his conclusions in action with a factual explanation of events. The ivory tower persona is real and crucial, bringing special authority with it, and special ideological consolations, but Dupin is not just an armchair detective.

The narrator is an important part of this bridge between the normal world and a lofty, isolated intellectualism. He is sufficiently like Dupin to be close to him, but like the audience enough to report his deeds with amazement. It is to him that explanations are made, through his eyes and ears the reader follows all, sharing his puzzlement and his helplessness when Dupin goes into seclusion to bring order to his data. When Dupin asks him what he thinks about the murders, he replies in symbolically collective ignorance: 'I could merely agree with all Paris in considering them an insoluble mystery.'

But the narrator is more than a dull background against which Dupin's genius is brightly lit. He is disposed, like the receptive audience of the stories, towards Dupin's values. He travels about with Dupin and does at times *almost* match him. As Dupin discusses the mysterious voice, the narrator says: 'At these words a vague and half-formed conception of the meaning of Dupin flitted over my mind. I seemed to be upon the verge of comprehension, without power to comprehend.' The hero brings the narrator and the reader that power . . . they are encouraged and they believe.

There is more still to the figure of the narrator. An individual who responds to his material and provides a figure of identification for the audience is in itself an emblem of individualism. Earlier texts had a neutral, objective narration that embodied the concept of an integrated society, as has been argued above in the case of *The Newgate Calendar*. Individualised and especially characterised narrators embody the concept that people know the world and exist in it as individuals, not as part of an integrated, mutually reliant society. The particular nature of Poe's narrator does, of course, contain aspects of an intellectual alienation that resembles Dupin's and relates to the overall theme. It parallels the developing bourgeois consciousness of the magazine readers who were Poe's audience and also that relatively small but highly trained and prestigious audience that has so much enjoyed and kept alive Poe's reputation and work in more recent years. The narrator meets Dupin because he too is a book-lover, and the opening of the story insists that they share a good deal. The invitation to join in the narrator's admiration of and closeness to Dupin is only really open to those whose self-concept is in some way like his.

Although there is, as I have tried to explain, a crucial illusion in that Dupin's unworldly powers are applied to real worldly data, this by no means makes the story as socially integrated with real life as the earlier stories discussed in Chapter 1. The alienation of hero and narrator is pervasive. The narrative remains in distant Paris and the nature of the crime and its resolution make the story an ideal example of how this approach can work, rather than being a down-to-earth narrative about crime and its control in a real, experienced community. The crime itself is grotesque, out of the ordinary. But perhaps more importantly, there is no punishment: it is not a real crime at all, but a freak occurrence, and in spite of all appearances no evil or aberration enters the story. The villain is an animal, behaving in a natural way. The extraordinary circumstances can hardly recur; the incident is isolated from the ongoing processes of life and death.

No presentation or analysis of the social causes of disorder is offered, it is merely suggested that strange and terrible things can happen and a clever man will be able to explain them. The crime and the resolution are without history, without recurring roots. This powerful and frighteningly delusive notion is still with us that desocialised, unhistorical understanding can, by deciphering iso-lated problems, resolve them. The whole tends towards an in-dividualist intellectual quietism; the real data involved, the specific knowledge and the action mastered by Dupin all simulate activity, but the story ultimately feeds back into the passivity of the opening description, and the life style adopted by Dupin and the narrator is validated. A comforting fable for skilled and dedicated readers is brilliantly fabricated.

So far the analysis has dealt with content, but the form of 'The Murders in the Rue Morgue' creates an overriding intellectualised epistemology which deals with actuality in a containing rather than an involved way. The most striking aspect of the form is structure; detailed style and presentation tend to follow the same pattern. The story opens with two pages of theory before Dupin is introduced. 'Analysis' is discussed, its lofty nature and its superiority to 'calculation' established, and Poe makes his first statement of the value and self-validating nature of this process: 'As the strong man exults in his physical ability, delighting in such exercises as call his muscles into action, so glories the analyst in that moral activity which *disentangles*.' Neither the strong man nor the analyst, it is clear, acts or feels towards others. The analyst's activity is described as 'moral' but this is passively idealist. The analogy of the strong man gives the illusion that we are moving from theory to reality; this effect develops as Poe moves on with the example of the chess and draughts paradox. Whist is taken as another demonstration. These are concrete examples of the ideal categories being discussed, but they are games, not real activities; the social interaction involved is competitive and self-gratifying, feeding individuality. The themes of this passage belong to the intellectual, subjective ideology of the tale, but the structurally important thing is the presence of this long theoretical beginning which asserts the primacy of thinking over doing by its own relation to the narrative to follow.

The structure of the story as a whole is organic, closely linked, moving to a climax of plot and meaning. The relations between the parts remain in Dupin's intelligence: the unity of the story enacts his power to order and control experience. Poe's comments on other crime fiction show how clearly he felt an overall intellectually-based unity was central to the form and meaning he thought it right to create. Dupin comments that Vidocq 'was a good guesser, and a persevering man. But without educated thought, he erred continuously by the very intensity of his investigations. He impaired his vision by holding the subject too close. He might see, perhaps, one or two points with unusual clearness, but in so doing he, necessarily, lost sight of the whole.' Poe grasps perfectly Vidocq's spontaneous, integrated approach, and indicates his own preference for an alienated, mentally (and artistically) holistic viewpoint. It is hardly surprising that Poe praised *Caleb Williams* for its structure, seeing its unity as much finer than Dickens' less organic form in *Barnaby Rudge*. Poe not only shaped a structure which validated his ideology;

he did it knowingly, with an appropriately conceptual grasp of his design.

The detailed style of the opening sequence dramatises the nature and value of a complicated intelligence, and shows the narrator speaking in a voice Dupin will use later in the story. The vocabulary is fairly learned; verbs tend to be passive; adverbs which assess sagely and inactively the state of things are quite common—and their assessments are personal insights, not the shared evaluations of a *Newgate Calendar* narration. All this creates a disengaged, wise tone. The syntax is extended but not noticeable for being highly subordinated or intricately ordered. The long complex paragraph, depending on one main clause and not unravelling its meaning till the very end, is not a feature of this story, not even in Dupin's most complex pieces of theoretical analysis later on. The complexity of the syntax rises from basically coordinate constructions that continue the flow of information: relative clauses, noun clauses, phrases in parenthesis. There is a balanced judgemental effect. It is more reminiscent of Johnson's solemnly accessible wisdom than James's intricately private insights.

For all its intellectualism Dupin's style, even at its most complicated, is not as fully private and cerebral as that of later writers—though cerebral and self-satisfied enough in its time. This is clear in the final sequence of the story where a dispassionate tone and elaborate syntax together place the action in a controlling frame, enforcing the central idea that disengaged thinking is the fit response to problems:

> 'Let him talk,' said Dupin, who had not thought it necessary to reply. 'Let him discourse; it will ease his conscience. I am satisfied with having defeated him in his own castle. Nevertheless, that he failed in the solution of this mystery is by no means that matter for wonder which he supposes it; in truth, our friend the Prefect is somewhat too cunning to be profound.'

This short sequence brings together the subtle-simple paradox motif with the image of Dupin as a lonely hero—the castle image is fascinatingly aggressive, competitive. The style of the long, intricate sentences ratifies Dupin's power, then this is finally pressed home in a paradoxical and bitingly élitist quotation—from Rousseau himself, high priest of rational romanticism. Poe's imagination works so well that it mobilises the themes and forms of romantic isolative superiority in a complex exuding power to convince readers of its ideological work.

When Dupin is actually 'analysing', the style is crisper: syntactic units are shorter, vocabulary more concrete, verbs much more often active and 'insightful' adverbs less frequent. There turns out to be more brisk reality in Dupin's speech (as in his action) than the lofty introduction led us to expect. In language as in thought-reading and subtle-simple paradoxes Dupin has both a superstructure of complexity and an actual structure of accessible inquiry. A minor pattern of stylistic change in the body of the story supports this greater directness. The narrator's opening shows him capable of speaking at a Dupin-like level, but when he speaks to the great detective he sounds more like the average man. Yet he, and so the self-concept of the audience, remains a little closer to Dupin than to the direct and condensed newspaper quotations and the plain style which represents the narrator reporting the sailor's statement.

The presentation of the material in the story conforms to the structural, stylistic and contentual patterns. There is very little direct action. The substance of the story passes through controlling, selecting intelligences. The events of the murder are reported from newspapers, but even this material, itself already mediated, is tinkered with to suggest meaning. The curiously note-like tone of these reports is not positivist representation of a bizarre contemporary news style, but is Poe's deliberate distortion by which he suggests the fragmentary, baffling nature of these 'real life' data, unsorted yet by an intelligence. Actuality is mediated into a scrambled version, to fabricate the need of an analysing mediator. Events, phenomena—even the people involved—all have no separate comprehensible being until the heroic intelligence processes them. The dissection of these reports is in Dupin's voice, and the actual events in the murder are also firmly mediated, reported by the narrator, from the sailor's account, itself prompted by Dupin.

Poe's presentation and structure work together to create a story which has already happened and which is only brought to us through individual minds which pre-organise it suitably. It is far from the unframed vigorously direct action of *The Newgate Calendar*, set in an ordered context by the shared values scattered through the text, or the excitements of Vidocq's *Memoirs*, perilously controlled by the hero's ever-ready cunning and energy. Poe's audience are listeners and readers, not watchers and doers, and the offered methods of understanding the world are passive responses to life. We

are shielded from raw events, even aberrations of coincidence—
Dupin can explain those away as well.

All these mediated events are linked for us into a single, knowable
pattern. In an interesting book, one of the few to consider Poe's
epistemology in any serious way, David Halliburton has outlined
'Poe's tendency to see every phenomenon in relation to something
greater than itself'. This presentation meshes with that dramatised
in the structure and the style, a unity of form and meaning that is
grasped by the individual, not left assumed and invisible in the
ambient world.

In both form and content Poe realises his ideology with such
imagination there are few signs of a fissure. Those that have been
identified arise more from later preconceptions than from any
contradictions in the realisation. Laura Riding, quoted approvingly
by Julian Symons in *Bloody Murder*, has found several faults with the
story. The police seemed too stupid, making success easy for
Dupin—would they really have left so may clues unnoticed? The
fact that Poe avoids this feature in the later stories might seem to
support the idea that here he makes Dupin too easily great, but
there are other reasons for the reduction in his physical exam-
inations, to be discussed later. In any case, early police methods
were very sketchy and forensic enquiry not at all developed when
Poe was writing: it is Dupin's special skills that bring them into the
story. Improbability has been found in the window that closes itself,
suggesting a mixture of the highly unlikely and the impossible.
Perhaps that is true, but the thrust of Dupin's force is in his theory,
not technicalities and so the criticism is tangential to the real issues.
Poe certainly wanted to make the mechanics sound possible, and he
made them seem so—to all but specialists in his audience. The aura
of technical conviction is important to the ideology, and Poe brings
that off successfully. It is not until Austin Freeman that the audience
can—or needs to—know that each solution has been tested in the
author's own laboratory.

For many modern readers the story's wordiness is a flaw,
especially in the opening sequence, and to some extent in Dupin's
more theoretical passages. This could be seen as a sign of strain, with
Poe swamping the topic in words to insist that verbal skills can
contain disorder. It is hard to be sure if this is an inherent feature:
Victorian readers were used to lengthy discussions in books and
from pulpits. Yet Poe does reduce the introductory and theoretical
passages in the two later stories, and it may well be that the difficulty

and, to him, the importance of the attempt has led to a certain verbose overkill.

E. H. Davidson sees in Poe a strain between mind and reality and, more damagingly, one between feeling and thought. Ultimately, Davidson thinks, 'The split was disastrous . . .'. In terms of the crime stories at least (and the other material too in my opinion) this view finds division where Poe in fact creates an imaginative unity from disparate elements. Whatever was to happen in 'Marie Roget', in 'The Murders in the Rue Morgue' his intellectual, analytic control kept the 'realistic' material of the narrative in its thoroughly mediated place.

The techniques of this control have been noted by some critics. Halliburton has explained how Dupin himself functions dually in 'creative and resolvent aspects'. He works by induction as well as deduction, has inner and outer, dream and observation aspects to his character. Halliburton sets out these dualities, but he feels they are balanced in tension; this fails to see the literary shape and affective force of the tale which throws the weight on to the internal, the isolated, the theoretical aspects of Dupin. A second critic comes closer to seeing how the illusion is shaped. G. R. Thompson calls the mixture of the emotive and the cerebral 'Romantic Irony', and traces its tradition. More importantly, he shows Poe's debt to Schlegel, who had argued that the author should objectively control the work where he has created subjective feeling. Schlegel called such a structure Arabesque—and Poe's full title for his first collection of stories was *Tales of the Grotesque and Arabesque*. The realistic detail in 'The Murders in the Rue Morgue' is certainly treated in a subjective way: the horrible crime, the baffling nature of the events make us feel the disorder directly, and the title itself gives emotive quality to a factual statement in the name of the street. This subjective material is, equally certainly, transformed by the containing treatment at the cerebral level, but this is quasi-objective only. Poe's ideology is not what Schlegel called an 'objective' treatment and found in Cervantes and Shakespeare; Poe presents nothing more than an intellectual and passive subjectivism which urgently persuades itself that its subtle and ideal nature gives it objective status and so validity.

The ultimate movement of the story, like the life-style of Dupin and the narrator, is inward, asocial, satisfied with comfortable alienation. This explains adequately the story's success with a well-educated élite audience over the years. But more specifically personal meanings arise from Poe's own individual anxieties which, naturally, may well also be relevant to the audience which shares the central ideology.

At a simple level it has been suggested Dupin is basically a wishful figure of the author. The book-lover, the aristocrat fallen on bad times, the supreme analyst who reaches the highest realms of the creative imagination—these are certainly aspects of the way Poe saw himself. He too loved creating paradoxes, enjoyed pontificating and showing how wide learning could resolve problems. Robert Daniel has argued that 'Dupin's function in society is one that allowed Poe to dominate society imaginatively when in fact society pretty much rejected him.' This presumably has truth in it, but it is a reductive interpretation that takes no account of the historical reasons why Poe felt asocial or why his presentation of this feeling had power and appeal. The newly isolated position of the artist in a bourgeois market economy, working without patronage, commissions, subscriptions or intimate contact with the audience is a crucial feature in the development of a hero who makes aspects of alienation into weapons of success.

A different insight into the personal pressures that shape the story is given in Marie Bonaparte's Freudian reading of 'The Murders in the Rue Morgue'. She argues that Poe's breach with his editor Burton early in 1841 reactivated his sense of the paternal crime, and this story is consequently drenched with symbolism from the child's anxiety. Chantilly, the stage-struck clown, is Poe's father David: the story rejects and ridicules him. The central action shows Poe's anger at his mother's imprudence in not keeping herself cloistered for him; the ferocious entry of the orang-outang represents the feared masculine attack on his mother, her beheading is the castration that the child both fears and wishes for her; jamming the daughter up the chimney represents a nightmarish return of his sister Rosalie to the womb, so resolving the fears that she was not his father's or even his own—child. A summary cannot convey the power of the argument; details may seem strained, but it is hard to deny that the story has a dynamic only a Freudian approach can explain, and easy to see, the central symbols may well have had similar meaning for many readers—after all, the locked room mystery has been an obsession among the more élitist mystery writers.

A reading of the tale which, at first sight, seems contrary to this has been offered by Richard Wilbur. He has noticed a set of parallels in situation between Dupin, the sailor and the widow and concludes that the action and detail of the story should be read allegorically as 'a soul's fathoming and ordering of itself, its "apprehension" of that base or evil force within it (the orangutan) which would destroy the redemptive principle embodied in Mme L'Espinaye and her daughter'. So Dupin—and by extension Poe 'uses his genius to detect and restrain the brute in himself, thus exorcising the fiend'. The fact that Wilbur presents this as an allegory should not alarm us or suggest he is therefore wrong. In spite of the modern distaste for the word and its connotations, the idealist conceptualisations Poe presents in the opening of the story and elsewhere in his work are fairly described as allegory, and theorists like Bertrand Bronson have shown that personified allegories (concepts like Beauty, Truth, Despair and so on) are only idealised, Platonic versions of what we happily accept as symbolism. The idealist analysis offered by Wilbur in itself has a methodology and epistemology quite akin to the intellectual world-view Poe advocates and dramatises.

The notion that the characters are split facets of one being is itself redolent of medieval allegory (as in *Everyman*, for example), and also of the symbolic treatment of the criminal and the detective as closely related—a feature which Wilbur finds here and is also clearly present in 'The Purloined Letter'. But there are limits to the validity of Wilbur's view. If we paraphrase the story his case seems a good one, but in terms of the story's affective force the heroic emphasis laid on Dupin fights against such a reading: he is not just an aspect of meaning, he is the dominant figure. It may well be that the symbolic anxiety, the potential identity of hero and criminal is a submerged theme in 'The Murders in the Rue Morgue', traceable only at the Freudian level and Wilbur's evidence is strikingly Freudian, coming through name-games and physical locations. This theme, so important in recent crime fiction as a whole, was liberated in 'The Purloined Letter' which is both more successfully imagined as a work of art and more completely internalised and self-conscious than this first story, where the arduous intellectual control may well repress an intuition of criminal kinship.

Elsewhere Poe determinedly asserts intellectual control over his imaginative intuition. His essay on writing 'The Raven' is a classic and relevant case: it claims the text was constructed backwards from the end, like a mystery story. Poe's need for a conscious human control of the threatening world was so strong he was not willing for the imaginative surge to seem inexplicable. In the same way, when through Dupin he first suggested the lonely mind would dominate the alarms of its environment, Poe laid on the cerebral analysis very thickly. Though so much of the action in 'The Murders in the Rue Morgue' is mediated and distanced, he felt the need to swamp it with explanatory words.

The artistic illusion Poe created still works. It remains an illusion, because to bring the story to a comforting resolution Poe, like other crime fiction writers, selected and arranged material that was more tractable than real life. By doing this he created a false dialectic of thought and reality, a bogus problematic that could convince the newly alienated intellectual reader that his own epistemology could stand as an ontology: that all this reading and thinking was a way to live. The fictional control, the illusion and the distancing of the material were essential from the very beginning for the fable to have the necessary ideological power. This becomes fully clear in the second Dupin story where Poe, believing he had created a valid response to life, used his detective's methodology to deal with reality. The failure of 'Marie Roget' is the best indication that 'The Murders in the Rue Morgue' is a powerful and illusory piece of ideological argument, manufacturing validity for a particular view of the world and the human being in—and out of—society.

II 'The Mystery of Marie Roget': A Sequel to 'The Murders in the Rue Morgue'

This story was written less than a year after 'The Murders in the Rue Morgue' was published. In 'Marie Roget' Poe applied Dupin's approach to a real crime which had defeated all attempts to resolve its mystery. Mary Rogers had been found dead in the Hudson River in July 1841. The details of the event and the contemporary accounts of it are laid out in John Walsh's book *Poe the Detective*.

Poe moved the setting from New York to Paris, providing French names and places. This change rose from his desire to make the story a sequel to the previous one, and the effect and much of the cause of the wholesale alteration of the story are related to the ideological pattern of 'The Murders in the Rue Morgue'. The Parisian setting provided the physical distancing basic to Poe's alienated world, and it meshed with the French authority on crime analysis. In the end, the fictional treatment would make it easier for Poe to resolve his difficulties by repudiating any relationship between Marie Roget and Mary Rogers. This neat closure shows how effectively an alienated attitude can sidestep the sheer difficulty of comprehending the stubbornly incoherent data of real life.

The similarities to 'The Murders in the Rue Morgue' are obvious. Dupin and the narrator are much the same; their intellectual seclusion has grown deeper: 'Engaged in researches which had absorbed our whole attention, it had been nearly a month since either of us had gone abroad, or received a visitor, or more than glanced at the leading political articles in one of the daily papers.' The 'researches' are not explained; it is enough that they are neither social nor political. Poe relies to a good extent on the situation created in the earlier story, just as he is content to remind his readers of the 'very remarkable features in the mental character of my friend'. This is not necessarily laziness on his part; in the opening of 'Marie Roget' he attempts a crisper pace than the earlier story offered. This one begins with a learned epigraph and a theoretical discussion as did 'The Murders in the Rue Morgue', but the sequence is much shorter and leads more sharply into the story: the coincidences discussed in such a lofty tone are in fact between this narrative and the actual murder. The opening tone is less slowly cerebral than before and the fact that the narrator tells us directly what happened creates a less mediated account of events. Only after he gives the basic facts does he explain how the Prefect introduced the friends to the case, and how the newspapers themselves were a source of knowledge.

This interesting change of presentation, reducing the complex distancing of the earlier story, is itself linked to the real—though transplanted—nature of the events. A more business-like and direct approach is the corollary of Poe's bold attempt to analyse a genuine problem. But as the story steadily insists on the power of thought there is a strong formal resemblance to the earlier pattern. Complex argument flows while Dupin assesses the newspaper accounts. First he gives a version of the subtle-simple paradox so common in the earlier story. Here, he says, the ordinariness of the crime has misled the journalists: they might dream up explanations easily enough, but 'the ease with which these variable fancies were entertained, and the very plausibility which each assumed, should have been understood as indicative rather of the difficulties than of the facilities which must attend elucidation'. His analysis of the reports and, especially, the flotation of corpses is long and intricate. Dealing with a real problem causes Poe to adopt an initially brisker tone and

then to flounder while Dupin attempts to control these mysterious
and now real events.

The narrator's verbal style has broadly the same pattern as
before, though with a shorter opening he does not show so marked a
change from lofty cerebration to a humbler, easily impressed tone.
The newspaper narratives are more varied than before. This is partly
because much of the material is literally quoted from real reports,
but even when Poe invents them (or parts of them – Walsh has the
details), he varies his style to suggest the lack of a uniform, lucid
voice. In the previous story Poe gave reports in a deliberately
crippled note form to emphasise their incoherence and Dupin's
genius. Here, where he hopes to explain real events, he gives the
news in a less manipulated form, but still emphasises its confusion.
Yet the way to resolution is implied in the variety, because a
relationship exists between elaboration and reliability. The more
complex narratives, as we might expect, are the ones Dupin finds
most valid when he subjects them to his scrutiny.

Dupin's own style is very much like that of the earlier story. His
language first implies special powers and then deals with material
issues in a more matter-of-fact tone. The early lecture on corpses in
water contrasts with the later exposition of evidence on the thicket
and the gang. This latter sequence, after Dupin's week of successful
reflection, is a nicely judged mixture of the authoritative and the
dramatic, with frequent emphasis to etch Dupin's mental power,
pressing busily on through the coordinate, ordering speech: 'But
would a *number* of men have put themselves to the superfluous
trouble of taking down a fence for the purpose of dragging through it
a corpse which they might have *lifted over* any fence in an instant?
Would a *number* of men have so dragged a corpse at all as to have left
evident *traces* of the dragging?'

The stress in this last sequence falls on the hard physical evidence;
the presentation develops from the theory-based understanding of
Dupin's early analysis to the firmly practical; the shift is just that of
'The Murders in the Rue Morgue', creating dramatically the idea
and the illusion that cerebral powers deal best with tangible
problems. The structure and presentation of this long central
sequence is well conceived: the reader is to be swept along and
convinced by its affective force that Dupin can bring order. But a
fissure is plain when the solution offered is less than convincing. And
indeed there are some signs of strain within the development of the
story that create this final failure; the supplied content does not

manage to ratify the pattern of meaning that the form here implies, and that the earlier story had completely fulfilled.

First there are inherent difficulties that Poe does not conquer in Dupin's analysis of events. Walsh has criticised some features of the argument. In particular he feels Dupin is wrong to say the gap between Marie's two disappearances 'is a few months more than the general period of the cruises of our men-of-war', and he dismisses the argument offered to prove that the deduced sailor must be an officer. Like the window mechanics in 'The Murders in the Rue Morgue' these are weaknesses, but in both stories they are glossed over by the force of Dupin's and Poe's presentation. They certainly reveal feebleness in the detective method—as Walsh argues, there is no 'general period' for cruises, and the class relationship of girls and sailors is less simple than Dupin believes. Yet successful detective stories work by an illusion of logic, not by being a reprinted police dossier.

The real weakness in Dupin's analysis is, as many readers have felt, that the story does not keep its illusory confidences going, that the argument falters. This shows in process the strain Poe felt in applying his method to these real events. It is clear in the discussion of floating corpses and the time of the murder, and to some extent in the final treatment of gangs and thickets. The indecisive tone of this latter section has a special cause, to be examined shortly, but as he tries to establish when corpses float and when the murder was committed, Poe simply flounders. This is emphasised because, as has already been argued, he here tries to sustain a learned speculative tone to validate Dupin's position as a real intellectual— the later shift to a simpler tone avoids this 'running on the spot' effect. The fact that the argument does not arrive anywhere makes the complex coordinate syntax seem all the more inconclusive. It may well be that Poe's contemporary audience did not find the movement as turgid as we do, being more leisured and more inclined to admire the relatively new phenomenon of a floridly cerebral forensic argument. But there remains the fact that as Poe does not know the answer to the problem he cannot shape a steady movement towards it with the elegance so effective in the other two stories. The wordiness that blurs the effect in 'The Murders in the Rue Morgue' is here more damaging: if the narrative is not a clearly resolved triumph any traces of indecision in the process of argument emphasise an uncertain effect.

Such a resolution is lacking; the end of the story suggests a naval officer is the criminal, but Dupin does not identify him, only suggests where further inquiries must be pursued. His own confidence and Poe's rhetorical skill work hard to assure us that the problem is solved: 'This boat shall guide us with a rapidity which will surprise even ourselves to him who employed it in the midnight of the fatal Sabbath. Corroboration will rise upon corroboration, and the murder will be traced.' A footnote Poe added suggests this did indeed happen, and though generations of literary critics accepted the statement without question, it is not at all the same as having Dupin's full resolution of the crime confirmed, as happens in the other two stories.

Poe himself makes it clear he was not fully satisfied, or was not willing to stake all on Dupin's resolution, when he writes another paragraph insisting this was all no more than a coincidental analogue to the tragedy of Mary Rogers. This picks up with organically united effect the epigraph and opening of the story. Walsh argues forcefully it was the final paragraph of the original draft, so ending with a lofty and obfuscating sequence about our inability to reason our way through to understanding in the face of Divine Omniscience: 'With God all is Now.' This quite contradicts the claim of the story, that inspired reason can resolve intractable difficulties—but the real difficulties encountered along the way were resolved by this unusually pious ending.

If Poe did, as is most probable, conclude the story this way and did not wish to rest too strongly on his offered resolution of the mystery, he showed surprising prescience. After he had completed the manuscript and it was already part published, news broke in the Rogers case which clearly pointed away from his offered conclusion. This led him to tinker with his ending, so weakening the literary and ideological effect of Dupin's final argument. He added some short remarks that make Dupin's judgements disconcertingly irresolute: 'We have attained the idea either of a fatal accident under the roof of Madame Deluc, or of a murder perpetrated in the thicket at the Barrière du Roule, by a lover, or at least by an intimate and secret associate of the deceased.' The point about Madame Deluc is quite unsupported by the argument: this and a series of similar remarks about her involvement rose, as Walsh indicates, from the fact that in November 1842 Mrs Loss, who owned the inn near the alleged site of the murder, appears to have made a dying confession of involvement in Mary Rogers' death—an abortion seems to be implied in some of the reticent contemporary accounts. This led Poe to hedge his bets in Dupin's summing-up, and in all probability to add two lengthy paragraphs at the very end, which deny more strongly than did the 'coincidence' paragraph, which presumably ended the first draft, that there was any suggested parallel between Mary Rogers and Marie Roget.

It is a fascinating development. Some of the slowness and uncertainty of Dupin's analysis came from the difficulty Poe found in dealing with the problem, but here the uncertainty rises from a rift between Poe's own solution and the apparent cause of the real death. Dealing with reality has not only made the material hard to resolve, but means it can take a sudden and disturbing turn. Poe felt he could give only a suggested conclusion to the story, but it gave itself a quite different one. The attempt to order life's disorder by cerebration has not only proved hard, but a genuine failure.

In his first paragraph of conclusion Poe fell back on the protective device of 'coincidence' he built in from the beginning. The crime in 'The Murders in the Rue Morgue' had been caused by sheer chance and this, as has been argued, allowed the story to ignore the social and historical realities of crime. Here coincidence is used, in a different but still ideological way, to protect Poe's recommended approach to reality from its evident weakness. But then in the final paragraphs he brushes aside his problems with an argument deriving even more directly from the world-view he has espoused. True 'analysis', he implies, stands back from petty detail, and does not compare similar cases like those of Marie Roget and Mary Rogers. Using a metaphor from mathematics—probability in dice-throwing—he dismisses studies that concern themselves short-sightedly with detail. He has sought to be accurate, to calculate in detail about genuine events, but is defeated and finally withdraws. With great rhetorical skill he uses the language of 'calculation', mathematics itself, to validate his rejection of such an approach. The answer is to move into the ideal, to ignore the detail that is our confusing everyday experience. Detail has frustrated his approach, so the intellectual theorises his way out of the problem.

The attempt to 'analyse' reality was not totally unsuccessful. One of the many notable features of 'Marie Roget' is that Poe did show real detective ability. His suspicions that the clothes in the thicket were false clues seem, in the light of the Loss 'confession', to have been both original and well founded; and for all their complication his remarks about corpses are full of the shrewdness lacking in the newspaper reports. He did successfully interpret some real events and he did make headway in ordering part of the chaos. But not completely: the man who could fairly claim to have predicted the outcome of *Barnaby Rudge* had here taken on life, not fiction, and the illusory nature of his ideology was exposed by the intrinsic complexity of reality and a perverse turn of events.

It was a serious effort, and this attempt to move outward from subjectivity towards an objective understanding of events is no doubt the reason why individualist critical interpretations that worked so well with 'The Murders in the Rue Morgue' are barren here. Bonaparte says 'Marie Roget' is a 'very feeble replica of the first story' and merely suggests it embodies Poe's sado-necrophile passion for his wife, the sailor representing basically his admired brother Harry. The argument is more far-fetched than before, because Freudian anxieties are obstructed by the non-subjective effort of the story. For the same reason Wilbur's allegorical approach finds no material here: the idealistic level is only fully invoked at the end, to extricate the author from the tangles of reality.

These scholars have more to say, though, about the last of the Dupin stories. It is hardly surprising that when Poe again dramatised a Dupin-like approach to resolve problems, he kept firmly within the bounds of fiction—and this time a fiction further removed from life than the grotesque but at least physical and tangible crime in the Rue Morgue. 'The Purloined Letter' is not only the most famous of the Dupin stories and the most dramatically successful, it is also the most purely fantastic, the one where intellectual powers are realised in a quite fanciful environment. It keeps well away from the disturbing actualities that had finally frustrated the brave attempt in 'Marie Roget' to employ the world-view developed in 'The Murders in the Rue Morgue' against the everyday challenge of genuine criminal disorder.

III 'The Purloined Letter'

Poe did not return to the detective story pattern until 1845, but 'The Purloined Letter' develops directly from his problems in writing 'Marie Roget'. This is plain in modern collected editions of the *Tales of Mystery and Imagination*, where the last words of 'Marie Roget' are closely followed by the epigraph of the later story. Too much detail obscures and misleads the analytic mind: that was Poe's formula to gloss over the failure of 'Marie Roget'. In 'The Purloined Letter' the point is made at once, and in appropriately elevated manner. No less an authority than Seneca tells us in the epigraph that 'Nil sapentiae odiosius acumine nimia—Nothing is more hostile to wisdom than too much cunning.'

The plot of the story dramatises this theme; the meticulous police searches are futile without Dupin's uninvolved, cerebrally powerful viewpoint. In 'The Murders in the Rue Morgue' Dupin searched better than the police and this revealed the 'acumen' on which his analysis was based. A detailed, data-involved type of investigation failed to feed theoretical investigation successfully in 'Marie Roget', and here Poe takes an approach whose determined intangibility enables the story to cast its comforting spell.

In keeping with this greater distancing of Dupin and this fuller statement of the passive, generalised force of his method, we here find modifications in both content and form from the earlier stories. Both the villain and Dupin are poets, and their special powers are generally associated with that status. The narrator, while still Dupin's friend, is more obviously in line with the Prefect of Police in character and attitudes. In the opening sequence the narrator is more forceful than before. He shares the confidence and the business-like manner of the Prefect, both of which Dupin destroys. The detective's greater isolation and authority in this story are implied in one vivid sentence. The Prefect proudly announces that the 'illustrious personage' has committed the matter to him: ' "Than whom," said Dupin, amid a perfect whirlwind of smoke, "no more sagacious agent could, I suppose, be desired, or even imagined." ' The superhuman voice in the whirlwind commands a highly intricate tone and also speaks in the indirect, innately superior mode of heavy irony. A reader who does not share Poe's ideology might feel the negativity of the tone and content in itself discloses the nature and value of the position.

There is another striking moment in the opening sequence, when Dupin realises the Prefect has come on business: ' "If it is any point requiring reflection," observed Dupin, as he forbore to enkindle the wick, "we shall examine it to better purpose in the dark." ' Love of the dark was present in the first story, but this initiative shows a crisper, more decisive Dupin. What in 'The Murders in the Rue Morgue' was a general mood of unease, preferring gloom, has here become a firm piece of method, part of a set system of enquiry. Dupin's statement might seem odd, even comic, but the complexity of the writing ('forbore to enkindle the wick') suggests that Poe, through the narrator, supports the intricacy of tone and the arch, unusual action. Dupin has begun to function in the caricature-like way of the heroes of formula stories, which briefly sketch the main symbolic features of the hero's power and then demonstrate with quick sureness his inevitable triumph. Such formulaic heroes are central to crime fiction; the thorough establishment of Dupin in the earlier stories has in this one been set aside for a comforting deployment of the ideological apparatus in confident action.

In this opening sequence Dupin's style and the presentation of his thoughts are by no means as elaborate and lengthy as in the passages of reasoned complex argument that dominated the two previous stories. A paragraph must be quoted to convey the effect. The Prefect says why he has come:

> ' . . . I make no doubt that we can manage it sufficiently well ourselves; but then I thought Dupin would like to hear the details of it, because it is so excessively odd.'
>
> 'Simple and odd,' said Dupin.
>
> 'Why, yes; and not exactly that, either. The fact is we have all been a good deal puzzled because the affair *is* so simple and yet baffles us altogether.'
>
> 'Perhaps it is the very simplicity of the thing which puts you at fault,' said my friend.
>
> 'What nonsense you *do* talk.' replied the Prefect, laughing heartily.
>
> 'Perhaps the mystery is a little *too* plain,' said Dupin.
>
> 'Oh, good heavens, who ever heard of such an idea?'
>
> 'A little *too* self-evident.'

The basis of what Dupin says is the subtle-simple paradox argued out at some length in 'The Murders in the Rue Morgue', present in the opening of 'Marie Roget' but submerged by the attempt to reason out the real mystery in detail. Here the theme is stated at once, repeated in a confident, almost insulting tone. Although Dupin knows none of the details of the case, he has assumed this is its nature. He is right; in fact he has already given the solution. The hidden object will be self-evident, nothing more than a letter in a letter-rack.

The scene states a crucial change in the detective's methodology that the rest of the tale will enact. He does not need to undertake lengthy inquiries, think possibilities slowly through to their only correct interpretation. The intricacies of reasoning, finally dismissed in 'Marie Roget' and excluded by the epigraph from the values of this story, have become unnecessary to the method. Dupin is now more seer than scientist, as the 'whirlwind' image and his status as poet symbolically make plain. What in 'The Murders in the Rue Morgue' was a tension between rational and imaginative has (because of the failure of the imaginative triumph to emerge from the rational methodology in 'Marie Roget') become a decisive rejection of rational procedures. Dupin knows—that is the meaning of this story.

Poe does not sever Dupin entirely from the world of thought. His lengthy speech to the narrator about the Prefect's mistakes shows both knowledge and rejection of the methods of 'acumen', of 'calculation'. It dramatically validates Dupin's position, his brisk attitude to the Prefect in the opening exchange. Dupin has become a superman of knowledge, and his progress from the first to the last of these three stories tells in brief the initial fascination with science and the ultimate rejection of it that is marked in imaginative literature of the nineteenth century. The ability of the great artist to sense and realise in art the inner dramas of his culture is evident and it is not surprising that an adventurous individual artist like Baudelaire felt Poe was writing sentences he had himself thought.

Poe realised this newly limited ideology in the form of 'The Purloined Letter'. Where the attempt to create a hero who is both imaginative and rational had committed Poe to long stories and extended arguments, his rejection of 'detail' now enables him to write a much shorter, more actively dramatic story. The process of fining down the lengthy and sometimes stodgy sequences of 'The Murders in the Rue Morgue' is already present in the opening of 'Marie Roget', but the intractability of the material prevented the crisp drama of 'The Purloined Letter'. We also find a precision of scene and imaginative detail that may rise from Poe's sense that he has mastered his topic and knew how the story should work. But the presentation, the epistemology embedded in the detailed information is just that mediated, cerebrally organised mode that was so clear in both the earlier works, now sharpened and increasingly individualised.

After a brief theoretical opening, the problem is presented directly with the voices of the Prefect and the narrator setting out in puzzled yet confident terms the apparent facts. Dupin reacts quizzically and negatively, rejecting any share in this approach. Facing reality, reporting it realistically, leads nowhere. He is quite distanced from them both and their method, though the position is sharply presented, not theorised at length; in rejecting their realistic mode Dupin deepens the mystification of his own position. His advice is simple—search again thoroughly. A month passes: previously the reader at least knew Dupin was making inquiries, but now the narrative is silent. The resolution here is to be quite mysterious, produced suddenly from the sage's arcanity after a short scene with the Prefect baffled and Duplin sarcastic. He teases him with a story conveying the arrogance and acquisitiveness of the professional man. Doctor Abernethy advised the miser to take advice, so outwitting him, asserting his own professional mystique and, presumably, gaining some of his money. The notion that knowledge is personal property, that the specially qualified man receives not only respect but cash for his private skills responds directly to the ideology of the bourgeois professional intelligentsia who were and still are the central audience for the cerebral detective story. Interestingly, Dupin is no longer the narrator's protégé; he has emerged into a world of cash payments, as the story soon reveals.

The resolution of the problem is explained entirely in Dupin's voice. There is no question here of the sailor's confirming narrative; Dupin's judgement now needs no external support. The story ends with the insulting intellectualism found at the end of 'The Murders in the Rue Morgue'—but again with a crucial difference. There it was the Prefect who suffered Dupin's wounding tongue; here it is the criminal, the real adversary in the story. Dupin is so much above the Prefect now that his final superiority is over the one character who did challenge him at his level, who was also a poet. The power of wit and hostility in the earlier story merely raised Dupin above the herd of investigators. Here, with Dupin's status as given, briefly sketched at the opening of the story, his wit and aggression are aligned against the agents of disorder: alienation is assumed now, victory is important. In this, as in so much of 'The Purloined Letter', Poe has brought the components in line with the increased force and confidence of his protagonist, an assured archetypal hero of the ideological fable developed in the earlier stories.

The fable element is clear in the setting of the story. The first was about murder, though hardly a realistic crime. After his attempt to analyse real crime in 'Marie Roget' Poe has withdrawn into a world of intangible fictions. No more has been lost than a letter, and we never know anything about its contents, or exactly how it was usable. Nor do we know precisely who the victims were   though, as in so many fairy-stories, they are royal. We move in a dimly perceived world of high romance—rejection of realism and detailed specific presentation together. This characteristic led Daniel Hoffman to call 'The Purloined Letter' 'a boy's tale'. The almost childish simplicity and the fantasy element release the narrative from the everyday and enable its essentially idealistic nature to work all the more credibly in its own terms. The criticisms that have been made of the story work on a quite foreign premise: it has been said that the husband of the 'illustrious personage' would have wanted to know what was in the letter and all would have come out. Equally it has been suggested that if the Prefect's search was so thorough, covering 'every square inch' then he must, in fact, have found the letter. But the sweeping conviction given to Dupin's own authority and the blurred fable-like setting quite dispose of such mean-mindedly naturalistic ideas. The presentation and argument are true to the ideology: the lofty romantic setting and vagueness of detail clear a way through the awkward incoherence of everyday life, and so the story enacts a romance about the power of the free floating super-intelligence.

That illusion is emotionally filled out by individualist, subjective elements of submerged meaning. Where Bonaparte had difficulty making much out of 'Marie Roget', her Freudian account of this story is a riot of gripping detail. Once again only a close reading can bring out her full impact, but essentially she sees the letter as a symbol of the penis lost in the castration which the child believes his mother has suffered: the chimney and the button from which the letter hangs represent the vagina and the clitoris. Dupin and D. fight an Oedipal battle not for the mother herself but her organ, hence a battle conceived in pregenital terms   a feature deriving from Poe's arrested sexual development.

As before, we do not have to believe in the Freudian analysis exclusively, or to accept every detail to acknowledge that much of the memorable strength of the story derives from the deep-rooted power in its imagery and suggestive detail. And such an in-terpretation is not without its social implications; it is within an individuated consciousness that such material becomes the sub liminal topic of art. The very absence of a shame-oriented consciousness, the weakening of the artistic superego brings the personal, guilt-oriented material into the range of the creative imagination of a writer with Poe's responsive power and here, where the story has moved quite away from any realistic topic, this theme is all the more free to be realised.

Just as before, the idealistic interpretation also carries weight and integrates with the individualist anxieties. The concept of duality is very strong; the themes that Wilbur finds hidden in 'The Murders in the Rue Morgue' are patent. D.'s name proclaims him a coded version of Dupin; he is a poet, a man of powers almost equal to the hero: his position as a Jungian 'shadow' is very clear. As the individual hero has emerged easily clear of the 'calculating' herd, the story directs his conflict towards the malign possibilities of his own powers. Poe perceives and realises in lucid form the superman's capacity for good and evil; the Nietzschean position is already imagined. This can arise because of the thoroughgoing individualism of the pattern: neither D.'s threat nor Dupin's resolution have any social relevance. The worst D. could do was to jeopardise 'the honour and peace' of the 'illustrious personage', and honour has no social function in the world-view of this story. Dupin's motives are personal triumph over a worthy, largely internalised opponent, and—by the way—a lot of money. The hero conquers the dangers inherent in his own powers and through such self-control gains personal glory and financial success: Dupin personifies so much in the Victorian view of what makes a great man.

Another aspect of the theme, closer to Poe's own profession, is that a letter is the central precious object; his own craft of writing provides the dynamic object that energises the mysterious romance. Jacques Lacan's 'Seminar' on the tale takes up the symbolism of the letter itself, and shows how the individual subject verifies its existence by purloining literary and linguistic media for its own ideology. He argues the letter is symbolically an alphabetical sign and develops his position that language is the central means by which the subject, personal and grammatical at once, conjures itself into being. Lacan's perceptions are far-reaching and the whole individualist epistemology and ontology of crime fiction are in accord with them. A point similar to the 'letter' ambiguity can be made about the crucial importance of newspapers in the earlier stories, and Walsh makes the interesting comment that the fascination of the Mary Rogers case itself depended on the self-consciousness New York papers had developed. But even the limited social awareness represented by reading newspapers is absent from 'The Purloined Letter'—and the title itself spirals in on the central single object.

In this story Poe created a powerful fable about a hero who brought intellect, imagination and self-consciousness to such heights he did not need painstaking study to cut through a problem that bemused others. The self-gratifying illusion of this fable for passive intellectuals is the more powerful because of the fabulous setting—the events are abroad, royal and only vaguely described in any case. The dynamic of the story is for and towards the skilled literate individual. The fable had force for Poe, of course, the troubled struggling man all too aware of his extraordinary ability and his relative failure. His own obsession with plagiarism (of his work and that of others) reveals the writer as an individual whose thoughts were the only property that can bring value and security. In the brilliant, acknowledged and lucrative success of Dupin in this last tale he created a figure who assuaged the anxieties he felt, and did so in the terms by which he viewed the world. The success of all his stories with the romantic symbolist poets in France indicates the figure he finally brought to a head in 'The Purloined Letter' was more than a personal totem. His own anxieties were those of a whole class of alienated writers and intellectuals of his time and of succeeding periods. Poe realised his theme so powerfully that although no later writer has been so completely asocial, his formal patterns have remained authoritative. This is clear in the work of his direct descendant and the great populariser of crime fiction, Arthur Conan Doyle.

REFERENCES

Text
Tales of Mystery and Imagination, Everyman's Library, Dent, London, reprint 1975.

Criticism
Poe discussed *Caleb Williams* in a review of *Barnaby Rudge* and other novels, published in *Graham's Magazine*, Feb. 1842, reprinted in the Virginia edition of *The Complete Works of Edgar Allan Poe*, AMS, New York, 1965 (reprint), vol. XI, 38–64. Poe's remarks on 'The Raven', also including some comments on *Caleb Williams*, are in 'The Philosophy of Composition', *Graham's Magazine*, Apr. 1846, also see *Complete Works*, vol. XIV, 193–208.

Marie Bonaparte, *Edgar Poe: Etude Analytique*, Denoel et Steele, Paris, 1933.

3 '. . . a great blue triumphant cloud'—*The Adventures of Sherlock Holmes*

No literary figure has a stronger hold on the public imagination than Sherlock Holmes. The name is a synonym for a detective; he has been parodied, imitated and recreated in all media with great success. The triumph of the figure made Conan Doyle wealthy, but forced him to keep writing Holmes's adventures and discuss him in public when he much preferred other topics. These pressures are irresistible proof of real social meaning in the stories. The embarrassing success depended on the hero's power to assuage the anxieties of a respectable, London-based, middle-class audience. The captivated readers had faith in modern systems of scientific and rational enquiry to order an uncertain and troubling world, but feeling they lacked these powers themselves they, like many audiences before them, needed a suitably equipped hero to mediate psychic protection.

When Doyle was trying to make a living as a doctor he took up freelance writing to earn more—the artistic activities of his male relatives were a stimulus and a model. He had some success with short stories and as a writer in search of sales he naturally enough came upon the detective story. In *Memories and Adventures* he recalls:

At this time I first thought of a detective—it was about 1886. I had been reading some detective stories and it struck me what nonsense they were, to put it mildly, because for getting the solution of the mystery, the authors always depended on some coincidence. This struck me as not a fair way of playing the game, because the detective ought really to depend for his successes on something in his own mind and not on merely adventitious circumstances which do not, by any means, always occur in real life.

Doyle has two premises: the rational scientific idea that events are really linked in an unaccidental chain, and the individualistic notion that a single inquirer can—and should—establish the links. He domesticates these ideas by his nerveless style and familiar asides—'to put it mildly', 'by any means'; and he uses game language to make an ethical faith in this ideology seem both pleasant and natural. Doyle's ability to popularise and naturalise rational individualism runs through the stories and is central to their success.

When he fashioned a figure to carry his meaning he turned, like many others who have drifted out of religion, to an academic intellectual model. He thought of his own outstanding teacher, Dr Joseph Bell, who gave demonstrations of 'deduction', diagnosing from mere observation his patients' characteristics as well as their illnesses. Even the physique of Holmes owes something to Bell. There may have been a stage when Doyle thought of making his inquirer a doctor. In his diary he records his reading of Emile Gaboriau's *M. Lecoq*, obviously one of the novels he hoped to surpass. On the same page he sketches the history of an army doctor, much like that given to Watson in the opening of *A Study in Scarlet*. It would have been odd for Doyle to conceive of his narrator before his hero; the implication that a doctor detective preceded Holmes fits Adrian Conan Doyle's statement that he had seen a draft of *A Study in Scarlet* which did not contain Holmes. It may also explain the curiously forceful name, Ormond Sacker, given to the Watson figure in a surviving note which sketches in the first details of the emerging figure of Holmes—who was then christened 'Sherrinford'.

When Doyle did decide on a detective hero, the medical link remained. Holmes is neither a languid amateur like Dupin nor a professional policeman like Lecoq; his position as a consulting detective is parallel to that of a medical specialist—and this is what Doyle then aspired to be. By the time he started the short stories he had set up as an eye specialist in Devonshire Place, round the corner from Baker Street. Holmes was a heightened version of Doyle's own ambitions; a man of science, acting independently, serving the community. Watson was a deliberately lowered version of Doyle himself, humourless and plodding but full of sound virtues. Between them Doyle would realise the virtues he, like many of his class and time, had most faith in—those of middle-class morality and individualised rationality.

Another model is Robert Louis Stevenson. His influence has not been noticed very often; unlike Poe and Gaboriau, Doyle does not make Holmes refer to him, presumably because Stevenson wrote no specifically detective stories. *The Rajah's Diamond* and *The Dynamiter* were published with success in 1882 and 1885 respectively and a good deal of plot material for the first two long stories came from them. More generally, Doyle borrowed their mood and setting: they showed young professional men encountering crime, surprises and love in modern London under the overall protection and guidance of the aristocratic, all-knowing and deeply ethical Prince Florizel of *The Suicide Club*, now made more accessible as the *patron* of a Soho cigar-divan. Such stories had obvious appeal to the young men who had, as economists now put it, disposable personal income. The first Holmes adventures, *A Study in Scarlet* and *The Sign of Four*, convey a less whimsical version of Stevenson's pattern. In them Watson discovers London, a wife and the amazing and comforting authority of Holmes. These publications did not have Stevenson's success, but then they did not appear in London periodicals; when Doyle had a major magazine outlet his less excitable, better controlled and more plainly ethical fables of adventure against disorder in London were to eclipse what Stevenson had achieved.

In the two novellas Doyle developed the characters of Holmes and Watson, the 'deductive' method, and the blend of a material and exciting presentation that was to be important to his success. In structure these first two works differ from the short stories which fully created the Holmes phenomenon. With their length and their retrospective elements they are slower and less organically united, less swiftly converging on a climax of revelation than the later adventures. The retrospective pattern derives from Gaboriau, and like him the novellas present the crime as being a largely justified punishment for past immorality. As a result they tend, like Stevenson's tales, to be a sensationalist inspection of crime from the outside, not the internalised realisation of aberrance that will appear later. The novellas are lively and original developments on the earlier patterns, but they do not fully dramatise the ideology so pervasive and so important in Doyle's great success. A grasp of the meaning of the Holmes phenomenon must come from a study of the material that first gripped a mass audience, and this chapter will concentrate on *The Adventures of Sherlock Holmes*, the collected reprint of the first twelve short stories.

By early 1891 Doyle had moved on from the Holmes novellas to historical novels. *Micah Clarke* had been well received and *The White*

Company, then appearing in *The Cornhill Magazine*, satisfied him deeply. Historical moralism was to be his mode. But these novels demanded slow research and to supplement his meagre income as an eye consultant Doyle turned back to Sherlock Holmes and submitted two short stories to the new and successful magazine *The Strand*. Greenhough Smith, the editor, was very impressed; he later recalled that he ran to the office of George Newnes, the proprietor, and told him excitedly this was the work of the best short story writer since Poe.

Newnes had established himself with *Tit-Bits*, a weekly paper which culled the world of news and literature for small interesting items. It aimed at the growing audience of literate but hurried readers who sought diversion and a sense of contact with a world that seemed increasingly complex. Then he moved on to *The Review of Reviews* which offered guidance through the world of serious periodical literature for those without the time   and probably the expertise   to master it. Newnes' strength already was to compress and popularise material for an urban audience aware of modern forces but unable to handle them adequately.

He struck his goldmine when, aiming between his earlier efforts, he designed a new magazine that had a bourgeois, middle-brow content and a satisfyingly modern format. *The Strand* started in 1890 and the first issue sold 300,000 copies. It cost sixpence (quite a small sum compared with other journals), was widely distributed through railway bookstalls to catch the commuting white-collar market, and was strikingly up-to-date in form. Newnes imitated the rising American magazines by having an illustration on every opening, using newly developed photographic and photo-etching techniques to lighten and dramatise the text.

The contents of early copies define the magazine's ideology: prominent are the biographies of successful men, stories about courage and adventure, features about new machines. But there are also stories that realise bourgeois sentimental morality, and sections for housewives and children regularly occur. The magazine was to be read and taken home by the white-collar man who worked in London. It was a central piece of middle-class ideological literature, oriented towards the family and respectable success in life. The cover of the magazine brought form and content into a masterly union: an etching from a photograph of The Strand itself, taken just where the head office was located. The busy and then fashionable street had rich symbolic meaning: it stretched from the city where the purchasers mostly worked to the West End where they might one day aspire to live. The anxious, alienated, upwards-looking white-collar workers of the capital were caricatured in the Grossmiths' tellingly titled *The Diary of a Nobody*; in *The Strand Magazine* they could find a validation of their morality and a prospect of all they could look forward to, in dreams at least.

There are many relations between the meaning of the Holmes stories and the world-view of *The Strand* and its purchasers. It is best to assess first how the form of the stories worked, how Doyle affectively created patterns that supported, even developed, the attitudes of his audience. With these formations in view, it will be easy to understand how the nature of the plot and detail shapes a problematic responding to the concerns of the audience and resolvable in comforting terms.

The titles of the short stories have the crisp materialism, the briskly objective, unemotive quality that Doyle first encapsulated in the title of *The Sign of Four*. This final version was itself just a little firmer and more mysterious than 'The Sign of the Four' the title of the original American publication, commissioned by *Lippincott's Magazine*. Most of the short story titles are briskly specified: 'The Beryl Coronet', 'The Noble Bachelor', 'The Blue Carbuncle'. Some titles use a material but unexpected qualifier to create an enigma: 'The Engineer's Thumb', 'The Five Orange Pips', 'The Speckled Band'. The early titles 'A Scandal in Bohemia', 'A Case of Identity' and 'The Boscombe Valley Mystery' include a less material term that suggests the genre of the stories. But they too have an objective aura, clearly abandoning the manipulative rhetoric Doyle sought in his first title 'A Study in Scarlet'. That was originally 'A Tangled Skein', a weakly emotive title, and the final choice is reminiscent of Gaboriau's melodramas, especially *L'Affaire Lerouge* (although Lerouge is the murdered woman's surname). The rejection of this emotive element is quite conscious: in *The Sign of Four* Watson refers to the 'somewhat fantastic title' of the previous adventure.

The early stories show a brisk attack from the beginning. Like *The Sign of Four* the first three adventures all use Sherlock Holmes's name in the opening sentence. The initial paragraphs are increasingly crisp and briefly suggestive. One of the motives is Doyle's conscious production of a series, encouraging regular purchase of the magazine; he assumed that readers of the later stories would know the established patterns and characters. But at the same time he wanted to grip the audience, plunge them into the matter with less of the narrator's comment than opens 'A Scandal in Bohemia'. The direct openings bring the hero into active involvement with problems, reducing his earlier aloof distance from the reader and his world. This effect is also created by the greater simplicity of the endings. In the two novellas and in 'The Red-Headed League' Doyle continues Poe's pattern, giving his detective a final comment, separated from the action both by its lofty, judging tone and its foreign language. In 'A Case of Identity' the comment is translated, and from then on they disappear; the final disengaging remarks, when they occur, are English and moralistic, not isolated pieces of intellectualism.

These features all tend to involve the hero in action, not isolate him in cerebration like Dupin. This model responds to the world-view of a basically uncerebral audience, and it is most fully created by the varied and dramatic action. The pace accelerates as Holmes comes to grips with his problem: the paragraph where he studies the King of Bohemia's notepaper is a fine example of a vigorous and object-dominated presentation which enacts the worldly involvement of the hero. Watson examines the paper and sees some letters in its watermark:

> 'What do you make of that?' asked Holmes.
> 'The name of the maker, no doubt; or his monogram, rather.'
> 'Not at all. The *G* with the small *t* stands for 'Gesellschaft', which is the German for 'Company'. It is a customary contraction like our 'Co.'. *P*, of course, stands for 'Papier'. Now for the *Eg*. Let us glance at our Continental Gazeteer.'
> He took down a heavy brown volume from his shelves.
> 'Eglow, Eglonitz – here we are, Egria. It is in a German-speaking country – in Bohemia, not far from Carlsbad. "Remarkable as being the scene of the death of Wallenstein, and for its numerous glass factories and paper mills." Ha, ha, my boy, what do you make of that?' His eyes sparkled, and he sent up a great blue triumphant cloud from his cigarette.

Details flow out, under the control of Holmes's supreme knowledge—did he know all the time, and just gave Watson a lesson in method? Or was he really looking something up? The passage does not make it clear: the method is a little clouded in mystery. Built into the passage are Holmes's special and amazing powers, and also information perfectly comprehensible to anyone with common sense. But the vitality of the passage, the expressive dynamism of the created personality, make us believe he has brought off a triumph. Where Poe expressed an almost prophetic mystery in the smoke that wreathed Dupin, Holmes's signal is of victory over a material enigma—and one located in notepaper, an object straight from the everyday experience of the white-collar worker.

The speed of the stories derives not only from a vigorous style. The fast-moving and interlocked plot has its own meanings. First, since nothing is accidental, and cause and effect control the relationship of events, the incidents converge with rapidity and increasing sureness on the climax of the story. This convergence brings all the satisfaction of organic unity, and true to the attitudes that lie behind the development of that structural pattern, discussed in the previous chapters, the convergence is only made possible by the power of a single intelligence. The hero—and behind him the author—is the individual understanding and resolving contemporary problems, so realising in shapely and persuasive fictions the motives that led Doyle to deplore Gaboriau.

Doyle's plots are not only organic and rapid; they also present many puzzling incidents in a short space for hero and form to resolve. They are dense enough to seem valid representations of the packed experience of everyday life. Doyle knew well that full and tightly connected plot was essential to his success, saying accurately: 'every story really needed as clear-cut and original a plot as a longish book would do.' Many later crime novels use less actual puzzle-plotting than Doyle puts into six or seven thousand words. His action and dialogue are rarely extraneous to the mystery; the long sequences of description, comedy or emotion that fill out a novel by, for example, Dorothy Sayers are absent here. The brief sequences of characterisation or setting operate in close connection to the central mystery and this strict sense of relevance etches deeply the effect of the stories. Doyle recognised the importance of a tight, stylised manner when he wrote of 'the compact handling of the plots' and said that Holmes's character 'admits of no light or shade'.

With a vigorous material style and a compressed, rapidly linked structure, the emphasis of the presentation falls all the more sharply on events and objects. These tend to be less exotic and essentially melodramatic than the phenomena of the novellas; even the royal romance of the first story centres on nothing more recherché than a cabinet photograph, and the objects used for deduction—a watch, a typist's sleeve, a letter—make the superior powers of the detective operate in a very familiar and real world. It is not only the evidence of the detail itself that establishes this; Doyle presses the point through Holmes himself. 'It has long been an axiom of mine that the little things are infinitely the most important' he tells Watson when discussing nothing further from the ordinary business world than a typewriter, in 'A Case of Identity'. The set of the stories towards enigmas of the ordinary world, materially presented, is given specific and authoritative expression by Holmes in the opening of the same story:

> We would not dare to conceive the things which are really mere commonplaces of existence. If we could fly out of that window hand in hand, hover over this great city, gently remove the roofs, and peep in at the queer things which are going on, the strange coincidences, the plannings, the cross purposes, the wonderful chains of events, working through generations, and leading to the most *outré* results, it would make all fiction with its conventionalities and foreseen conclusions most stale and unprofitable.

The passage is fascinatingly double in its tone. The image of flying and the notion of peering into other people's lives reveals an alienated intelligence dramatising its own isolated power; the romantic artistic consciousness is created, and ratifies itself not only in the image but also in the final reference to Shakespeare—and that to Hamlet himself, prince of alienated intelligence. Yet the interest is real, and the subtle mind elevates the everyday. The power of Holmes is not only to resolve the problems of ordinary life, but to make that life seem rich in itself, and therefore emotionally fulfilling.

A world is created where people enmeshed and to some extent daunted by the puzzling and the mundane nature of their experience can find comfort both in the Holmesian resolutions and in the aura of grandeur, the sheer heroism and enrichment he brings with him. In terms of epistemology we have a materialistic model, which can read off from physical data what has happened and what will happen. The succession of incidents in explained and necessary relationship to each other expresses the ideas of material causation and linear history so important to the Victorian world-view. The perception of these patterns by the heroic individual manages to balance those essentially deterministic attitudes with the basically contradictory idea of the individual as noble and free, untrammelled by the laws of material causation. A deeply satisfying and heavily ideological view of the world is made in the stories by concealing the fissure between heroism and materialism; this illusory resolution will be discussed further in terms of content but it is brought to life in the crisp and compressed creation of those two forces by Doyle's mastery of lively and suggestive writing.

The structuring of the narrative units within an organic, convergent model is in some ways simple, in others quite complex; here too the effect is dual. At its barest, analysis of the Holmes story would have three parts: relation, investigation and resolution of mysterious events. This reveals an unchanging basic structure, but, like a lot of structural analysis, tells us little about what the stories mean as they are communicated. In the early Holmes stories there is surprising flexibility in presenting relation, investigation and resolution. Not until later stories does a fixed pattern emerge, the structural system so well remembered. In that formula, the story opens with Holmes and Watson at Baker Street; a client arrives; Holmes deduces from the client's appearance; the problem is outlined; Holmes discusses the case with Watson after the client leaves; investigation follows—usually some is conducted by Holmes alone, but most occurs at the scene of the crime with Watson and the police looking on; Holmes identifies what has happened, normally in action of some kind; Holmes explains all to Watson, back at Baker Street. This formula is used in the skilful pastiches by Adrian Conan Doyle and John Dickson Carr, but it is by no means a constant pattern in *The Adventures*, nor even in the second book of stories, *The Memoirs of Sherlock Holmes*.

As you read through *The Adventures*, the elements often seem familiar but there is no sense of formulaic repetition; each story has something different in its structure or in the context of some of the structural units. The effect is much more lively, varied and interesting than the usual remembered model which is established in the later collections. Two of *The Adventures* never go to Baker Street at all—'The Boscombe Valley Mystery' and 'The Man with the Twisted Lip'. These variations are outside the basic pattern of relation, investigation, resolution and include them, but within those bare categories there is also much variety.

The dominant pattern in relation is for the client to explain what has happened, but in three cases Holmes himself outlines the problem—'The Boscombe Valley Mystery', 'The Blue Carbuncle' and 'The Man with the Twisted Lip'. Investigation has a whole set of variable features. It can be very sketchy, when Holmes thinks about events taking their own course, as in 'The Five Orange Pips', 'The Man with the Twisted Lip' and 'The Copper Beeches'. Or he may just put himself in the right place to find the answer, as in 'A Scandal in Bohemia' and 'The Blue Carbuncle'. Other stories present detailed investigation and so approach the later 'clue-puzzle' where a great amount of detected data is put before us, but only the detective can see the pattern that gives the answer—'The Red-Headed League', 'The Boscombe Valley Mystery' and 'The Speckled Band' are of this sort, and 'A Case of Identity' as well, though in it most of the data comes out of the relation.

If the intensity of investigation varies, its methods also have considerable flexibility. There are three types: armchair analysis at Baker Street, often with the use of reference books; Holmes goes alone to make inquiries, sometimes in disguise; Holmes and Watson go together to the scene of the crime. No story in *The Adventures* has all three of these methods; most have two, a few rely entirely on a joint field investigation. You gain a sense of a common pool of methods, of familiar patterns being re-enacted, but the reader of *The Strand* would not have found this month's story quite like the previous one. This commercial skill has wider meaning. Holmes's abilities are flexible enough to make him a convincing respondent to the variety and difficulty of the problems he tackles; the varying form creates an aura of spontaneity, of resourceful vigour that strengthens the hero's authority.

The resolutions of the stories are formally more similar than the investigations, but two differences can be seen, one of context, one of content. As to the first, five of the stories are resolved at Baker Street and the dénouement of the others occurs in the field. This is merely a non-significant varying of pattern, but the second, contentual variation has considerable impact on meaning. In some stories Holmes is not fully triumphant: he understands the crime but has not brought the criminal to justice. At the end of 'The Five Orange Pips' comes a report that the ship carrying the criminals has sunk; justice has been done, but not through Holmes's hands, and the story also shows his failure when John Openshaw is murdered after consulting him. This reduced control by the hero appears in 'A Scandal in Bohemia' and 'The Engineer's Thumb' where the perpetrators escape. This does not necessarily weaken the hero's authority: an analysis of the content-meaning of these endings will be offered later, but here it should be noted that Holmes's relative uncertainty can itself be an element of variety in the narrative.

The overall structural pattern is one of fairly intense variation within an unchanging order; in no story do the three basic units, relation, investigation and resolution, change position. Even in 'The Man with the Twisted Lip', where Holmes has worked on the case off-stage for days before explaining the problem to Watson, his successful investigation occurs in the story, as he sits up all night and smokes his way to the resolution. Overriding order and intrinsic variation are common enough features of popular story, of course. V. I. Propp has shown in his well-known analysis of Russian folk tales that 'functions' (the controlling actions) come in the same order, and while some may be omitted, the normal series will continue in order from where the story picks it up. In this way Holmes's solitary investigation, if it occurs, will come before the climactic field investigation with Watson. The compulsive order causes some slightly odd plotting in 'The Boscombe Valley Mystery', where Holmes has to visit a prison at night because fieldwork is scheduled for the next morning. This order creates the ideologically important meaning of a hero whose individual, isolated action in response to problems is always a means towards a social end; his lonely researches must be realised in the setting of a public inquiry, shared with Watson who represents the public, and with the ineffectual police authorities looking on. This rigid order emphasises the active movement of the story and hero from knowledge of a problem towards its resolution. A dynamic model of applied intelligence is created in the structure, quite different in its vigorous, engaged effect from the retrospective explanatory structures that Poe and Freeman (especially in his 'reverse' stories) were led to create by their valuing of the quite isolated intelligence.

And if the permanence of structural order is meaningful, so is the consistent absence of a feature ever-present in fairy tale. The stories Propp discusses and most of those that have come down to us from the past have an essential 'Provider' function. That is, as the hero is about to undertake his quest or has just started on it, a 'Provider' gives him a magical object which will help him in a crisis. This is obviously present in the James Bond stories where the armourer gives the hero items of technological magic to rescue him from danger. The 'Provider' helps heroes who need supernatural aid to bring order to a troubled world. But Holmes is his own provider: self-help, that great Victorian virtue, is embodied in his power to succeed with no more than his own abilities.

Skilful variation within the structural order itself emphasises that resourceful independent power. The emphasis may arise affectively, as from changes of location and from the variety in presenting the relation and the resolution; or it may be directly created by the varied ways of investigating. In both cases the strength and ideological force of the figure come together with the inventive variety to please the audience.

A modern audience's pleasure in innovation is not a free-floating phenomenon. The idea that originality in art is a virtue is itself modern, rising from the concept that the individual artist communicates something of a special, private and inventive nature. It also relates to the market-place situation of the artist, needing to distinguish one product from another to sell his wares for cash. The copyright act which recognised originality in law was passed to cover the situation of emerging market-artists like Hogarth: uniqueness was not sought or even much approved in earlier work, just as the idea that a human individual could triumph alone was not then entertained. Repetition formulae and supernatural assistance together are actively pursued and applauded in art outside the consciousness of bourgeois individualism, like the stories of Gaelic shanachies or the narratives of medieval chroniclers.

In its varied, original-seeming construction, in its materialist presentation and in its stylistic vitality Doyle's art found formal patterns that were valid fables about a problem-solving hero who works in a recognisable world with essentially graspable and credible rational methods. The linked plotting, the driving pace and the dominance of the hero over the action (patterns which were fully developed in *The Sign of Four*) have been compressed in a short story form to combine richness with speed into a mixture both ideologically satisfying and easily readable for people who bought *The Strand* and who subscribed to the values the stories ultimately dramatise and support. These values are specifically realised, the formal energies are channelled, by the selection and the details of content, and it is now appropriate to examine this process, starting with the characterisation of the hero himself.

The notes Doyle first jotted down about his detective establish some crucial features. Holmes has a private income of £400 a year— a decent, but not enormous sum, enabling him to live in reasonable comfort without relying on his chosen profession for support. He is in, but not enclosed by, the world of bourgeois professionalism. The notes also imply Holmes's arrogance and commanding nature: a brief piece of dialogue is given: ' "What rot is this," I cried—throwing the volume petulantly aside . . .' This forceful, quasi-professional hero is qualified for success by his mastery of science. The opening pages of *A Study in Scarlet* made the point at length, but in the first short story Doyle works more subtly, realising these qualities in images rather than action. Watson describes Holmes as 'the most perfect reasoning and observing machine that the world has seen'. This power involves a certain distance from human normality; in particular, feeling would damage the scientific force: 'Grit in a sensitive instrument, or a crack in one of his own high-power lenses, would not be more disturbing than a strong emotion in a nature such as his.'

The importance of science—more exactly, of the aura of science —in Holmes's methods is well-known; it mobilises for the audience's fictional protection the contemporary idea that dispassionate science was steadily comprehending and so controlling the world. But Holmes's power does not only reside in his well-known romatic scientific insights. The steady collection and analysis of data was in itself the basis of nineteenth-century science and a strong feature of other areas of thought—such as Doyle's own beloved history. And Holmes, it is less well-known, is also a master of the data of his subject. He has collected thousands of cases, can remember them and see the patterns of similarity in new problems: this power is in itself part of the Victorian romance of knowledge. Holmes does not 'deduce' in a vacuum; he understands through his materialist, association-based science the probable meanings of physical data and through the patterns of criminal action. This latter part of his armoury is, like his science, expressed in detail in *A Study in Scarlet* and touched on more lightly, but insistently, in the short stories.

The dispassionate isolation arising from Holmes's scientific powers meshes with his aloof, sometimes arrogant personal qualities. His drug-taking was, at that time, seen as an excitingly dangerous means of elevating and isolating the consciousness, closely bound up with the romantic artistic persona. His moody reveries, strangely atonal violin-playing, arrogant, dismissive tone to Watson are all other parts of the model of a superior being, a superman whose world differs from that of limited and often baffled people like Watson. The trenchant style Doyle gives to Holmes realises this aspect of his personality well, as does his occasional sarcasm, threatening Watson, and the audience, that he might cut himself adrift from their mundane realm. But he does not; Holmes is never the self-indulgent dandy American and French presentations of his figure have made of him, he is that familiar figure in English fable, the stern, distant yet ultimately helpful patronising hero.

The importance of this figure in nineteenth-century culture has been documented in W. E. Houghton's chapter on 'Hero Worship' in *The Victorian Frame of Mind*. Great emotional value was found in an individual who seemed to stand against the growing collective forces of mass politics, social determinism and scientific, super-individual explanation of the world, all of which appeared as mechanistic threats to the free individual. A figure like Holmes, who treated all problems individualistically and who founded his power on the very rational systems which had inhumane implications was a particularly welcome reversal of disturbing currents. Aloofness, self-assertion, irritation with everyday mediocrity were not merely forgivable—they were necessary parts of a credible comforting hero.

The crucial device by which Doyle makes this figure so effective is the limit he sets to Holmes's distance. The passage quoted above, where Watson tells how this machine-like scientist avoids emotion, ends by almost reconciling him with ordinary human feeling: 'And yet there was but one woman to him'. The story tells how Irene Adler can not only match his skill, but inspire something suspiciously like affectionate admiration in the hero. The whole characterisation of Holmes contains many dualities of this sort, that assert both his isolation and his contact with normality. He chooses to be a lone agent, but he takes cases, neither a mundane policeman nor a self-gratifying amateur. He is a self-confessed Bohemian, yet he lives in busy professional London, not in a Dupin-like romantic hermitage. He shares his lodgings with Watson, being neither a solitary nor matched by a partner. For all their eccentricity his rooms are cosy, filled with masculine gadgets for comfort. He will not eat when the hunt is up, but good meals are available, with a decent English housekeeper to provide them. He travels in normal conveyances, not some special heroic vehicle, yet his movements are sudden and dramatic. His atonal violin playing can give way to amusing Watson with favourite sentimental pieces, and he is a keen concert-goer—for him music is both private incommunicable reverie and social activity. His chemistry is smelly and dangerous, but can be practical and applied. His explanatory language, for all its learned aura, remains materialist, never withdrawing into the idealist intellectualism of Dupin. He works alone, often in disguise, but will use agents and the street arabs of the Baker Street Irregulars, so revealing his demotic touch. His world is modern, real London, not some imagined or mistily foreign city.

These details make the critical link across the fissure between the special hero and the 'dull routine of existence' that at his most isolative he claims to abhor. The action of the stories sets this dualism in motion. In 'A Scandal in Bohemia' Holmes's reasoning is interwoven with active investigation, disguise, play-acting and the dramatic activity of smoke bombs and mock blood. The thoroughness with which Doyle makes Holmes a dual figure is clear when he examines his client in 'A Case of Identity': 'he looked her over in the minute and yet abstracted fashion which was peculiar to him'. It is his special power to embrace both detail and analysis. The mixture of modes is constant and intimate: Doyle's hero is never bogged in mundanity or lost in etherealness. Doyle never lets the audience forget either aspect of the hero.

The special, distant features of Holmes's personality are threaded through the stories. He has a copy of Petrarch on the train in 'The Boscombe Valley Mystery', he quotes Cuvier in 'The Five Orange Pips'. Yet neither writer is so abstruse to be unknown to the average reading man; the spread of science and the medieval tendency of much Victorian art made both figures known generally as the sort of thing knowledgeable people comprehended. The physical aloofness that authorises Holmes's greatest efforts is also touched on. He does not eat all day in 'The Five Orange Pips', he thinks with his eyes firmly closed in 'The Red-Headed League', he smokes all night in 'The Man with the Twisted Lip'.

Holmes's heroic quality is exerted in a professional direction. He accepts fees for his work, though only unusual rewards tend to be mentioned. But this mystification of his income does not mean he will not work for the public. Where Dupin's heroic action made him strangely, passively transformed, Holmes is enlivened when he engages with human problems. His eyes glitter on the chase in 'The Boscombe Valley Mystery', they sparkle through the smoke when he cracks the enigma of the notepaper in 'A Scandal in Bohemia'. Activity is often quite hectic, even when he is following, rather than elucidating events. Withdrawal is the state in which he activates his special resources of knowledge and insight, but these episodes are only the inspiration and impetus for busy, involved implementation of that almost oracular knowledge.

Apart from Holmes's involvement in ordinary life there are many occasions when he openly shares the values of his clients. To the lady typist in 'A Case of Identity' he shows 'the easy courtesy for which he was remarkable'. He often belittles his own ability with a proper English modesty and feels the threat of failure in a very native way. In 'The Man with the Twisted Lip' he says 'I think, Watson, that you are now standing in the presence of one of the most absolute fools in Europe. I deserve to be kicked from here to Charing Cross.' It is a demotic, physical, London-based self-deprecation. Holmes can feel restrained chagrin at a degree of failure; in 'The Five Orange Pips' when he hears of John Openshaw's death ' "That hurts my pride, Watson," he said at last. "It is a petty feeling, no doubt, but it hurts my pride." '

This human side of Holmes is shown in his deference to Irene Adler, and he often has attitudes like a normal man about London. As the King of Bohemia arrives at Baker Street, he says 'A nice little brougham and a pair of beauties. A hundred and fifty guineas apiece. There's money in this case, Watson, if nothing else.' And as he reads the biography of Irene Adler from his files he deduces her status as a retired mistress with a slightly prurient amusement: ' "Contralto hum. La Scala, hum. Prima Donna Imperial Opera of Warsaw, yes. Retires from operatic stage—ha. Living in London— quite so." ' We find in Holmes many signs of the 'knowledge of the world' that he praises at the end of 'A Case of Identity', and we also find disenchantment with aristocrats—a feature shared by many middle-class people, who felt both attraction and jealousy towards those of the undeniably upper-class. He is drily sharp to Lord St Simon in 'The Noble Bachelor':

> 'I understand you have already managed several delicate cases of this sort, sir, though I presume that they were hardly from the same class of society.'
> 'No, I am descending.'
> 'I beg pardon?'
> 'My last client of the sort was a king.'

But as the story develops we find this is not just an instinctive dislike of a lord; St Simon has dismissed a mistress with the inhumanity of the King of Bohemia. Holmes's rudeness turns out to be a moral evaluation, just as his ironic shaft at the King of Bohemia has a critical basis. The king asks of Irene Adler ' "Would she not have made an admirable queen? Is it not a pity she was not on my level?" ' Holmes's reply has fine irony: ' "From what I have seen of the lady, she seems, indeed, to be on a very different level to your Majesty," said Holmes coldly.' It is highly likely that this royal figure, like that in 'The Beryl Coronet' is a transparent disguise for the Prince of Wales. Holmes is the agent of middle-class feeling against the manipulative, immoral hedonism of aristocrats. Sir George Burnwell in 'The Beryl Coronet' is another; he leads both son and daughter astray and, according to his suggestive name, is headed for the everlasting bonfire.

Holmes's power to evaluate is ratified by his wide experience as well as his personal authority. He is in touch with all levels of society. In 'The Noble Bachelor' a letter from St Simon, the son of a duke, reminds Watson that the morning's letters came from a fishmonger and a tide-waiter, that is a beachcomber in the tidal mud of the Thames. The extraordinary breadth of his experience, the story suggests, is one of the sources for Holmes's insight, just as he can turn street urchins into an effective force of detectives.

This contact with the lower reaches of London life is really a rhetorical flourish on Doyle's part, not crucial to the plotting; it is an extension of the complex by which Holmes is partly an ordinary man, partly a very superior figure. A similar piece of rhetoric, taken effectively from Poe, is the simple-subtle paradox, as when Holmes speaks of 'those simple cases which are so extremely difficult'. These are finishing touches to the solidly created dual figure, aloof and yet available, who is constantly recreated and was clearly in Doyle's mind from the opening of the first story. The situation is put lucidly in 'The Red-Headed League', when Holmes says ' "My life is spent in one long effort to escape the commonplaces of existence" ' but he is reassured by Watson, high priest of the commonplace, ' "And you are a benefactor of the race." ' Doyle himself has sent up a cloud of triumphant characterisation, a smoky illusion concealing the real nature of detecting crime and the difficulty of controlling contemporary threats to order. To read further into the appropriateness of Doyle's image of Holmes, his cigarette smoke was blue, and the whole creation fulfils the implications of that colour in the period. The aura of chivalry, of patronising autocracy and essential conservatism is a pervasive feature of the heroic personality and its function.

The effect is not only Doyle's work. Sidney Paget's dramatic illustrations of the hero did much to create the incisive and consoling image. He provided the legendary deerstalker hat that naturalised Holmes's hunter-protector element, and by the time of 'The Boscombe Valley Mystery' Doyle had altered his earlier description of Holmes's features to fit Paget's authoritative version. Paget's flair linked Doyle's imaginative creation to the exciting new force of the illustrated medium, and he caught exactly the aloof nobility and material bourgeois setting so important to the duality that is central to the power of Holmes as a figure. Paget used as his model his elder brother, in itself a relevant image of authoritative familial guidance. His brother was the man Newnes had meant to commission for the illustrations, but by a most irrational error the job went to Sidney instead. It is a fine revealing irony; inside the all explaining image are fragments of human chaos: beneath the production of the text lie the strains the text is dedicated to resolving.

The creation of Watson does not have the weight that the more overt feeling and greater length of the story gave him in *The Sign of Four*. In the early stories Watson is married, but by various plot devices is with Holmes through most of the action. From 'The Speckled Band' on Doyle goes back in time before Watson's wedding. This does not diminish him as the representative of family solidity and bourgeois morality: Doyle has settled down for a long series of stories and presumably did not want to explain each time how Holmes and his narrator came together.

Watson personifies the virtues of middle-class manhood: loyal, honest and brave—these features come out especially in 'The Red-Headed League', 'The Speckled Band' and 'The Copper Beeches'. Holmes explains all to him, and so to the audience, but Doyle avoids letting Watson stand as the presence of the audience in the story. His characterisation enables the reader to see him as a little foolish, and so to by-pass him and construct the one-to-one relation with Holmes that the underlying individualist epistemology requires. Doyle achieves this delicate and important effect largely through a careful modelling of Watson's voice. At times it is a hopeful imitation of Holmes's decisiveness, a deferential recognition of his mastery; but he can also be sharp enough to remind Holmes of the values of common humanity. But between these two tones that indicate the limits of Holmes's dual personality lies the tone that is Doyle's triumph, the one that Watson adopts to comment at a story's beginning. It is the voice of a mildly self-satisfied bourgeois who feels he has a mastery of things: a slightly wordy style, a little too much insertion of the first person pronoun and his own self-conscious opinions, along with a delicately banal rhythm. The opening of 'The Beryl Coronet' is a good example: ' "Holmes," said I, as I stood one morning in our bow-window looking down the street, "here is a madman coming along. It seems rather sad that his relatives should allow him out alone." ' The fussy inversion of 'said I', the flat prepositional phrases that follow, the carefully limited 'rather sad', all sketch the figure with almost subliminal effect. The reader can like him, admire his virtues, but also can suspect the situation is more complex and threatening than Watson can really handle. The hero's greater incisiveness is needed to control anxieties. The closeness Watson has to Holmes links the detective firmly to the actual bourgeois world; the crucial difference between them, the definite diminishing of Watson through his own mouth are the features which make the hero distant from and also immediately, personally accessible to an anxious, individualist bourgeois audience.

The major effect of Doyle's characterisation is a duality of the familiar and the exotic: this exists between Watson and Holmes and within Holmes himself, as has just been demonstrated. It is no surprise, then, to see that the methods by which Holmes solves problems are themselves dual in effect, a set of fairly simple procedures within an aura of elaboration. In the novellas Doyle carefully described 'The Science of Deduction'—a chapter heading in each book—and established Holmes's credibility as a master of scientific and criminological knowledge. Then he went on to show him making fairly straightforward, commonsense deductions. In the short stories a similar illusion is at work, but the higher qualifications are not clearly realised. There are general statements like 'He was still, as ever, deeply attracted by the study of crime, and occupied his immense faculties and extraordinary powers of observation in following out those clues, and clearing up those mysteries, which had been abandoned as hopeless by the official police.' This appears in the opening of 'A Scandal in Bohemia' and sets the tone for the series in *The Strand*. Later on, in 'The Five Orange Pips' Watson mentions 'those peculiar qualities which my friend possessed in so high a degree'. Less stress is laid on science and information, more on 'those deductive methods of reasoning by which he achieved such remarkable results' (in 'The Engineer's

Thumb') or 'severe reasoning from cause to effect' (in 'The Copper Beeches').

Doyle gives this process the elevated name of 'deduction' and claims it is both highly scientific and also a means of ordering the confusing data of experience. Both of these claims are illusory. Firstly, if Holmes really were finding patterns in facts he would be practising 'induction': in reality he has a knowledge of what certain phenomena *will* mean, and is practising deduction, that is drawing from a set of existent theories to explain new events. Doyle's wish to protect old values, ideas and their social setting is innate to his hero's methodology; the weakness of his own reasoning is clear in misnaming his hero's methodology. The dress of modern materialist science is used for conservative thinking, for a failure to face the real, disorderly experience of data: Doyle's own process and the needs of the bourgeois audience faced with threats of disorder are quite the same.

But, secondly, even the genuine, conservatively based deduction that Holmes does practise is not carried out at the abstruse level that Doyle asserts; an effective illusion allows the average reader contact with the hero's method. The contexts of medical science, the chemistry and the exhaustive knowledge of crime are only gestured at, and we are actually shown no more than a special rational process. This is, of course, closer to the powers of the mass audience, and so makes the detective more accessible in his heroism. It is a corollary of the less melodramatic plotting we find in the short stories, and the new direction of the crimes and criminals, as will be discussed later. In *The Adventures* the scientism of the early Holmes is contained, and deduction alone offered as his method in action.

Yet there is still an illusion present, because the resolution of the mysteries often does not depend on the deduction itself, or not very much on it. Doyle was aware of this sleight of hand. He spoke in his memoirs about 'clever little deductions which often have nothing to do with the matter in hand, but impress the reader with a general sense of power'. In 'A Scandal in Bohemia' the 'deductions' about Watson's watch merely validate Holmes's power; the only 'deduction' involved in the plot itself is that a woman will fetch her most treasured object in a fire. Other early stories are less illusionary. In 'A Case of Identity' there is a good deal of reasoning from the details of the case after an initial smokescreen of irrelevant 'deduction' about the client. 'The Red-Headed League' also involves sharp analysis, and Watson himself realises he has all the data but can make nothing of it.

But this thorough analysis is not always basic to resolutions. In 'The Blue Carbuncle' the elaborate interpretation of Mr Baker's hat has nothing to do with tracing the stone itself—Baker answers an advertisement for the hat, and in any case he knows nothing of the carbuncle. Holmes finds James Ryder, the thief, by something suspiciously like a coincidence when he visits the poultry-stall just as Ryder returns in search of his goose. In a story like this the reader is asked to believe—and does so readily enough—that the skill Holmes demonstrates with the hat ratifies the luck that leads him to the solution. Similarly, the penetrating and confident analysis Holmes gives Watson of what has so far happened in 'The Man with the Twisted Lip' validates the fact that he can just sit down, smoke a lot and resolve the whole puzzle. The stories only rarely provide all the details, as in 'The Red-Headed League' and 'The Speckled Band'.

The reduction in *The Adventures* of Holmes's sheer scientific expertise might make ordinary people think they could imitate the master. Doyle forecloses this possibility, and makes sure that accessibility does not become identity when Jabez Wilson, whose head seems as thick as it is red, reacts unfavourably to the explained deductions: '"Well I never!" said he. "I thought at first you had done something clever, but I see that there was nothing in it after all."' The trace of foolishness in Watson also helps to keep Holmes, close as he is to commonsense reasoning, a crucial distance away from normality. The proximity to the thinking powers and the epistemological grasp of the man in the street that develops in *The Strand* stories is very important to their success: the hero is less distant than he once was, though he still trails clouds of powerful cerebration and withdrawn intellectual force.

This development is parallel with a change in the central ideological aspect of the stories, their treatment of crimes and criminals. Disturbing events are not now caused by past and foreign-based immorality, but represent dangers present in contemporary London and so both credible and fearful. The threats and their perpetrators are now conceived within the limits of bourgeois ideology.

The crimes that underlie the mysteries in the first twelve short stories are not in general as melodramatic or exotic as those in the two novellas. In only two stories is a murder actually committed, and they both resemble the previous pattern. In 'The Boscombe Valley Mystery' and 'The Five Orange Pips' the disorders stem from past misdeeds, and in neither case is the villain punished by law—the Ku Klux Klan murderers drown in a storm and Mr Turner, who kills his old blackmailer at Boscombe Valley, dies a natural death like Jefferson Hope in *A Study in Scarlet*. These two stories do not follow directly on from the novellas, and their plots may well have arisen because Doyle was short of invention. Before they were written he had produced three stories where not a blow is struck, not a drop of blood is spilt (apart from Holmes's simulated blood and blows in 'A Scandal in Bohemia'). Indeed, in two of the first short stories no crime at all has been committed; of the later stories 'The Man with the Twisted Lip' and 'The Noble Bachelor' are simply misunderstandings, and there may not be any specific crime in imprisoning a stepdaughter in 'The Copper Beeches'.

From a modern distance it may seem odd that the greatest detective of all established himself so successfully with so little contact with violence, and even relatively little with crime itself. But the unexotic nature of these problems is crucial to the stories' success; Doyle, aware as usual of the essential elements of his work, lets Holmes and Watson present the issue. At the beginning of 'The Blue Carbuncle' Holmes is looking at the hat that has turned up, and Watson naively suggests 'this thing has some deadly story linked to it'.

> 'No, no. No crime,' said Sherlock Holmes, laughing. 'Only one of those whimsical little incidents which will happen when you have four million human beings all jostling each other within the space of a few square miles. Amid the action and reaction of so dense a swarm of humanity, every possible combination of events may be expected to take place, and many a little problem will be presented which may be striking and bizarre without being criminal. We have already had experience of such.'
>
> 'So much so,' I remarked, 'that of the last six cases which I have added to my notes, three have been entirely free of any legal crime.'

The problems are little, city-bred—but also whimsical and bizarre; in some the lack of any criminal action makes the issue inevitably one of moral and family disorder rather than any external criminal threat. A daughter's freedom and property are under attack in 'A

Case of Identity', the fragility of a respectable man's grasp on his professional role is examined in 'The Man with the Twisted Lip' and both the sensuality and arrogance of the upper-classes are dramatised in 'A Scandal in Bohemia'. 'The Noble Bachelor' and 'The Copper Beeches' are modified reprises of the themes of 'A Scandal in Bohemia' and 'A Case of Identity' respectively. These five stories deal expressly with family irregularities, and something of the same effect is found in the two stories where Doyle uses the 'past crime' plot of the novellas. In 'The Boscombe Valley Mystery' and 'The Five Orange Pips' the evil done in the past not only destroys its perpetrators but disturbs their innocent families in the present. The natural logic of a marriage between James MacCarthy and Alice Turner is upset by the past of their parents (though it should be noted that James MacCarthy, like Thaddeus Sholto in *The Sign of Four*, has some of his father's irresponsibility). In 'The Five Orange Pips' John Openshaw is completely innocent, and what was in the novellas a distant, almost symbolic treatment of evil, insulated from being a pressing concern by its very pastness, has become a vividly realised threat to family life in the present.

In the seven stories just mentioned, allowing for the different emphasis in those based on the older plot pattern, it seems fair to say that the dynamic meaning of the plot is disorder threatening the normative morality of bourgeois, respectable England. Breaches of fidelity are central; these may involve interfering with another's property—that of women in particular—but financial greed itself is not a major motive. The disturbance arises from selfishness and a failure to respect the rights of others.

The five remaining stories specifically involve a crime for greed in the present. Two of them also concern undervaluing of respectable family order. In 'The Speckled Band' Dr Grimesby Roylott interferes with his stepdaughters' right to life and property, so the story has links with the group already discussed. (His own colonial origin and the off-stage murder of the elder girl also give it some resonances of the two 'past-crime' stories.) 'The Beryl Coronet' shows an aristocrat subverting a family—the son is distrusted by his father and the daughter loses her sense of family and self-respect. In a rather savage ending Holmes expresses the Victorian distaste, not without a touch of prurient sadism, for the fallen woman— 'whatever her sins are, they will soon receive a more than sufficient punishment'. Neither of these stories concerns everyday crime; in each of them a disorderly, selfish influence disturbs the order based in one case on rightful inheritance, in the other on expertise —those twin pillars of augmenting and protecting income and property in the middle-class Victorian world.

The three other crime-based stories deal with types of professional villainy; a bank robbery in 'The Red-Headed League', a jewel theft in 'The Blue Carbuncle' and coining in 'The Engineer's Thumb'. There was a great deal of organised crime in nineteenth-century England, especially in and around London; records show, perhaps surprisingly, baby farming and forgery as the most common detected offences and robbery with assault—mugging— the most commonly known in ordinary experience. But Doyle selects his crimes, aims the threats at bank deposits, jewels and coins, the tangible forms of property, the totems of an acquisitive and money-conscious society.

The presentation of the criminals is even more ideologically selective than their crimes. They are not unregenerate members of a professional gang, or part of those 'dangerous classes' who genuinely did threaten bourgeois London. They are respectable people gone wrong, turned aside from their proper roles. The fact that these are 'real' crimes, not family disturbances, places most of the criminals outside the ring-fence of middle-class family structure, but in one way or another they are marginal members of that society, and should have respected its values. James Ryder in 'The Blue Carbuncle' is a superior servant who succumbed to 'the temptation of sudden wealth so easily acquired' Holmes judges, and feels able to let him go, sure that 'This fellow will not go wrong again'. The coiners of 'The Engineer's Thumb' are an English doctor and foreigners who mislead him and seem themselves to be middle-class renegades. They all get away, and though 'from that day to this no word has ever been heard' of them, this does not suggest that they were reformed—there are other reasons for the equivocal ending to this story that will be discussed below. The remaining criminal, John Clay of 'The Red-Headed League' is a professional who has been in jail and is arrested. Yet even he has an oddity that conflicts with criminal reality. He is the grandson of a royal duke, and he has been to Eton and Oxford, so partly represents the weak aristocrat figure. Even in him the mundane reality of crime is avoided.

The economic or psychological origins of crime are not recognised: the stories assert that if decent people pulled together, did their duty and fulfilled their moral roles these disorders would not occur. The ideas are not unlike those basic to *The Newgate Calendar*, but here a secular and fragmented view of the world makes a heroic agent of order necessary, and also causes the mystery to be presented in terms of one person's experience. Holmes can only expose the errant and restore order through the channel of a normal, innocent person who is involved in and damaged by the crime, so symbolising the personal threat felt by the individuated audience. Jabez Wilson in 'The Red-Headed League', Henry Baker in 'The Blue Carbuncle' and Victor Hatherley in 'The Engineer's Thumb' are innocent bystanders drawn into disorder by accidental contact with the criminal process. Of the three, only Hatherley is physically damaged, and his is a rather special case, to be discussed below. The other two, though ruffled by their experience, continue ordinary life, but it is interesting that both are presented in a critical light: Wilson is rather stupid and Baker has fallen into bad habits. It seems as if the very fact of being involved in such a business must cast doubt on the individual—and so shelter the self-consciously upright bourgeois from the threat of the such contact.

Pierre Nordon is one of the few critics to have discussed Doyle's work along socio-cultural lines; he has pointed out the special selection of the crimes involved, but his analysis of the situation seems over-simple. He suggests a line is drawn between the rich and the poor, and that villains in the stories before 1910 tend to be 'the calculating enemies of order'. There are figures who emerge in the second collection of stories who fit such a description, notably Charles Augustus Milverton and Professor Moriarty himself. But these ogres simplify Doyle's meaning by naturalising evil, giving it an incorrigible presence in dedicated villains, and in the opening volume of stories that first gripped the reading world things are not so simplistic. The evil that arises from selfishness in *The Adventures* is often expressed in calculating terms and does usually seek money; it is also certainly a threat to order as well as property. But Nordon's summary wrongly identifies an embattled class seeing and facing enemies outside itself. Doyle is more self-conscious, more attuned to middle-class worries about the ability to protect and reproduce itself. His stories do not present the foreign, loathsome enemies encountered by Sexton Blake, Bulldog Drummond or, in the modern period, by James Bond. Doyle offers fables in which the class whose language, epistemology and values are enacted can examine the dangers that arise if its members are untrue to its codes.

It is important to recognise that doubt and fear are firmly directed at other members of the class, their potential failure to remain faithful to the shared morality. Yet none of the stories imply a sense that the individual might himself fail to maintain these standards; this is achieved through the absolute trustworthiness of Watson and the clients who bring the problems to Holmes. Watson never fails in morality, however inadequate his intellect might be. Through him the stories express self-confidence in bourgeois ethics and by recognising his limitations they clarify the need to know more, to improve the educational skills of the audience to defend their personal moral fortresses. The clients who invoke Holmes's special intellectual force are always puzzled, but never dishonest or immoral. Agatha Christie will develop a sense of disquiet about the self by using unreliable or criminal narrators, and Raymond Chandler will isolate the hero by making his clients untrustworthy. But here a series of respectable people experience disorder, and an unfailingly honest narrator and a comforting reliable hero close ranks with them. At the same time, the stories never invoke intelligence in the clients, never suggest the reader can match the hero's intellectual power: he is accessible, but not imitatable. Later writers allow the reader to doubt the existence of a shared and automatically restorative morality and also suggest the reader can match the intellectual skill of the hero; the next chapter will discuss this pattern.

The only enemy clearly identified outside the class is the aristocrat who does not subscribe to middle-class values—an interesting corroboration of the fact that through the nineteenth century the upper-class had steadily become more bourgeois in outlook. Here too Doyle could sense and realise the forces of his period. This fear of a distinct aristocratic class and its different values is a part of the uncertainty that arose from the middle-class awareness that it had 'made itself', and that its successful position depended on vigilance, on a sustained defence and propagation of the virtues that seemed central to its continued security. The fact that they 'seemed' central is important. Doyle's stories are concerned with property and money, but they do not show acquisitiveness and protection of money as virtues in themselves. Money and property are considered the natural result of correct ethics, and failure in morality causes the attack on property and even on life. Dr Roylott, the memorable villain of 'The Speckled Band', is an eccentric irascible man as well as greedy for his stepdaughters' property; John Clay is a renegade gentleman and a thief; James Ryder is weak and so tempted by the great carbuncle; Sir George

Burnwell is a profligate first and a thief second—and the nobleman who puts the beryl coronet in pawn and triggers the whole crime has himself acted badly to come to this state.

Weber argued that protestant ethics were a substantive cause of bourgeois financial success; others have agreed with Marx that the pervasive bourgeois morality was an ideological screen for the acquisitive and self-defensive instincts of a newly self-conscious class. Whatever the truth of the dispute, Doyle's stories dramatise the dialectic effect of that morality: it both justifies the possession of property and is shown protecting the possessors in their comfort.

The nature of the resolutions themselves is an important part of the ideology of the stories. Only rarely does the legal system operate at the end of a case. An arrest is made in 'The Red-Headed League' but we hear no more of the criminals; they are out of sight and out of interest. Comprehension of their attempt has been enough to dissolve their threat. In 'The Blue Carbuncle' and 'The Boscombe Valley Mystery' for Holmes to know all is for him to pardon: one criminal dies naturally, the other is set on what we are asked to believe will be a life of reform. In several stories punishment is autonomous, rising from the machinations of the criminal. The grisly fates of Dr Roylott and Jephro Rucastle, attacked by their own savage animals, are satisfying self-created judgements, and in 'The Five Orange Pips' the stormy weather that broods over the whole story is the indiscriminate agent of fate, sinking the ship *Lone Star*—apparently with all hands, innocent as well as guilty. In 'A Scandal in Bohemia' and 'The Noble Bachelor' no actual penalty falls on those who have directly caused the disorder; Holmes's scorn punishes the aristocrats judged to have been most at fault—and this kind of resolution operates in 'The Beryl Coronet' as Sir George Burnwell gets away with a mere £600 for his boldly immoral crime and feels Holmes's contempt. Doyle, like many middle-class people, cherished ideas of his family's past grandeur—his mother was obsessed with heraldry, especially that of her family. His scorn for aristocrats who failed in their moral duty was strong and expresses both the middle-class dislike of and impotence towards the classes they admired and sought to join. Such class values cause Holmes's contempt for James Windibank in 'A Case of Identity'. He has shown improper greed and broken familial ties; the threatened beating is the traditional punishment for a man who betrays a woman. The only criminals who escape unscathed are the coiners of 'The Engineer's Thumb'; the destruction of their press is certainly a handicap to them, and it may be the real purpose of the story, as will be discussed below.

Selection of setting is a crucial ideological feature in crime fiction, and the physical world in which Holmes operates is basically that of the natural audience of *The Strand Magazine*. The vivid pieces of London life in 'The Blue Carbuncle' and 'The Red-Headed League' move around the fringes of the City of London itself; though there is no 'Saxe-Coburg Square', the Jabez Wilson country is familiar enough and many streets are those the readers would walk through to catch their trains. A few precise details set each story in the world of contemporary experience, however much they may now seem to be charming pieces of nostalgia. But much of real London is omitted; there are ideological absences in the treatment of the setting. Watson's perception of the gloomy menaces of London and its darker areas, strong in the novellas, is not now usually present. Watson himself does not go into these areas, with the exception of 'The Man with the Twisted Lip', which has a special significance, to be discussed below. The real threat to respectable life posed by the grim areas where the working-class and the 'dangerous classes' lived is thoroughly subdued. Just as the stories have mastered a problematic which locates disorder in the failure of middle-class people—and some aristocrats—to be faithful to their moral roles, so the story omits that more real criminal pressure from dispossessed, outcast London in a period of economic depression. When the plot needs to recognise such people and such areas, which is not often, Holmes goes among them, frequently in disguise, but the story does not go with him. He returns with his messages of comprehension and comfort and the actual contemporary threats are omitted from the story. Here, as in the treatment of crimes and criminals, selection and omission build up the ideological pattern of the story.

The grim London weather seems in the novellas to be an emotive displacement of the potential disorder of London life, but here this element is much reduced. Only one story deals to any extent with bleak weather; this is 'The Five Orange Pips', already shown to be harking back in structure and theme to the earlier patterns. It has developed a new, consoling element though: the bad weather may express affectively a displaced sense of fear, but it has become the agent which punishes criminals that even Holmes cannot reach.

The treatment of the setting in the short stories expresses a greater sense of illusion, a firmer grasp on imaginary ideological comfort of the stories. To describe Holmes's problems as 'whimsical little incidents'—a motif repeated in several stories—itself implies that all disorders can readily enough be mastered. In one striking passage Doyle suggests to his audience that life in London is not really as bad as it may seem. Holmes and Watson take the train down to Winchester to sort out the mystery at The Copper Beeches, and when Watson admires the country houses Holmes retorts:

> 'You look at these scattered houses, and you are impressed by their beauty. I look at them, and the only thought which comes to me is a feeling of their isolation, and of the impunity with which crime may be committed there.'
>
> 'Good heavens!' I cried. 'Who would associate crime with these dear old homesteads?'
>
> 'They always fill me with a certain horror. It is my belief, Watson, founded upon my experience, that the lowest and vilest alleys in London do not present a more dreadful record of sin than does the smiling and beautiful countryside.'

Perhaps the passage engages the anxieties of Doyle's prosperous country readers and the increasing number of city men who commuted a good way into London—many of the later stories are set in the country, where Doyle lived in prosperity. But the main point of Holmes's claim is to draw the sting of the threats of city living, and it demonstrates how far Doyle is from presenting a realistic account of the sources and patterns of real crime in late nineteenth-century England.

The emphasis here has been to establish the social meaning of the patterns of form and content in Doyle's stories. This crucial aspect has been too little observed. But as with Poe's stories, the ideology, however much a shared one, is essentially that of personal achievement and personal morality threatened in a subjectively perceived way—and ultimately defended by an individualistic hero to whom the audience relates on a one-to-one basis. It would be surprising, then, if there were not some resonances in the stories of Doyle's own anxieties. One obvious channel for these, so clearly present in Poe, lies in the hints that respond to Freudian analysis. Neither the space nor the expertise is available here to identify these features in any satisfactorily full way, but two aspects of male anxiety seem to thread their way through the stories.

Loss of masculinity is the fear behind some details. For all his vigour the King of Bohemia is crucially weakened because Irene Adler (her name in his own language means that rapacious bird, the eagle) has locked away a power totem in her most secret compartment. Jabez Wilson, whose head is aflame with virility, is suborned in his own house, and his betrayers penetrate the bank, that fastness of security, by a suggestive back passage. The vigorous, phallic-necked animal that would make James Ryder as powerful as his surname implies, is found to be empty of its stone. Victor Hatherley loses his thumb, a prime phallic symbol; Neville St Clair becomes hideous and deformed in the quest for money; Lord St Simon finds his wife has disappeared and belonged all the time to someone else.

This last case perhaps moves away from sheer loss of masculinity to the other main anxiety, the fear of supplanting that is most firmly felt by the father for the daughter; several stories act out this family drama. James Windibank not only desires his stepdaughter to stay at home and allow him to control her person and property, he actually provides a suitably weak-voiced and unthreatening rival to himself. Dr Roylott goes so far as to attack his stepdaughter with a snake, forced through a hole he has pierced in her wall. Alexander Holder (a tenacious man?) finds his daughter's virtue is stolen along with the jewelled coronet that symbolises it as well as wealth and honour; the tug of war between the supplanter and the son who, though suspected by the father is still his own image, shatters the perfect circle. 'The Copper Beeches' also presents a possessive father whose neck, well-known phallic object, is savaged by the beast kept in his own home as his daughter is finally lost. There may well be many more such details, and a close analysis would chart the meaning more fully. But the presence of such material can hardly be denied; here too Doyle has the power to realise the fears and urges that seethed in the respectable personality and that needed to be contained by normative influences like the unperturbable yet comprehending hero Sherlock Holmes. If there were any doubt of Doyle's artistic sense of these topics, they would be dispelled by a glance at his novella *The Parasite*. Written in 1894, this vivid case-study of a man possessed by the id only achieves the triumph of the superego by the foreclosing coincidental incursion of Victorian moralism. The vicar arrives just before the hero is about to destroy his proper, respectable lady friend for the sake of the ugly but powerful and sensual woman who has possessed him.

There was a very strong response to the stories that appeared in *The Strand* in 1891 and 1892 and Doyle found himself committed to a hero and a story-type he had intended as an occasional potboiler. 'It was still the Sherlock Holmes stories for which the public clamoured, and these from time to time I endeavoured to supply', he remarks in his memoirs. His attempts to disengage himself from Holmes are well known. He asked more for a second set of stories, but Newnes paid up happily. Then Doyle killed Holmes off; the firmly entitled story 'The Final Problem', where Holmes and Moriarty plunged together down the Reichenbach Falls was published in 1893, made even more vivid by a particularly fine full page illustration by Paget. After great pressure Doyle wrote *The Hound of the Baskervilles* in 1901, but set it back in time, before the liberating death, and the story is notable for the absence of Holmes for six of its fifteen chapters. Finally he resurrected Holmes for the stunning sum of £100 a thousand words, but reluctance persevered. After the *Return* stories were published he called the next series *His Last Bow*, but another volume, *The Case-Book of Sherlock Holmes* was forced out of him in 1927, not long before he died. In the last of the novellas, *The Valley of Fear* written in 1915, he used a long Gaboriau-like retrospective section, found before only in *A Study in Scarlet*, and so limited Holmes's place in the narrative. This all shows how the wide acceptance and need of the figure of Holmes operated against the very wishes of his creator; the facts press a social meaning upon the success of the stories. But Doyle's distaste for Holmes developed surprisingly early, and there are signs of its operation within the first series.

When *The Adventures* had been running for only six months Doyle wrote in his diary 'Holmes keeps my mind from better things'. But even before this his interest in Holmes was limited. After completing 'The Boscombe Valley Mystery' Doyle had a bad attack of influenza, and on recovering decided to be a full-time writer. It was not the Holmes stories he saw as his métier—his mind was on another historical novel, to be *The Refugees*. But he did complete the promised half-dozen Holmes stories. The next was 'The Five Orange Pips' where the strong resonance of the past-crime plot of the novellas suggests the barrel is being audibly scraped and where Holmes comes close to failure. The sixth story was 'The Man with the Twisted Lip'. In this and 'The Engineer's Thumb' Doyle appears to be dramatising his dislike of the Holmes phenomenon,

his sense that it weighs him down and interferes with his real work
and his self-respect.

The two stories are linked by unusual structural features—which
first drew my attention to them as a pair. In both stories Watson
controls the opening action, pushing Holmes into the background in
a surprising way and when he appears his powers are considerably
reduced, as they were in the preceding adventure. He is mistaken
for most of 'The Man with the Twisted Lip', saving himself by a
quite unexplained piece of overnight deduction, and in 'The
Engineer's Thumb' he makes only one simple piece of analysis (that
the villains drove round in a circle). Holmes's limitations and
Watson's added weight suggest a doubt in Doyle's mind about the
validity of the hero. The symbolic meaning of the stories' content
makes it clear that this arises from Doyle's unusual element of self-
expression.

'The Man with the Twisted Lip' tells the story of a respectable
reporter who, in the course of a special commission, finds he can
earn more disguised as a deformed, sharp-tongued beggar in the city
than in his real employment. When he is short of money he takes up
the role again and begging becomes his livelihood. Ultimately his
wife sees him in circumstances that will reveal his shameful state.
He is unable to reappear as himself, and so is accused of his own
murder.

The parallels with what Doyle felt he was doing are obvious. A
respectable writer, for the sake of gaining large sums of money in a
way he has accidentally discovered, degrades himself and takes
profits made in the street from City workers. Doyle, *The Strand* and
the Holmes phenomenon are effectively symbolised. The beggar
reveals Doyle's projected fear. A handsome body is distorted and a
mouth that should produce decent speech is twisted into a sneer to
bring in more cash; this shameful practice amounts to a murder of
the real self, a betrayal of the family. 'It was a long fight between my
pride and my money, but the dollars won at last' says the disgraced
man. When Holmes finally sifts the matter he wipes clean the soiled
face, restoring honour and clean upright life to the money-dazzled
reporter.

It is a fascinating allegory, revealing Doyle's growing dislike of
what he saw as vulgar potboilers which kept him from the scholarly
and overtly moralising work of his historical novels. Watson's
introduction itself offers an even more alarming model, a respectable well-connected man who, becoming a drug-addict was 'an

object of mingled horror and pity to his friends' and was no more than 'the wreck and ruin of a noble man'.

Apart from these patent traces of meaning and the reduced power of Holmes himself, there is a quite unusual intensity of feeling in the writing. Doyle rarely works with imagery, but this story is rich with motifs of light and dark more intense even than those of *The Sign of Four*. Holmes and Watson drive through 'sombre and deserted streets' across 'the murky river' through 'a wilderness of bricks and mortar' and the reporter's wife stands 'with her figure outlined against the flood of light' from her warm respectable house. When he begins to grasp the case Holmes says 'the clouds lighten' and when he has cracked the problem he and Watson go out into 'the bright morning sunshine'. This sort of emotional landscape has been used generally in the novellas, but here it is locked into the meaning of the man defined by his own situation, by his own filth that is washed away and, above all, by being called Neville St Clair. The aristocratic Christian name and the holy light of the surname have been besmirched in shameful money-grubbing—the fact that it came as a sudden, unexpected and eventually troubling gift-may well be subconsciously expressed in his beggar's name, Hugh Boon.

The problem is still resolved by Holmes, limited though his powers might be. This clarifies Doyle's ambiguous relationship with his hero. Though he is still writing stories he dislikes, he actually uses the distasteful hero to resolve the problem that, symbolically at least, has been set by that figure. In his own anxiety Doyle employs the absolving force of the hero who combines isolated intellectualism and social service: in the story Holmes does for Doyle just what he did for Doyle's kin among his audience.

Having worked out his feelings in this manner Doyle refused to provide more stories. But as the public and Newnes clamoured for more he weakened, demanding £50 a story in the hope of a refusal. Newnes agreed gladly and Doyle had to set to work again. His professionalism and the relief found in the previous story set the next two, 'The Blue Carbuncle' and 'The Speckled Band', among his most brilliant efforts, vigorously written and inventively plotted. Yet the shadow of Holmes was not so easily dispersed, as the later events reveal, and as is plain in 'The Engineer's Thumb', a more deeply troubled story than 'The Man with the Twisted Lip'.

Here Holmes is distanced further from events at the start of the story, as Watson actually brings the case to him. Watson is himself consulted and acts with Holmesian decisiveness. This reduction of

Holmes's force in the action leaves an emotive gap filled by Doyle himself: the figure of Victor Hatherley, the client, is very much like the author. Hatherley is a consulting scientific specialist with few clients, seduced by a lucrative offer that turns out to be disabling. The Doyle who has just decided to give up his specialist's role for writing, but who has Newnes's money to weigh him down is clearly enough presented. More sharply still Hatherley has shown the link between his own engineering knowledge and medicine in his ability to treat his wound; his 'suit of heather tweed with a soft cloth cap' and 'strong masculine face' could come straight from a surviving photograph of the young Doyle. The client's disturbing involvement is not, as was Neville St Clair's, a matter of impersonation and losing self-respect. The threat is deeper and more damaging; Hatherley has been seduced into dealing with people who, for all their vigour and apparent respectability, are criminals, and their crime is literally to make money with a press—of all things. The covert reference in the villains to the respectable Greenhough Smith and the Newnes who brought foreign know-how into his press operations to coin money is quite irresistible. The physique of Colonel Lysander Stark is remarkably like Greenhough Smith's, and Dr Becher has a general resemblance to Newnes in his portly, comfortable English appearance.

The plot tells how the press closes in on the young idealist just as he discovers the false villainy of the whole operation. The light he has, literally, brought in burns down the press but though he escapes with his life he leaves behind his thumb—a clear sign that he has lost his masculinity in the process. The story has the wish-fulfilling power to illuminate and destroy the whole of Newnes's establishment, but the villains themselves are untouched. They do vanish: they are exorcised from consciousness at least, but not destroyed. True to the legends of Victorian manhood, a good woman has saved the hero; but the crippling wound remains. Holmes has watched all this happening without any real act of analysis, but the authority of his final words gives comfort to the client as if he really were an author: 'you have only to put it into words to gain the reputation of being excellent company for the remainder of your existence'.

This final comment shows Doyle's anxiety to avoid being the shameful outcast pictured twice in the earlier story, and his desire to gain and hold respect through his chosen profession of author. The greater disturbance of this story, compared with 'The Man with the Twisted Lip', is shown by the increased obscurity and distancing of the symbolism, by the client's career being that of the Doyle who was not a writer, and in the failure of Holmes or any other agency to find the villains. There is no renewal here, just a wished for destruction of the press, and a remaining sense of emasculation. The debilitation that gave rise to the story seems to have lasted; the next, 'The Noble Bachelor', continues the theme of impotence though it is distanced further from Doyle because the client is a feeble aristocrat. In spite of this partial recovery, the story shows how Doyle was exhausted by his exegesis of anxiety: it is one of the weakest of all the Holmes stories, as Doyle later admitted.

The pattern covertly present in these two stories is fascinating. Firmly in the grip of contemporary moralistic ideas about what was good art, Doyle could not see the ideological function for a particular audience (including himself) of his work. Critics can be as blind as authors; Charles Higham, in his recent book *The Adventures of Conan Doyle*, can do no more than trace these two stories to fairly similar events in contemporary news reports. This approach, itself reifying and fragmenting the force of fiction, belittles both the imaginative power Doyle possessed and the neurotically urgent pressure of the stories.

Doyle's financial commitments and the comparative failure of his other work in critical and market terms kept him returning to the figure he had created better than he knew or wished. But as time went by Holmes and the stories changed a good deal. Like so many of his readers, the young Doyle lived close to relative poverty and to class disgrace as a result. The dialectic force of respectability as both perilous state and a power for its own defence is strongly felt in the early stories—and beneath their surface there bubbles the muted force of a vigorous man's sexuality and the accompanying anxieties, channelled into family strains by the period's taboo on acknowledging extra-marital sex. The conflict between money and morality is another of the realised tensions that invigorate the early stories.

The older Doyle was a much more prosperous and prestigious man, and the later Sherlock Holmes becomes more respectable, more certain—less expressive of the strains that the younger Doyle and his readers felt. Holmes gives up cocaine, goes for healthy walks, gets on better with the police and is much less barbed towards Watson. A reduced individuality is structurally reified as the story-patterns become formulaic and Holmes even narrates some of his own stories: previously Watson had been essential to mediate his quicksilver aloofness.

The later stories are more concerned with murder and crimes directed against property, without the mystifying concealment of property-ownership behind morality, so important in the early stories, as has been discussed. This development is visible in *The Memoirs*, even before Doyle killed off his hero. The emergence of master criminals as threats which are naturally evil also steers the stories away from the anxious enactment of a class's suspicions of its own kind into a world where right and wrong are clearly defined, enemies easily identified and confronted by the unfragmented force of bourgeois morality and law. The settings, the characters themselves and the large sums involved tend to move the stories into the environment of upper-middle-class prosperity where Doyle now moved. The lossening grip on a problematic of moral anxiety and this movement towards one based on a simple aggressive defence of prosperity causes Doyle, as Nordon has well shown, to replace the earlier self-conscious tensions with grotesque detail and sensational crimes. Excitement is manipulated into the stories, rather than rising from innate patterns of plot and from Holmes's delicately balanced duality.

A similar artificiality comes from Doyle's habit of giving comic titles to Holmes's unreported cases. This is an ironic revenge on the hero that deliberately trivialises his meaning, where originally listing of other, serious cases made his power seem denser and more all-embracing. The structural form also becomes less varied, more formulaic and perfunctory. The restless dramatisation of the 'whimsical little incidents' of the average Londoner's life is much less in evidence; stylisation hardens into caricature as the earlier realised moral dialectic tends to become a clear cut fight between right and wrong, between the immutable good characters and the naturally evil agents of disorder. It is interesting to notice the same development in the Brigadier Gerard stories; the first volume, published in 1893 has a double dialectic based on the forbidding yet fascinating power of Napoleon and the admirable yet foolish chivalry of Gerard. In the second volume, published ten years later, Gerard has become much more a buffoon, Napoleon a more clearly admired man of strength.

In spite of these changes, the brand-name qualities that Holmes had gained through the early period survived to the present. There is, for all the weakened force in the later stories, more vigour and concern with bourgeois morality in them than in most of his competitors. Chesterton and Freeman today seem cold and clever ratifications of very narrow approaches to reality, while even the last Holmes adventures have a mobile and inventive application of the power of materialist, moralising thought that still gives them convincing ideological force to many.

The Holmes stories, especially in the period when Doyle's success and Holmes's nature were formed, are a contemporary analogue to a series of folk-tales, or a set of epic lays in which a figure fitted to be a culture-hero of his period was presented in a medium and form technologically and epistemologically valid for a contemporary class. The function of epic and folk-tale has been well described by anthropologists and folklorists; a most succinct account of their social meaning, along with other human behaviour, has been given by Clifford Geertz (who describes himself as an anthropologist of culture). Man, he says, is an uncompleted animal who completes himself through culture. Through his habits, rituals and fictions he explains the world to himself and justifies his place and his actions in that world. Month by month in *The Strand Magazine* readers could see, through the plots, the crimes and the criminals of the Holmes stories, an account of what they felt might go wrong in a world that was recognisably theirs and which was, through the force of omissions and the formation of its problematic, one where their own sets of values would work. The consolations were great, and the wit and verve of Doyle's writing give those comforts the illusory vitality of a living system. The essential functions of folk-tale are to explain the world, to protect the folk against psychic and physical threats, to offer escapist entertainment and to be socially normative—to urge that these values will keep society on an even keel, resist discommoding change. All of these functions are manifest in the Holmes stories: we find scientistic and rational explanation of a materially known world; the psychic protection of a powerful hero and the exclusion of real physical threats from the plots; lively dialogue, wry jokes and sensually sharp presentation of admired objects and valued feelings; and above all central bourgeois values which operate through Holmes as the tools of maintaining order, and through the victims as the qualities that earn Holmes's care and deserve the correction of disorder about them.

Holmes was a hero shaped for a particular class in a particular time and place, but like many other heroes he has survived out of context as a figure of heroism. Such characters, equipped with memorable details that symbolise their methods and the setting of their

greatness, retain a central core of meaning made newly valid in
other periods. Arthur with sword and round table meaning martial
fraternity, Robin Hood with bow and greenwood setting to
symbolise the force of anti-authoritarian morality are two major
British examples. Holmes with magnifying glass and London fog has
attained the same status, epitomising the rational hero who resolves
urban disorder. A fine irony is that by killing Holmes off and then
resurrecting him, Doyle gave his hero one of the constant features of
the heroic pattern. Lord Raglan was the first to identify the fact that
mythic heroes tend to exhibit a group of identical features; the
descent into apparent death and miraculous return is a crucial
stage. But it may not be just an accident; Joseph Campbell has
traced the recurring patterns of the hero's career to archetypal
patterns of human need, and the final struggle where Holmes gave
his life to defeat mankind's foe is, as in the case of Beowulf and
Roland, mythic whether the hero returns or not. The patterns of
human imagination and story were there, working in the author's
imagination at the time; made dynamic by Paget's stirring
illustrations and Doyle's vivid realisation they can retain their
force.

As time and socio-cultural patterns change the Holmes myth may
itself be demoted by a new force, as in Nicholas Meyer's pastiche
The Seven Per Cent Solution where the hero of a different culture,
Sigmund Freud, is 'the greatest detective of them all'. Holmes may
survive as a symbol of rational enquiry and rational superiority as in
many an English advertisement, or as a standard totem of detection
in passing references or jokes. The quality of the realisation and the
far-reaching nature of the print medium made the detective's name
a household one—and that domestic metaphor is perfect for a hero
whose name emerges from Doyle's imagination to imply that we
can, in fiction at least, have a sure lock on our homes.

One particular formation of the Holmes myth is of more than
passing interest for a writer and academic. Intellectuals and
professionals have cultivated the myth in clubs and quasi-scholarly
journals, and in particular have tried to fill in the background of the
life of Holmes, to explain the many inconsistencies that Doyle
carelessly and uncaringly created. Completion is a common process
in mythical development—the life of Christ attracted commentary
and clarification from an early date; the vulgate Arthuriad on
which Malory partly based his work was a scholarly attempt to
bring inconsistent stories into a corpus that replicated the en-

cyclopedic, knowledge-ordering instinct of the thirteenth-century cleric. The academic professional mind tries to tidy Holmes up as if he were the subject of a Ph.D. thesis or a formal biography, and so finds in its own reworking of the myth a realisation and a validation of its own values—especially those of trivial research and tidy unitarian structures that organically justify the narrow concern with a single subject. Even Doyle's interest in rationalism and organic structures was not so obsessive, so opposed to the tumultuous confusion of real life; he made his stories a bridge between the disorderly experience of life and a dream of order, by containing both aspects in a graspable, contained and controlled form.

The figure of Holmes was so well created and attuned to its time and audience that it has survived to the present. But as different realities have emerged, new ideologies have been required to contain and conceal them. New formations of the detective and ways of presenting and controlling crime have been necessary to appease disquiet. And new detectives, often owing much to Doyle's inventive and imaginative creation, have appeared, to be read as new encapsulations of socio-cultural responses to the ambient world. Agatha Christie made a crucial remodelling of the detective in form and content and redirected rational analysis towards a different audience in a different medium. Her detectives Hercule Poirot and Jane Marple provide ready access to the attitudes of the respectable middle-class novel-reading public of the 1920s and 1930s in England.

REFERENCES

Text
The Complete Sherlock Holmes Short Stories, Murray, London, reprint 1971.

Criticism
Doyle's comments on his work are found in *Memories and Adventures*, Hodder and Stoughton, London, 1924. His manuscript note and various quotations from his diaries are reprinted in John Dickson Carr's *The Life of Sir Arthur Conan Doyle*, Murray, London, 1949, and in W. S. Baring Gould's *The Annotated Sherlock Holmes*, Murray, London, 1968.

Joseph B. Campbell, *The Hero with a Thousand Faces*, Pantheon, New York, 1949.
Clifford Geertz, *The Interpretation of Cultures*, Hutchinson, London, 1973.
Charles Higham, *The Adventures of Conan Doyle: The Life of the Creator of Sherlock Holmes*, Hamilton, London, 1976.

4 '. . . done from within'— Agatha Christie's World

In the fiction room at Foyle's London bookshop two large signs direct customers to the books most often sought. One proclaims Sherlock Holmes, the other Agatha Christie. Her reputation as an author has become as prodigious as that of Doyle's detective. By 1979 her sales, in all languages and formats, were approaching five hundred million copies. Forceful marketing and a steady output have played their part, but Christie's product obviously has the power to compel and satisfy readers.

Her stories realised the attitudes and resolved the anxieties of many people, especially women, whom earlier crime stories did not interest or satisfy. Three features of her own formation were basic. As a woman she had no interest in the active male narcissism common to much crime fiction; being of upper-middle-class background she firmly believed and recreated the values of the English property owning bourgeoisie; having almost no formal education she offered nothing more difficult than sharp observation and orderly thought as the systems by which crime was detected and disorder contained.

These patterns of content were realised by a suitable style and presentation but, more importantly, Christie perfected a structure, best called the clue-puzzle, which invited and empowered the careful reader to solve the problem along with the detective. The individualism and the sense of isolation inherent to the audience who shared the basic bourgeois values were themselves activated by the overall form of the novel. It is true that many readers could not solve the puzzle, and hardly tried to do so; indeed some novels are not quite fairly open to such solving. But these facts do not remove the crucial ideological force of the clue-puzzle, which marshalled the simple skills of a respectable, leisured, reading public and applied them in their own personalised defence system, with an inquiring agent to represent the reader who could only aspire to such observing and ordering powers.

Christie's original audience was quite small, as Elizabeth Walter records in a recent collection of essays, *Agatha Christie: Queen of Crime*. In other pieces from the same book Colin Watson and Julian Symons locate her basic readers among respectable suburban people, especially women. The private lending libraries were a fortress of Christie reading. Her huge later sales testify to the number of titles she has produced and the increasing book buying habits of the people, in all countries, to whom she basically appeals. At the same time, the reputation she has gained among a class well equipped to give authority to their tastes has certainly taken her readership beyond the original and continuingly central audience that shared her ideology and was eager to have it confirmed.

The young Christie, like so many girls of her class, was a dilettante of the arts; most interested in music, she also wrote poems and invented stories. Her elder sister encouraged her to write and suggested crime fiction—the original stimulus itself, like the threat in the stories and (symbolically at least) its detection, came from within the family. Christie knew Doyle's work well and had enjoyed Maurice Leblanc's logical puzzles. Her first novel, drafted by 1916, alters Doyle's pattern towards a passive problem-solving that rejects romantic male heroism as a protecting force. Hercule Poirot is a fussy, unheroic figure. His physical vanity is foolish but his brain works well: what is of value in him is not tied to masculine stereotypes. As a Belgian he combines the French-speaking tradition of close detective analysis with the contemporary idea of Belgium as a 'brave little' country. Even his name suggests a redirection of male heroism. By implication he is a Hercules who is also something of a 'poirot', a buffoon. Christie, fluent in French, would certainly have known the word.

Poirot is an alien: in *The Mysterious Affair at Styles*, the first of Christie's novels, he is a retired Belgian detective exiled to Britain. His dress, speech and manner remain, through all his appearances, foreign to the setting and the characters among whom he moves. The effect is important. Doyle implied, in Holmes himself and through Watson's mediation, that a certain class can be protected by a natural leader, but Poirot is not a socially integrated culture-hero, not even through his early narrator, Captain Hastings. He only symbolises certain ways of thinking; we can never identify with him, but merely recognise the success of his methods.

It may well be that Poirot's vanity and oddity distance and subtly downgrade that cleverness the English bourgeoisie slightly distrusts, but at the same time must partly respect. A clearer feature, persistent through all of Christie's work, is that from the first she neither finds nor offers comfort in an active, heroic, male stereotype. Individualised heroism and special intelligence are both suspect to her; Poirot has some reduced, contained elements of both, but in her later work Christie rejects even such limited special power and isolated heroism as Poirot possesses. Miss Marple, whom Christie preferred to Poirot, is clearly a typical figure of the respectable classes, exerting familiar powers of observation and reflection.

In some of the later novels, including the ones she thought her best, Christie moved even further away from a single resolving figure and derived solutions from autonomous applications of observation and orderly thought by people actually involved in the problems. This is a pattern that readers addicted to Poirot and Marple do not fully applaud, but Christie consistently displays distaste for too much individualism, even in her unspecialised and slightly mocked inquiring agents. I will return to this topic, as it relates to Christie's formal methods. Here it is relevant to notice that, within its narrow social range and allowing for its deep conservatism, Christie's pattern is essentially less authoritarian than Doyle's, or that of most crime fiction. Her urge to generalise detection presumably arose partly from her class's sense that it was in control, with no need for heroes; partly from her feminine distrust of masculine narcissism and its associated individualistic heroics. Her attitude meshes extraordinarily well with the overall clue-puzzle structure, suggesting that the individual reader may equal the enquiring agent; Christie shapes an imitatable method, not a comforting élite personality.

In the first Poirot novel his inquiry is meticulous, its method and overall rationale based on observing events, gestures, objects and words, and reasoning out a pattern which explains them all. The facts and their observed interpretations are, it is fascinating to notice, very domestic ones, rising from the world of a woman's experience and understanding, at a time when women were largely restricted to household activity. A broken coffee-cup, a fire lit in summer, freshly planted begonias, the need to tidy a mantelpiece: these are the sources of information. Women also wrote—letters, diaries and even novels—and the minutiae of handwriting, the implications of written words are important. Like the plan of the house that became traditional in the clue-puzzle, the scraps of writing are laid into the text for the reader to interpret along with Poirot.

The Mysterious Affair at Styles offers little mystification of Poirot's method, no real illusion to aggrandise and also simplify his system of inquiry. On several occasions he states that his method is the observing and ordering of facts. Once he goes further, saying 'instinct' is needed, and he does finally show an intuitive understanding of love—though this is itself based on close observation of the apparently hostile pair. It is in the second Poirot novel, *The Murder on the Links*, published in 1923, that Christie begins to weave illusion about the meticulous pragmatic method. Hastings, the limited narrator she borrowed from Watson (but was soon to discard), admits 'Order and Method' were Poirot's gods, but separates him from the mere plodding of police work.

> He had a certain disdain for tangible evidence, such as footprints and cigarette ash, and would maintain that taken by themselves, they would never enable a detective to solve a problem. Then he would tap his egg-shaped head with absurd complacency, and remark with great satisfaction: 'The true work, it is done from *within*. *The little grey cells*—remember always the little grey cells, *mon ami*.

The internal cerebration that Christie emphasises is shown, by the action, to be successful; the audience can share Poirot's satisfaction and complacency, while recognising, and smiling at, his immodesty. It can all be done within the head: we do not need the busy, object-dominated expertise and exertions of detectives like Giraud in this novel or the neat, professionally competitive sleight-of-hand of Holmes. The thoughtful, passive readers who sat and slowly read through the novel could feel assured that peaceful reflection would resolve problems and restore the 'order' that is, by an effective ambiguity, both the overt method and the covert purpose of the analysis. Hard work, activity, professionalism and the positivistic mysteries of contemporary forensic science (which Freeman had made crucial in his Dr Thorndyke stories) are all thrown out together. Yet Christie does not rely on arduous intellectualism, as Poe did. The wished for resolution requires only patient and minimally testing thinking in the agent and, potentially, in the reader. The illusion of effective self-help and self-sufficiency is a crucial part of the story's meaning, and the exclusion of detailed police-like activity is a major step in shaping the ideology.

Later in the novel Christie offers another illusion when Poirot speaks knowingly of 'the psychology of crime'. This is merely a name for the inward cerebrating already established as the method, no more than comprehending people in a general, untested way. Poirot says of Madame Renauld, the victim's wife, 'I recognised as soon as I saw her that I had to deal with a woman of unusual character.' Poirot never shows any fuller grasp of psychological process; in later novels Christie firmly rejects the approaches to crime that developed from investigating the criminal mind. As Thomas Narcejac has argued, 'psychology' has no real presence; the term is merely used to dignify and reinforce a very simple set of methods and, especially in the thinly plotted and reasoned later novels, to justify intuitive short-cuts in the detection. There is a contemporary sheen to the word, and to the quasi-medical insistence on little grey cells, but the reference to modern science is much more perfunctory than the ones Holmes made; the withdrawal from it to ordinary human methods is even more complete than Doyle's process of humanising Holmes's special powers. And— an important feature of Christie's strength—Poirot's actually simple methods are less illusionary than Holmes's because they are firmly supported by the detective's advocation of simple orderly observation and by the possibility, offered in the clue-puzzle structure, that a reader may solve the problem.

The early novels that developed this detective and this method were reasonably successful—*The Murder on the Links* was well reviewed by the *Daily Express*, acknowledging Christie as a respected new author. But sales were by no means big, and Christie was not committed to the form at all; in this period she also wrote *The Secret Adversary*, a melodramatic spy thriller, filled with patriotic suspicion of the foreign manipulators and the misguided Labour politicians who threatened England's security and prosperity. But, as the title suggests, a greater threat still is the highly placed barrister, a traitor to class and country. In both the early Poirot novels the crime, like the detection, was done from within, in the sense that a member of the victim's family, with other inside help, was guilty. In the spy thrillers she continued to write Christie gave national scope to the idea of a concealed enemy within the circle of shared values, breaking its mutually protective security. The means of detecting such national betrayals remain internal: normal powers are sufficient to unmask the deviant threat, though the free-flowing action makes activity and courage the required virtues rather than close observation. But in spite of the mobility and physicality of the drama, Christie again avoids a heroic male model: her investigators are a young couple—and Tuppence, the girl (named for money, not femininity), is the more effective of the pair. Christie enjoyed her thrillers because they were easier to plot than the clue-puzzles, but her audience responded most to those crime novels where a specialised inquirer modelled the power of normal thought. Hercule Poirot and Miss Jane Marple remain her most successful creations. In order to see how Christie created forms that successfully realised her ideology, this chapter will concentrate on the archetypal Poirot story that made her a best-seller, *The Murder of Roger Ackroyd*, and will then comment briefly on the slightly different later archetype seen in the novel which introduced Miss Marple, *The Murder at the Vicarage*.

1926 was a memorable year for Agatha Christie. Her husband planned to leave her for a friend's secretary and her own consequent disappearance was covered sensationally by the national press. Exactly what happened remains unclear; in her autobiography Christie says she had a nervous breakdown and amnesia. The events left her exhausted and, to judge from following novels, with a distaste for charming young men and attractively efficient career girls who jointly outraged honest women. But in the same year Christie herself had caused disturbance. Some reviewers thought she went outrageously far when the narrator of her new novel turned out to be the murderer. The extreme reaction suggests genuine alarm rather than literary disapproval: though Christie's earlier novels had taught the reader to think anyone in the family circle was capable of murderous disorder, here she cast doubt on the very conventions of narrative fiction. It was a brilliant structural device, enacting the fear the respectable bourgeois held that disorder within society, threats against the self might be caused from within the charmed circle, and by someone who seemed most trustworthy. But the structural audacity went further than this. The murderer spoke throughout as 'I' and this may well have woken, especially in those who complained the most, an awareness of possible deviance within the reader's self. Guilt, like disorder and detection, could be 'done from within'. Freudian interpretations of the classic clue-puzzle argue that criminal and detective represent the id and the superego, the urgent hostile drives of the self and the controlling, socially responsible force that represses them. The power to trace the criminal by oneself responds to personal doubt. This level of anxiety, lurking beneath the more overt fear of a concealed enemy of the self, is touched sharply by Christie's bold plotting; Doyle kept it at bay through his treatment of both victim and detective.

Apart from this deep-seated relevance to the audience, the plot creates the more conventional and acceptable suspicion of those we should be able to trust. Not only is the murderer a narrator, that privileged figure of the traditional novel, he is a doctor, the very man to be trusted with the individual's bodily secrets and hope of continuing life, the emerging figure of wise authority in an increasingly secular society. The pastoral duties he should have pursued are implied with Christie's usual economy in his name, Shepherd.

The controlling power of a Christie novel lies mainly in the selected plotting, the way in which the content detail moulds the ideology. The form of the story is very important to her success, validating the reader's quest for self-generated comfort in the clue-puzzle structure, and through style and presentation Christie gives a strangely impersonal authority to the ideology of the content. But where Poe's ideal intellectualism and Doyle's vigorous materialism were themselves lucid and shaping aspects of the ideological defences embodied in the hero, the formal meaning of a Christie story, with its essentially passive, unfocused quality, is best understood after the content patterns are set out.

Dr Shepherd is a friend of the victim, Roger Ackroyd, and appears from the opening of his narrative to be a reliable man, full of common sense. He quotes Kipling on the first page, establishing a solid, reliable tone. He reminds Poirot of Hastings, which suggests honesty if not intelligence. His irritation with his sister Caroline's trivial gossip implies an upright, serious-minded manly persona. Christie invokes the evaluative connotations of male-dominated literature in this way, but takes them to a deliberately exaggerated degree when, in Chapter Two, Shepherd wonders if Mrs Ferrars left a suicide note, and so incriminated him. He decides she has done, because he knows how women cannot resist stardom, even in suicide. Such a narrator is pompous, even unreliable. And he is wrong: she acted with modest determination, sending Ackroyd the fatal letter. The story shows how Shepherd's self-indulgence led him on to abuse his position in just the callous, dismissive and eventually stupid manner he adopts here. A murderer develops from a normal, responsible professional man.

Yet Christie does not make this murderer fully evil. The threat is muffled, the ideology never lets deviance seem too irrational, destructive or uncontrollable. His first victim, Mrs Ferrars, had poisoned her husband —not, in her exculpatory turn, without some justification. And Shepherd's motives are seen as weakness rather than as virulent evil. Opportunity, greed and moral uncertainty led him to blackmail Mrs Ferrars, then press her to suicide and finally kill Ackroyd to cover up his original wandering from proper behaviour. Shepherd's sister has sensed the weak strand that is in him. Poirot uses the same idea (so tightly and simply closed is Christie's ideological scheme) in the speech where, already knowing Shepherd's guilt, he explains to the brother and sister how the unnamed murderer drifted into crime: because his morality is weak (his better nature cannot win) and so succumbs to temptation, fails to maintain the high and, it is recognised, difficult road of right moral behaviour.

Even in his deviant state, Shepherd retains aspects of a doctor's proper morality. As he proudly says at the end, there is no falsehood in his narrative, though there are some omissions. His description of events in Ackroyd's study at the time of the murder is ambiguous, only clarified at the end of the novel, and through the narration Christie scrupulously charts Shepherd's reactions as Poirot closes in. The murderer keeps a record without lies: his last fidelity is to the truth of literature, that medium which the readers themselves trust in for comfort. And when finally confronted by Poirot, he does the decent thing and takes veronal as Mrs Ferrars had done. The criminal who has strayed from bourgeois morality is contained by it: he is trapped by its intrinsic skills of watching and thinking, and himself subscribes finally to its moral force as he has throughout the narrative to its cerebral values. Emphasis is thrown on the self-denying courage needed to maintain bourgeois values and order, and the plot ultimately values highly the successful endurance of the people, like Caroline, Shepherd underrates and mocks. They avoid temptations to be selfish, they respect the moral imperatives that hold respectable society in orderly stasis.

Greed for the wealthy victim's money is often a major motive in Christie, and the murderer is very often someone who will directly inherit. Yet the villainy is never presented solely in terms of greed, and as a result Shepherd's crime is not as far from those of the family murderers as it might seem. The essential offence of those who kill to inherit is that they break natural fidelities to a relative, while acting the part of familial loyalty. Shepherd has broken a bond of great weight to his friend and patient, betraying him while playing the role of a trustworthy man. Money (from Mrs Ferrars) is involved in this breach of morality. The quest for more money than is one's due is the central feature of crime in Christie; in her world, as in Doyle's, money is the natural accompaniment of good morality and it rewards proper living; physical comforts bless those who conform to the bourgeois value-system.

Christie's plots show how easily people can be deceived by those who are only acting the part of propriety, especially by those who are closest—and this betrayal always takes the form of murder. This is of course the ultimate threat in an individualistic world-view, and the Freudian reading of crime fiction shows killing to be the authentic wish and fear of the reader. At the same time, the partly sympathetic treatment of a figure like Shepherd shows how easy it is to stray, the element of acquisitive immorality in the audience is invoked, confronted and fictionally put to silence. This system of closure, the novel's power to raise but defuse issues, is very clear in the emotionless way in which Ackroyd's death is treated. The threat of sudden death is euphemised like that of guilt, and the protected reader can contemplate the fear of receiving or of causing such a crucial disturbance to individual life.

Ackroyd sits neatly and bloodlessly in his chair, stabbed in the back—of all things. Nobody grieves much for him. The emotionless treatment of death is a constant in Christie, after the abnormally painful and naturalistic death of Mrs Inglethorp in the very first novel. But Ackroyd's death is all the more unmourned because he is not presented as a very admirable man. He was mean, and this, Christie implies, came from his vulgar business background. Although he has the position of a squire, he is not authentically part of that important network of power and patronage in the English counties. His Yorkshire surname itself connects him with the industrial north, and Shepherd spells his background out in Chapter Two, saying that he is not a true landed gentleman because he made his fortune building something like cartwheels. So Ackroyd is a bogus authority, and the doubt about just what he manufactured itself shows the 'respectable' person's contempt for those soiled by trade.

The male victim in *The Murder on the Links* had a disreputable background like Ackroyd's; it is a curious feature in Christie that the female propertied victims are always more admirable than their male equivalents. Men in Christie are rarely quite innocent, apart from those who conduct the inquiries.

The characters assembled at Fernly Park, Roger Ackroyd's extended family, are limited to the upper-middle-class; their servants are the only people who work for a living, apart from the doctor. The family lives on income from capital. This does provide a ready motive for them to need an inheritance, but the leisure the characters enjoy is also a real picture of Christie's own background and the wished-for state of most of her audience. All of these characters come under suspicion in turn, including the servants— though little lengthy or serious suspicion is directed at them. The threat in Christie rarely emerges from below the central class, and then (as in *Sad Cypress* or *After the Funeral*), the interloper can have an unrecognised link to the family. The real focus of suspicion is the class that provides the victim, and in turn the novel inspects the family and their friends for traces of the crucial weakness.

Major Blunt, a supporting character, is never a serious candidate for deviance. His inarticulate Englishness, embodied in rank and surname, give him high credibility; he is basically present to provide the romantic resolution common in Christie novels. Many of her stories end not with the solution to the problem but a final linking of two lonely lovers. Plainly borrowed from romantic novels, this is not only a gesture to feminine feeling. It asserts that a new family order can rise from the family disturbed by murder; it has a healing, renovating effect similar, in its often bathetic way, to the final sequence in a Shakespearean tragedy when the emergent controller of the wounded state speaks in calm, ordered tones. In this novel, where the form demands that the narrator speaks the last words, the love between Flora and Blunt (a splendidly simple English allegory peers through the names) is organised before the end, and as usual the detective helps to create this resolution as well as showing where suspicion should rightly fall.

But even Blunt is, for completeness, included in Poirot's inquiries. And Flora herself comes under strong suspicion, partly through her apparent relationship with Ralph, principal benefactor under Ackroyd's will, and partly because she is involved in one of the secondary actions with which Christie habitually thickens her plots to create suspicious behaviour all round. Flora's theft from

Ackroyd's bedroom, Ralph's secret marriage with Ursula Bourne, Miss Russell's drug-addicted illegitimate son, Parker's former activity as a blackmailer are complications which flourish around the main action and lead their characters to act strangely.

Christie's highly ornate plots make a testing, intricate puzzle, and that in itself replicates bourgeois thinking. Success in competitions is valued because it implies the unaided personal solving of life problems, dramatises self-sufficiency and calibrates personal achievement. But the complications also express a sense of ever-alert suspicion of all other competing individuals; the characters bear the reader's fear and distrust of his or her own equals and associates.

Many of the characters are morally weak. As the sub-plots reveal, they can be led to breach the moral conventions that hold this society in 'order'—and the word is ambiguous. It not only means both the method and the end of detection, but also implies the static ranking of society, that frame within which these characters live and the readers inspect their morality. None of the erring characters has gone quite as far as Shepherd, and the courage that Miss Russell, Flora and Ursula all show in the trying circumstances that have led them to breach normality allows author and audience to absolve them. Even Shepherd, as has been shown, remains in some ways within the moral system; Parker, who has reformed, and Ralph whose charming weakness only leads him to conceal and so abuse his wife, are deviants still safely within that world. Christie's reversal of masculine-centred morality is clear. The women are unwillingly forced to dubious action, as Mrs Ferrars was herself; the men are specifically weak and selfish in their unforced errant activities.

The setting of *The Murder of Roger Ackroyd* supports the class limitations and the moral perspectives embodied in the characters. Kings Abbott is a village immune to the industrial and social realities and turmoil of the mid-twenties. A pleasant environment and neutral weather are the undisturbed backdrop for the minimal activity of a workless, unproductive cast living on interest and through servants only seen in relation to the main characters. Abnormalities in the rigid patterns of class and behaviour are explained away, as in the case of the 'lady-like' parlourmaid Ursula and the murderess Mrs Ferrars; or are, as in the case of Ackroyd himself, used for a specific euphemising purpose in the affective structure of the story. The world of the Christie novel, as has often been noted, is a dream of bourgeois rural living without the heights, depths or conflicts of real social activity. It is a projection of the dreams of those anxious middle-class people who would like a life where change, disorder and work are all equally absent.

The narrator frequently denigrates this village living, but this does not proceed merely from his own selfish and anti-feminine animus. The lengthy scene where a game of Mah-Jong is played among confusion, gossip and small-scale pretension mocks the village environment outside the narrator's voice, and the same feature is found in most Christie treatments of her chosen setting. This mockery should not be mistaken for dismissal: it is a defensive presentation of this life style as being foolish, whimsical, hardly worth sharing . . . yet also assented to, and deeply supported with that self-satisfied quasi-humility, characteristic of English bourgeois self-protection. The false mockery itself is seen as part of the honesty of the self-denigrator and passes for an ability to see oneself in real terms. A wry, comic version of self-criticism can be a strong force to obscure the reality of one's position, to defend by stasis a hard-won position of advantage. The belittled virtues eventually triumph. The plot tells us that village values work, that Caroline does have good sources of information, and that her instinct about her brother was right, for Poirot consults Caroline in detail and his own methods are shown to be very close to her own system of understanding the world.

The fact that Poirot has come to live in Kings Abbott is one way in which Christie makes the detection more resident in the community, more autonomously produced, less an isolated and invoked force than previously. So she moves even further from the romantic heroic model that gratifies male fantasies so much in crime fiction. Poirot is still clearly a foreigner, a distanced representative of certain valued methods; his odd language and appearance separates both such intelligence and such special heroism from the society he helps. But Christie's conception of his methodology is moving closer to techniques resident at the heart of the village community, as is shown in an important exchange in Chapter Thirteen when Poirot explains to Shepherd how it comes about that his despised sister tends to be right about so many things. He analyses feminine 'intuition': it appears to be a mere invention that is miraculously correct. But in fact, Poirot continues, women have unconsciously noticed many little facts which they are able, still unconsciously, to process and so produce a correct analysis at the conscious level.

That is a telling description of the domesticated epistemology which actually gives the solution in a Christie plot. But this system is not overtly accepted yet; the process of mystification, of illusory authority in the detective, is still present. Poirot, a man and a superior hero of sorts, elaborates the real situation by saying that *he* obtains the same correct analysis by 'psychological' means. This, like the notion of the unconscious, belongs to his position as an authoritative inquirer, to be trusted by the reader who cannot personally work out the puzzles, however fairly they may be laid out. But Christie is clearly approaching a system of inquiry which is self-consciously female, and also fully rational. The women call it 'intuition', yet their knowledge has real observed bases. This will be typified in Miss Marple; at present it is no more than a curious and rather uneasy link, making Poirot a distanced and somewhat narcissistic projection of these methods.

He makes mystifying gestures elsewhere, telling Shepherd his own business is to examine human nature, and he repeats to the police in Chapter Eight that the psychological aspect of crimes must be studied. But at the same time he says if you organise the observed details with method, the answer will be simple: at once Christie covers his directness with mystification as he hurries on to speculate on the personality of Ackroyd's fatal visitor. Yet, as before, the real detail of discovery is precise, material and again exhibits knowledge and concerns usually associated with women. Poirot gains a major insight because he knows laundries do not put starch in handkerchieves: the fragment discovered comes from an apron. Moving a chair from its accustomed place is a central piece of tangible evidence; a dying fire, Ralph's boots, a crucial phone call and the implications of an overheard voice are other specific interpreted details. The world of objects and knowledge about household order and management, the nuances of human interaction, such fragments of the material, interactive world known and scrutinised by the anxious bourgeois personality will provide both the data and the methods for identifying the source of disorder.

The other crucial element in Poirot's detection is rigid attention to an objectified sense of time and place. A plan of Ackroyd's house is given, and throughout the novel time keeps ticking away. Shepherd took too long, in his narrative, to move from the front door to the gate of Ackroyd's house: he was up to something else, as we discover through Poirot's superior attention to the clock and the map. Not only objects have proper places and uses; people too can be located, any deviance from ordinary orderly movement can be traced. The relation of people in time and place is usually the central issue in Christie. The murderer somehow misrepresents himself against the map, the clock or, because of their tight interrelation, frequently against both.

Meticulously calibrated personal time and location is an important part of the bourgeois world-view. A part of the reified consciousness is that the person is conceived against objectified conceptual measures of time and place. Time is not gauged in the length of a task, the changing of light and season; place is not felt personally, known as an organic set of relations to the senses. The phenomena are themselves made absolute and positive. But both, in Christie, can be interfered with; their apparent reliability in locating the self—and, most importantly, other rival selves—can be distorted for the threatening purposes of the deviant individual. Christie's sense of the dominance and the fragility of bourgeois ideas of time can be judged from the excitement (recorded in her autobiography) she felt on reading Dunne's *An Experiment with Time*. His dislocation of industrial man's diachronic time stimulated her, offering a new set of self-locations that seemed liberating and also meshed with her archeological experience. In the fully bourgeois world of the crime stories she realised the crucial importance of defending the ideas of time and place central to contemporary epistemology. She made threats to that system a basic part of the criminal's assault on what her ideology presented as normalcy. In this novel, Shepherd's own movements, his use of a dictaphone (technology against its own temporal creation) and Flora's coincidental confirmation of his devices all disrupt the real timetable of events. Shepherd's hiding of Ralph and his use of a sailor to place a phone-call (machines again) without a traceable caller interfere with the expected normalities of place. These mechanisms are not only part of an intricate and teasing puzzle; they are ontologically vital to an audience whose reality depends on a consistent and externalised sense of clock-time and map-place.

It is Poirot who conducts the inquiries that reveal these and other ways in which the murderer distorts order and, by extension, reality. Because of this leadership, this archetypal exercising of the basic method of inquiry, Poirot retains some heroic proportions. Shepherd says in Chapter Fourteen only Poirot has earned the honour of having fitted all the details together. However, on other occasions Shepherd's mockery reduces Poirot's heroic status, links him with Caroline in our sympathy; and he has become to some extent naturalised by living in the village. These processes in themselves move him further away from the figure of the lonely, admirable hero so common in other crime fiction. He is not present from the beginning of the action and the narration does not treat him objectively as in the earlier books: these facts also diminish his already weak potential to be a Holmes-like leader. He is still in many ways an initiator, a figure who resolves puzzles and the reader's anxiety: yet Christie is holding back that aspect of him, and this restraint will take other forms in later novels. Many readers, of course, retain their taste for a male authority figure, women as well as men. It may be, ironically, that Christie's distaste for the forceful masculine heroes and her limitation of Poirot's place in and control of the action has actually shaped a hero in keeping with self-conscious bourgeois needs. Where Doyle's readers accepted an authoritarian hero (though one Doyle took care to make accessible), Christie and her readers, being in general better educated, more leisured, more often female, find hero-worship indecent and over-enthusiastic, reductive of personal dignity and authority. So they assent to Poirot as a transmuted reduced version of leadership. He symbolises the inactive, cerebral skills of a low intellectual order which, in so many cases, are the powers and work experience of members of the bourgeois class, whether they actually live off their property or merely aspire to do so.

The form of a Christie novel has usually been denigrated. The structure is acknowledged as clever, but the style and characterisation condemned as plain and boring. Such value-judgements come, of course, from ideological expectations and needs in literature foreign to Christie and her audience. A literary simulacrum of vitality, originality and constant variety is not part of the equipment these novels offer their readers; but her formal patterns are consistent and controlled, powerfully supportive of the ideology dramatised in the stories.

The narrator's style is in general composed of familiar phrases and banal rhythms. The word 'conventional' is a fair summary—but a revealing one. Conventions only come about because they have generally accepted force (including the convention that one must be unconventional). Shepherd's voice expresses the collective certainty of a particular class in a particular period; what seems ludicrous and stuffy for some readers is for the central Christie audience a comforting and valid means of interpreting events.

The second paragraph of the novel is a good example, as Shepherd returns home from Mrs Ferrars' deathbed. The way he presents his actions creates a model of respectable confidence. The narration is precise and also trivial; he tells the reader just how he opened the door, just why he wore that particular overcoat. The language is full of unsurprising collocations, and the whole statement of Shepherd's actions and attitudes is structured by conventional responses. The even, muted flow of clichés and trivial information, the unconceptual syntax all state the unexamined values of bourgeois life. The reader is drawn in to trust the narrator, find him blandly consoling and so overlook the cause of his stated worries. It is both a skilful opening to the puzzle and a tonal establishment of the mode of response to the world that will eventually resolve that enigma in similarly even, comforting tones and by similarly limited cerebral methods.

Although the narrative is by a character—and, above all, by the deviant character—this does not affect the basic meaning of the style. Shepherd's tone is no different from Christie's normal narrative mode, dry, even, informative and imbued with shared values. Apart from this overlap, there is an added factor to validate the narrative tone. In spite of his crime Shepherd is, in literary matters, reliable. The voice does reveal itself as the criminal, if we are sharp enough to read through its double meanings. The genuinely comfortable tone of the narration, a trusted voice to guide us to a resolution of present enigmas, does of course make the final resolution the more shocking. But it never makes us feel such voices are untrue: it is merely that Shepherd has failed to sustain the values embodied in his mode of speaking and seeing. His style, like his final return through suicide to bourgeois values, represents the even, untroubled path from which his weakness made him stray.

For a first person narrative the novel, like all of Christie, contains a great deal of dialogue, and is notable for simply related action without narrative comments or evaluations. Shepherd is not, for obvious reasons, the controlling intelligence of the story—Poirot and the reader, potentially, fill that role. Generalising action beyond a single character's control is common in Christie. She lets the characters speak, the action occur before us in its puzzling complexity. No single narrative voice mediates and explains as it did in the classic nineteenth-century novel, and even Hasting's inarticulate version of this intelligence is soon dropped.

There is no sense of constant control, merely a final release as the puzzle is crisply closed. Even when Christie uses first person narrative the events are not ordered from the narrator's viewpoint; he too appears puzzled and the heavy use of enigmatic dialogue and objectively related action makes this convincing. The story simulates the bemusing ragged ends of experience in real life. This presentation excludes the dream of a heroic, all-subduing sensitive intelligence that the traditional novel made privileged; and the use of simple shared evaluative categories about people rather than deep and subtle insights in itself replicates the clumsiness of real human evaluations—and, importantly, maintains that the people who do not fit these shallow confident judgements are themselves deviant from the prevailing value system.

The dry, objective writing and use of brisk dialogue have other effects which tend to obscure the intrinsic artificiality of the plots. The sudden events, the twists of motivation and personal history are calmly inserted, the frenetic action that surrounds the murder is stated plainly in a calm, bald manner. Emotion is removed and takes incredulity with it. The narration sounds so much like a train timetable we accept it, without considering its unlikely intricacy and naivety. A suddenly discovered fact—like Miss Russell's illegitimate child—does not ruffle the smooth, arid flow. It is noted, it takes its place among the other scattered jigsaw pieces. The low-toned formulaic language effectively conceals the emotive starts of real people and the sheer complexity of values and motives; it is both materialist and naively evaluative and in this way facilitates the extraordinary plots and replicates the mechanistic and simply certain view of the world held by author and also held—perhaps uncertainly—by audience.

In the period that shaped her success Christie's titles have a firm, unexcitable clarity. She immediately abandons the overtly affective 'mysterious' element suggested in her first book, and simply states a fatal event and, usually, the place where it occurred. Typically 'death' or 'murder' are coupled with a prepositional phrase: 'on the links' 'in the clouds' 'on the Nile' 'at the vicarage'. Occasionally the death or murder is personally located—of Roger Ackroyd or Lord Edgeware for example. This pragmatism gave way to a more playful way of euphemising the emotive subject in titles like *One, Two, Buckle my Shoe* and *Five Little Pigs* (many of which were changed for the American market which did not share the children's rhymes from which they were drawn). And later Christie sometimes imitated the literary distancing typical of intellectualising writers like Dorothy Sayers and 'Michael Innes'—*The Pale Horse* and *Endless Night* are examples. These art-based ways of euphemising the threat in the material are foreign to Christie's early material and approach.

Presentation of character is shallow and naturalised. A few details are given, and a general summary of the person's nature suffices. In the description of Ralph Paton in Chapter Three he is said to be selfish, both indulging himself and respecting no-one else. But at the same time, and with no explanation, he is loved and admired by his friends. That presentation at once admits and forgives the weakness of individualism; but it is also curiously, and crucially, non-individual in its flat simplicity. This sort of cursory but confident assessment given to all the characters. No depth is sought and no change occurs to them in the story. If discoveries are made they resolve enigmas in the original presentation—as with Flora, Ralph, Ursula, Miss Russell and Parker. Just as character is flat and single-faceted so when all the details are collected motive is uniform and simple. People do not undergo changes of mind, are not in dialectic with others or themselves. Ralph's concealed marriage is explained by his 'weakness', not by any perceived tension between personal desires and family pressures. The individual is conceived as a unit, guided by his or her own intentions and responding to, not controlled by, external forces. The relevance to the bourgeois idea of self is obvious; both the forces beyond the individual and the fissures in the private personality are concealed. We wait for each character to be given its brief notation— charming, efficient, nervous, servile and so on. Bizarre secrets and humble characteristics are narrated in an undifferentiating, and so antiseptic way. Marionettes are provided to play out the extraordinary complicated action, the puzzle plot is made possible, suspicion of all can be created without probing the real roots or mechanisms of unsocial behaviour.

This technique is easily scorned as formulaic, naive, unlike the complexity of real human interaction. It presents a very simple world where criminal deviance is equally plain, a 'weak' straying from the path of self-control and socially acceptable, mutually protective behaviour. In spite of the totem of Poirot's psychology this interpretation is a long way from the insights of mental science, and Christie later on (especially in *They Do It With Mirrors*) extricates herself with some vigour and animus from psychological interpretations of behaviour, preferring a simple right and wrong, good and evil model of human action. But to condemn her system from one's own self-consciously complex standpoint can too often lead to the conclusion that her system is ingenuous and therefore without validity for anyone. In fact her presentation and her evaluative technique are, like her dry, formulaic style, typical of well-known and enormously popular forms of communication, powerfully meaningful for many people. Her novels read like folk-tales or children's stories and, apart from their structural closure in a resolved narrative, like gossip.

In all these forms characters have a few crucial features, motivation is simple and only explained in terms of deviance from good; style is decidedly plain; resolutions are consistent, often highly artificial and deeply comforting. Gossip is a narrative form in so far as it recounts what people do; it may even include an implied closure—'she'll come to a bad end' or the ironic 'good luck to him' are typical examples. The naivety of the method matches many people's anxious need for simple comforting answers. Perceiving complexity, as most politicians know, is not a common or a popular activity. Christie's power comes at least in part from her own simplification of issues. She recreates familiar folk patterns within a specific social setting. If that sounds an unworthy role for a writer, perhaps one should hesitate to be censorious, remembering that much intellectual industry devotes itself to asserting naturalised value in complicated insights. The novel is resolved, the thesis completed as a means of justifying a sophisticated approach to life: a programme for action emerges as rarely from intellectualising work as social self-awareness and true self-criticism occur in a Christie novel.

To see the formal methods in the context of folk-tales, children's stories and gossip is to see both the authority and intrinsic authenticity of Christie's work. She charts a familiar world with no surprises, no senses that its detail might be foreign or alarming. Divagation from normalcy is limited to the crime and the puzzle surrounding it, and this is resolved by familiar methods. Even the crime itself is a demotic one; Shepherd is a doctor, but he merely stabs his victim. And though the first Poirot story had an intricate and specially informed—though entirely accurate and possible—way of poisoning, Christie's later crimes are quite ordinary in technique however complicated the embracing action might be. Through Shepherd Christie explicity mocks those élitist crime stories where elaborate poisons are used to manipulate mystery into being. *The Murder of Roger Ackroyd* is totally unrealistic in its limited setting, its blinkered view of reality, its extraordinary plot, but at the same time remorselessly realistic and accessible in its basic mechanics: the bizarre and the bathetically ordinary mix in a bland illusion that can both excite and console.

In structure the novel is, like all effective clue-puzzles, double. In one way it is an organic structure, moving steadily through events to a conclusion, and the ideological forces of such structures, discussed in previous chapters, operate to assert the validity of the account. Indeed, the notion that reality is being charted is pressed urgently on the reader by the insistent naturalism of time and place. Every chapter in *The Murder of Roger Ackroyd* either continues immediately from its predecessor or indicates in the opening sentence when its action begins (Chapter Fifteen is an exception as the time is given in the opening of the second paragraph, but even then a general reference to time occurs in the first sentence). As the clock ticks away the characters move within a delimited area, based on a plan of Ackroyd's house and a topography of the village. The physical location and interaction of the characters is carefully reported.

The traditional novel matched its organic form with a lucidly developing theme, but that comforting sense of a developing comprehension is foreign to this genre, where the reader must undergo puzzlement. Because some actions, speeches and actions are ambiguous or obscure in meaning the novel has another, thematic structure. The meaning of the action does not become clear as the novel proceeds, the climax is only prepared if we, like the detective, decipher the events. The rigidity of the time and place structure emphasises the obscurity of the thematic shape, challenges us all the more urgently to decode it. The dual structure enacts the central drama of the novel, a threat to order that only careful observation can resolve. Christie's art at its most effective makes both structures extreme: the one is strictly rigid, the other very baffling. Each new event or conversation, firmly realistic in its own mode, suggests new facts and new ways in which the information received might settle into order. The thematic structure is partly hidden by a mass of acts, many of which will be irrelevant. The secondary action of the sub-plots in particular obscures the answer to the puzzle, but other confusing details are also offered, like the enigma of Ralph's shoes.

There is a highly artificial quality to the complicated, even frenetic activity which surrounds the time and place of the murder. Some of the motivation is contrived to the point of flimsiness—the reason for Ralph's disappearance is particularly slender. This elaborate complication is basic to Christie, and gives a certain aesthetic pleasure from its sheer complication, like the self-congratulatory wit of crossword clues. At the same time, the artificiality of the puzzle-creation, so willingly accepted by readers, in itself euphemises events. The game-like features of the novel are forceful enough to dilute the real strength of the threats that are played with. Only the most technically and aesthetically strained processes can present so complete a puzzle, and this in itself suggests ordinary life will not be so testing and allows the reader's fears of others—and even of the self—to exercise and dissolve themselves in a controlled, hygienic environment. The tendency to use playful titles in crime fiction, and even in books about crime fiction, is another aspect of this feature, but in her early titles and her scornful attitude to the Sayers type of self-indulgence Christie puts a firm restraint to the extent of this escapist tendency in the genre.

The clue-puzzle structure in itself has immediate relevance to an audience deeply imbued with anxious individualism, but the stunning structural device of making the doctor-narrator the concealed criminal gives great formal energy to the distrust of other respectable people basic to Christie's novels and to bourgeois self-consciousness; and as has been argued it even invokes the sense of potential deviance within the self. A class whose very ascendancy is based on individual competition, on self-creation and self-protection, cannot rely, as *The Newgate Calendar* did, on a sense of cooperation to extirpate criminal threats. A class whose literary anxiety is personal extinction cannot easily trust anyone whose hand might be raised against them, when any dagger, gun, rope or paperweight might be the instrument by which the treasured private life may end. At the same time a class which is very aware of its own powers to govern itself, which does not happily agree to autocratic leadership, which evolved the highly complex system of popular representation that we know as democracy, is not as readily charmed as *Strand* readers were by dreams of a single figure who justifies his authority by extending protection. At best Poirot is a reduced and partly despised hero; he symbolises the values and methods which will fictionally bring order, but is never given the adulation that the thrusting authoritarian detectives of crime fiction are accorded by their less self-conscious, less self-made readers.

Although the main early readership of Christie's novels can be identified as a social class, that owned or aspired to own property and had a clear structure in itself, the fact that the victim is always a person of property and position is not, in my view, a sign that the stories have any conscious grasp of social patterns of authority. The stories do not enact a sense that social structures can be weakened by criminal incursion, that removing the head of the family weakens the social unit. The novels show so little consciousness of hierarchy that this essentially political interpretation of the murder is not realised. The victim owns property because property-owning is the personalised wish and self-knowledge of the bourgeois man and woman; the enemies to life and the property-conscious existence are already within the family or the trusted circle, like the family doctor. The individualised nature of bourgeois life explains the consistent presence of murder as a crime, and the direction of this threat towards property owners enacts the reader's own fears for his or her own property and also, as the Freudian interpretation shows, traces a reader's own envy towards those seniors who block his or her way to a fuller grasp of property and rank.

The pervasive individualism of bourgeois feeling and epistemology is, as has been argued here, crucial to the whole edifice of the clue-puzzle in crime, detection and literary structure. Yet at the same time the style, values and presentation of the material are curiously depersonalised; the upholding of group values, a duty to conform, is very powerful in Christie's work. I believe this confrontation between a basic individualism and a collective value system and style is a crucial meaningful fissure. It reveals the central reason for Christie's success, her almost mesmerising power over readers. She offers a dream of collective security which is based on fully individual systems. The whole construction denies that crime is a natural product of individuality; the threat of anarchy is removed from the pursuit of personal freedom. Through the notion of duty and normalcy, freely chosen not socially imposed, Christie presents as proper a system of living which can promise respectable people the continued enjoyment of the life-style they or their forbears have personally earned by successful conflict with others.

The problematic rejects real and contradictory material. The progress of others is excluded; erratic self-indulgence is minimised to trivial and harmless deviance; the internecine struggle among respectable people for property and money is confronted, put down to 'weakness' and brought to silence. The means of balancing this extraordinary tension between individual and collective systems is to select plot detail and organise the events so skilfully that ordinary powers of observation and orderly thought paper over the fissure, and are themselves a sufficient way of identifying the deviant. The saving methods are watching and listening, paying especial attention to objects, behaviour, gestures, verbal innuendo and, above all, to movement and time—all the skills which bourgeois people exercise as weapons to make a living, reproduce their class and pass their leisure time. Beneath the surface of the fiction the reader can exorcise fears that he or she could show 'weakness' and act self-indulgently against the interest of the class, be personally a model of the deviance that is feared. The whole construction provides illusory comforts of considerable power, worked out with an even and meticulous skill.

In *The Murder of Roger Ackroyd* Poirot is the symbolic projection and proponent of the detecting skills. Many of Christie's audience have continued to feel the need of such a figure, a hero with much reduced machismo. But as Christie went on she tired of Poirot. Market forces kept him alive and functioning, but she did not make Doyle's attempt, itself a futile display of individualism, to remove what she called her albatross. She did invent a detective closer to her own developed ideas, a woman who represented bourgeois village life much like Caroline Shepherd, who observed people and objects closely and in particular who could apply the lessons learnt in ordinary life to the threats of murderous deviance.

Jane Marple first appeared in *Murder at the Vicarage* in 1930, and she represents just the feminine method Poirot outlined to Shepherd. Her judgements of people seem intuitive but are quite sense-available in basis. An elderly spinster, much given to gossip, but kind as well as shrewd, she is in some senses a bourgeois anti-heroine, a little person who succeeds where others fail—notably the police and her posturing nephew Raymond, a writer of fashionable intellectual crime novels. This last feature, and the scorn for the press, come straight from Christie's personal feelings, but being authentic class feelings they merge successfully with the general ideology of the novel.

The meticulous density of detail and plot, the fully developed and innovative persona of Miss Marple have made this a favourite book, and it demonstrates well many of Christie's most important features. The viewpoint remains outside the detective. Here the narrator is the vicar; in later Marple novels Christie will use third person narration for this effect, or a multiple viewpoint form, with letters or explanatory epilogues to fill out the information. The detective is merely one of the forces in the novel, without the privileged position given to first person detective narrators, or achieved by the mediation of a Watson or Hastings in the early Poirot novels. The romantic element remains and the vicar's own relationship with his wife is the love-interest, sealed at the end by a pregnancy Miss Marple is the first to detect, so implying investigating skills are as effective in the context of life as in death.

The plot is labyrinthine; the complexities of time and place in the few houses around the vicarage are quite dazzling both in affective impact and in the skill with which Christie continually rearranges possible resolutions. Secondary actions abound to make characters act oddly—there are two different thefts, the victim's dying wife has returned to the village, and various interpersonal hostilities thicken the mystery. The victim, for all his money and authoritative position, is as unappealing a character as Ackroyd. The objective scenes of dialogue, framed by the vicar's calm moral clichés, give the hectic activity a gloss of normality to assist and conceal the euphemising force innate to its artificiality. The presentation slides blandly over some extremely strained plotting, as in the near murder of the unfortunate thieving curate. Miss Marple's busy, humble personality enacts with great success the idea of domestic watchfulness, though she is something of a leader, much better at observation and analysis than the other spinster watchwomen: only she sees the significance of a certain potted plant, a stone too large for her rockery, a piece of affectionate interaction between the criminals.

By making these ordinary skills tangible and unmystifying, Christie finds room to dismiss the psychology on which Poirot prided himself. A running debate occurs in which the doctor argues that crime is not derived from evil but a sickness; this view is dismissed, neatly rather than convincingly, when his pity for the attacked curate makes him eager to punish the murderer sternly. The theme remained important to Christie, and she spoke openly on the topic in her autobiography.

Miss Marple brings into focus the tendencies clearly present in the early Poirot novels, and in the following years Christie continued to work them out. Occasionally she offered bravura performances, as in *Murder on the Orient Express* where all the characters are villains, and its equally skilful reverse *Ten Little Niggers* where all are victims—the murderer presents himself as one of them. However much a large part of her audience remained indebted to the leadership qualities shown by Poirot and Miss Marple, Christie herself tried to make detecting deviance an even less individualistic process than her two protagonists embodied. Many of the later novels are without a detective at all, and this includes two of the three she chose in her autobiography as her favourites, *Crooked House* and *Ordeal by Innocence*. In both novels a family disrupted by murder casts up the destructive force with the help of a neutral outsider drawn into events. The third novel she chose, *The Moving Finger*, involves a brother and sister with murderous disorder in a village; only at the very end does Miss Marple appear and give a decisive analysis of their experiences. In these and similar stories Christie tried to make identification of crime within the power of ordinary people from her special social range.

The collection of short stories that she specially favoured dissipated individualistic detective authority by giving it supernatural status. Harley Quin, a deliberately thin disguise for Harlequin, the spirit who avenges the dead, appears magically to identify a murderer and sometimes supervise his punishment. The stories have an odd effect, for in spite of his unusual authority and power Quin's methods are restricted to observing and interpreting physical data. Christie does not turn to the supernatural for special insights into crime, but to naturalise and so defuse the way in which the process of detection singles out the practitioner, lifts him or her from the even tenor of bourgeois life and so shapes an unsettling authority in the detective.

The tension between an individual and society is, as sociologists like to say, itself a bourgeois perception. But it is also a dominant perception, part of what Raymond Williams would call the structure of feeling in our period. The resolution of the tension has occupied writers whose approach varies as much as Erich Fromm and Jean-Paul Sartre. Christie's instinctive literary concern tended towards anodyne and artificial resolutions of the tension rather than urgent exposure of its mechanisms. But there were some occasions when her own thoughts confronted the issues directly and with less simple or comforting resolution.

In her very guarded autobiography Christie records three moments when she was gripped by intellectual excitement. One was the contact with new ideas about time. They seemed to free her imagination from the onward progress to death, that extinction of the individual consciousness which is the inevitable conclusion of one's own relation with diachronic time. In fiction she did not deal with this alternative idea of time, though her ancient clue-puzzle *Death Comes as the End* seems, especially with its revealing title, a gesture in such a direction. In the equally ominously titled novel she wrote last, *Postern of Fate*, Christie made the positively decrepit Tommy and Tuppence Beresford put their great age to good use in solving a mystery as notable for its antiquity as for the creaky joints in its plotting.

The other two exciting occasions show Christie realising the solitary personality's relation with others, not with the immanent forces of time. She reports that she once had a sort of epiphany, realising that all other people were individuals, just like her. It seemed a profound insight and reconciled her greatly to the blank mysteriousness of other peoples' lives. It was clearly her own conscious formation of an ideological bridge between a totally personal viewpoint and a strange collective individualism, that pattern that she had already begun to construct inside the patterns of her fiction.

The third cerebral excitement is recorded in a 'Mary Westmacott' novel which she urgently wrote in three days, far from her usual craftsmanlike plod through a manuscript. Most of the Westmacott stories are fairly conventional romances, about a dutiful girl finally finding happiness with a man who will neither let her down nor lean on her. But *Absent in the Spring* is different. In it Joan Scudamour reflects over her life while marooned in the desert—the situation in which Christie had her 'other people' insight. She realises that she has always been too insistent on her own and other peoples' duty to let them—especially her husband—have full personal development. The title and the setting emphasise the sense of aridity she feels. She decides to be less restrictive; but when she meets her husband again only slips back into her old pattern.

The novel debates the problems of individual freedom, realising the dampening effect of a dutiful restrictive influence like Joan. Yet in the very last scene Christie seems to record her final sense of the limits of individuality. It is her initial and conclusive sense too, because, relying on her detective story technique, she wrote the last chapter first. The closure of the plot, the thematic structure which emerges from the mysterious hints shows Joan's husband buried in unreality, as selfish and manipulative in his own private pleasures as his wife is in her authoritarian collective pressures. Here Christie leaves in uneasy tension those opposites of duty and freedom that she had managed to resolve in the illusions of form and content in her crime novels.

The novel shows Christie was capable of bringing her own concerns into successful fictional realisation. It therefore seems all the more likely that she is a genuine channel for the anxieties and the ultimate self-consolations of her class and sex. The determinedly unartistic approach she took to writing does not mean she could not imaginatively activate themes immanent in her experience and environment. She saw herself as a story teller, but through the ages such naive, unpretentious artists, like Doyle in his Holmes stories, have been able to weave patterns that both raised and dissipated the fears of their audiences.

Christie's central audience was leisured, relatively unskilled but also competitive and self-conscious—the classic anxious bourgeois class. For them she fashioned a form that ratified conservatism, the duty others owe the self, and ultimately the ability of very ordinary powers to cope with the disorder such people faced, in the world and within themselves.

The banality and passivity of her investigations, the limited and artificial nature of her plotting were inherent to her ideological force. They did not satisfy everybody in her period. This was made very clear by the scornful treatment Raymond Chandler gave her work as he came to shape a very different fable of a hero confronting crime in what passed for a realistic and newly intelligent way.

REFERENCES

Texts
The Murder on the Links, Pan, London, reprint 1960.
The Murder of Roger Ackroyd, Fontana, London, reprint 1957.
The Murder at the Vicarage, Fontana, London, reprint 1961.

Criticism
Christie's own comments appear in *An Autobiography*, Collins, London, 1977.

Erich Fromm, *Escape from Freedom*, Farrar and Rinehart, New York, 1941.

Thomas Narcejac, *Une machine à lire—le roman policier*, Denoel, Paris, 1975.

Jean-Paul Sartre, *The Search for a Method*, Vintage, New York, 1968.

Julian Symons, 'The Mistress of Complication', in H. R. F. Keating (ed.), *Agatha Christie: First Lady of Crime*, Weidenfeld & Nicholson, London, 1977.

Elizabeth Walter, 'The Case of the Escalating Sales', in *Agatha Christie: First Lady of Crime*, op. cit.

Colin Watson, 'The Message of Mayhem Parva', in *Agatha Christie: First Lady of Crime*, op. cit.

Raymond Williams, *The Long Revolution*, rev. edn, Pelican, London, 1965.

5 '. . . a hard-boiled gentleman'—Raymond Chandler's Hero

The calm spell of the clue-puzzle entranced many readers in the twenties and thirties on both sides of the Atlantic. In the USA Erle Stanley Gardner reproduced Christie's arid certainty, while 'S. S. Van Dine' and Rex Stout matched Dorothy Sayers and Margery Allingham in creating an intellectualised, languidly triumphant detective hero. But even in Britain clue-puzzlers did not dominate the market, great though their prestige became. Simpler reflexes of Sherlock Holmes like Sexton Blake or the Saint had wide appeal to an audience younger, less cerebral or more naive than the clue-puzzle addicts, and Bulldog Drummond's violent defence of British respectability gave widespread satisfaction. In America the clue-puzzlers' authority was never so strong, partly because their natural socio-intellectual base was not so powerful in the opinion-making media, but also because a readily identifiable alternative genre arose, the tough-guy or hard-boiled thriller.

Dashiell Hammett is usually held to be the founding force of this kind of writing, bringing the independence and isolated rectitude of the old frontier hero into conflict with urban crime of modern America. The semi-factual novels ghost-written for Allan Pinkerton, the American equivalent of Vidocq, have been cited as a key fact in this development, especially by William Ruehlmann in *Saint with a Gun*. But this view makes literary relationships dominate real life—Hammett, himself a Pinkerton agent, was capable of realising his own experience in the American heroic tradition. He was the most influential of the writers on the tough-guy pulp magazine *Black Mask*; other contributors were urged to imitate him and their material was subedited to resemble his clipped, objective yet emotive style. His own radicalism, which brought him towards the Communist Party and to jail in the McCarthy period, saw urban corruption as the mainspring of much crime, and shaped an unromantic, realist hero in a style that seemed fully materialist.

Hammett remains an interesting figure, not least because each novel is different from the others. His restless mind avoided formulae, but after his socially limited, puzzle-oriented *The Thin Man* he fell silent for the last thirty years of his life. Hammett's techniques make him an attractive and comforting writer for partly investigative readers, but for an ideological study Raymond Chandler, who readily admitted his debt to Hammett, is more revealing. He did write to a formula, did create a constant hero, and so has a more uniform direction: he repeats in form and content the patterns that shape the meaning of his texts. His apparent realistic modernism conceals a conservative and elitist position, giving a classic example of the way in which illusion can operate in a popular fictional form.

Chandler's education and, to an extent, his social position suggest he might have become a writer of intellectual clue-puzzles. Born in America with a mother of respectable Irish family and an obscure American father, after his parents separated he was educated at Dulwich College in South London. This school avoids the aristocratic contacts and pretensions of Eton or Harrow; it is an upper-middle-class institution with age, culture, delightful setting and urban contact to fix it in the metropolitan power-structure sustained by that class. Characteristically enough, Chandler went into the civil service on leaving school; he continued along predictable lines by writing reviews, poems and short pieces of opinionated aestheticism for genteel London periodicals. A career as a minor poet and perhaps a series of clue-puzzles—under a discreet pseudonym—seemed to await the fluent, sensitive young man.

But Chandler became dissatisfied. Later he would say that English arrogance and high-handed manner irritated him. The early essays show a distaste for the more languid certainties of contemporary English intellectualism; it is a literary version of the same discontent. He borrowed money from his Irish uncle and returned to America—partly to retain American citizenship, and so reject the life-style that beckoned in England. Chandler served as an infantryman in the last stages of the war—a grim and disturbing experience which surfaces through Terry Lennox in *The Long Goodbye*. Afterwards he settled into an American businessman pattern as an oil company accountant, but his sense of exile seems to have been partly responsible for his restlessness—he constantly moved house and drank a good deal.

His own edginess and the economic depression together put him out of work in the early thirties, and he turned back to writing. He used Hammett and Gardner as models. From Hammett he drew a writing style and a sense of urban corruption; the link is strongest in the early stories. Hammett had stopped writing before Chandler began and they only met once; he gave a starting-point Chandler moved away from, and critics have overstressed their relationship. Gardner offered his plotting skill and the even tone in which he set out unlikely events and intricate action. Chandler's own ideology is some way from Gardner's narrow WASP business ethics, but the two men were friendly, and there was always a hard business side to Chandler. His work is an intellectualised literary mirror-image of Gardner's contented bourgeois world, rejecting it and also using it to define the valued self by that negation.

A number of Chandler's short stories were printed in *Black Mask* from 1933 onwards. In them a detective hero, who is sometimes presented in the third person, discovers by his physical presence and insight more than by detailed detection the real nature of a criminal event. The hero observes, suffers and also inflicts violence; the plot normally includes a final surprise as an unexpected villain is revealed, or a surprising piece of motivation is given for an obvious criminal. The setting is contemporary California; the tone seems objective, relying on staccato colloquial dialogue and brief direct accounts of the physical setting. The model of an adventure hero, an up-to-date knight errant has been noted by many critics who seize with some pleasure on the clue Chandler gave once by naming his hero Mallory. Sir Thomas Malory's *Le Morte Darthur* was the sort of thing people were enjoying in the literary London of Chandler's youth: Rhys's Everyman edition came out in 1906, just before Chandler joined the civil service.

The standard critical response to Chandler, basis of many articles and some books, is to see him merging Hammett's tough-guy tone with the more arty atmosphere of romance—even medieval romance if the critic has read widely. This describes some surface patterns in Chandler, but it does not examine the implications of the romance genre, nor wonder why Chandler made the union: the coincidence of aesthetic London and realist California seems enough of a shaping force. But Chandler had his own cultural attitudes to impose on his location; when young he dismissed realistic literature in favour of idealist, romantic writing as his essay 'Realism and Fairyland' shows. He continued to dislike naturalistic writing like James M. Cain's, especially when he was writing the film-script for *Double Indemnity*. In rejecting England and its culture he shed Georgian poetic trappings, but never altered his premise that real writing was based on romantic individualism. Hammett's approach had the virtue of seeming valid and contemporary, but Chandler consistently adopts an individual viewpoint. He breaks up the genuinely objective stance that Hammett worked for, and sees contemporary disorder from the position of a disgusted and disengaged persona, whose own values are defined by his rejection of a social world viewed as a hostile and corrupt unit.

If Chandler's work is examined in terms of its underlying ideology reasons emerge why it has generated praise from university graduates in English and people of similar tastes and needs. The pressure of the form and the content suggests that an isolated, intelligent person, implicitly hostile to others and basically uninterested in them, can verify his own superiority by intellectual means and create a defensive withdrawal. He can resolve apparently puzzling and personally threatening problems by thoughtful, passive inspection and so continue his lonely life—and earn a living in the process. A richly satisfying message is fabricated for the alienated person of some education, and the natural audience has not failed to find Chandler comforting. This has given him considerable sales—though nothing like those gained by Christie or Gardner. But what Chandler's natural audience lacked in sheer numbers it made up in its hold on literary prestige and opinion-making; he has gained special status as the most literary, and so the most respectable of the crime writers. Even Edmund Wilson, who despised the genre, attuned as he was to more sophisticated and roundabout systems of cultural self-validation, agreed that Chandler had merit, and *Farewell, My Lovely*, at least, was an interesting book.

This is the novel I will discuss in detail in this chapter, though all of them would provide a good source for analysis. After working on stories for some years Chandler, like Hammett and Gardner before him, moved up to the novel with *The Big Sleep* in 1939. This involved a more extended plot and expanded scenes. It also had a higher price—and a rather different market if the contrast between the cheap format of the magazines and the sleek bulk of a Knopf first edition is to be a guide (though Knopf were Hammett's publishers they did not specialise in crime fiction at all). The change of medium implies a change of attitude, and Chandler's technique and meaning alter a good deal, as is shown in his new treatment of previously published material. *The Big Sleep* was based mainly on the earlier story 'Killer in the Rain', with more material from 'The Curtain' and some small pieces from elsewhere. The novel was well received, though some reviewers found it violent and obscurely elaborate. It sold about 10,000 copies in a year, a reasonable success for the time, and Knopf were keen for another. *Farewell, My Lovely* was published in 1940, developed from three short stories: 'Try the Girl', 'Mandarin's Jade' and 'The Man who Liked Dogs'.

Chandler consistently thought it his best novel—he said it was 'the top', feeling the 'bony structure was much more solid, the invention less forced and more fluent' than in the other books. He was clearly aware of the interrelation of formal force and the selection of content detail: Chandler's critical remarks are often formally acute, though he usually stops well short of considering what the ideological direction of the form and content might be. Not all readers have agreed this is the best book: some have favoured the brio of *The Big Sleep*, the overt feeling of *The Long Goodbye* or the distaste for Hollywood in *The Little Sister*. *The Lady in the Lake*, which was largely written in tandem with *Farewell, My Lovely* and is very like it in tone and density, has had many admirers, and some (Philip Durham and Blanche Knopf for example) have even praised· *The High Window*, which Chandler thought poor. Only *Playback* seems universally condemned. It is much thinner than the other novels and Marlowe plays an unusual role in it; indeed he was not in the original film-script version. The other books are, in meaning and performance, very coherent, and so evaluative preference among them rests on quite random personal decisions. Any one of the novels will reveal the basic patterns of Chandler's form and content, and it seems reasonable to study his own favourite, a book written before his debilitating engagement with Hollywood and long before the illness of his wife. *Farewell, My Lovely* avoids the self-indulgence of the later novels and the unevenness Chandler felt flawed *The Big Sleep*: in it his art is fully formed and can be most fairly examined to see the ideological patterns he shapes in all the novels.

In commenting on his books Chandler consistently put great emphasis on style (which he often called 'writing') as a quality of his work, convinced it was his principal means of raising the crime story to respectable artistic levels. He is a conscious and obvious stylist.

Christie's style was a recessive and almost subliminal verification of an ideology more easily visible in her patterns of content; Chandler's manipulations of style and presentation are immediately evident and offer the most accessible path into his ideological construct, delineating patterns that a study of structure and content will confirm.

Chandler offered himself as an objective writer; he disowned 'the fuzziness that seems inseparable from the subjective approach' and told Knopf 'Insofar as I am able I want to develop an objective method.' Durham and other critics have been content to accept the style as objective, seeing it usually in the context of Hemingway's apparently neutral narrative method. The emotive implications of Hemingway's style are well known—Walker Gibson's book *Tough, Sweet and Stuffy* gives a good summary of this 'tough' rhetoric. And even Durham has to admit that Chandler's word-choice and images 'have a subjective force'.

The notionally 'objective' style creates an illusion. It suggests the material presented has absolute value, but at the same time the persona's viewpoint is insistently stressed; his own evaluation of the material is itself given a quasi-objective status, made valid by association. The positivist note is caught in the frequent clipped, unanalysed pieces of action like: 'The big man took me by the arm and we went over to the little elevator. It came up. We got into it.' Chandler was well aware of this positivism as a distinctive and gesturing style; he wrote a very funny pastiche of Hemingway, 'Beer in the Sergeant Major's Hat', and in *Farewell, My Lovely* he acknowledged the rhetorical nature of this technique when Marlowe calls Galbraith 'Hemingway' because of his repetitive laconic speech.

In the opening pages of the novel this style manipulates feeling; an apparently factual mode of narration is only the persuasive background to the foregrounding of a sensitive, discriminating persona. The novel begins with a calm, communicative tone: 'It was one of the mixed blocks over on Central Avenue,' but the sentence goes on to elucidate and predict: 'one of the blocks that are not yet all negro.' Repetition brings analysis, not cumulation of facts. This analysis is not, like Christie's, relying on clichés and collective wisdom; it has the power to explain and specify with sensitive precision, as the following narration shows. First, a simple statement again: 'A man was looking up at the sign too'; simple, but itself privileging the hero, because he was there looking first. That pre-

eminence is now created through verbal and analytic sophistication: 'He was looking up at the dusty windows with a sort of
ecstatic fixity of expression.' The persona then expands with a
confidently American simile that evaluates as it appears to describe:
'like a hunky immigrant catching his first sight of the Statue of
Liberty.' Subtlety of mind and vocabulary, clear and penetrating
observation, are emotively linked with the totems of American
independence and freedom: a ground-bass to the whole
Chandlerian ideology has been sounded.

Throughout this opening sequence the narrator raises the tone of
his description with confident, self-conscious metaphors: 'alligator
shoes with white explosions on the toes', 'from his outer breast
pocket cascaded a show handkerchief'. This self-aware analysis is
brought to a head in the closing simile: 'Even on Central Avenue,
not the quietest dressed street in the world, he looked about as
inconspicuous as a tarantula on a slice of angel food.' Chandler's
similes are a powerful element of his style, and this is a famous one.
Its sheer ingenuity draws attention to the speaker's—and writer's—
special abilities rather than giving merely a heightened description
of the topic. The extended, confident syntax stresses the polished,
literary power of speaker and author. In so far as the comment does
treat its subject, it conveys the speaker's fear and a sense of threat, an
alarmed recoil from a hostile body. Marlowe's reaction to people in
general is vividly communicated in the very words parading the
nimble subtlety of mind which provides his personal defence against
the threat of others.

This is far from being the objective style that many readers
would, in order to have faith in his ideological meaning, like to
identify in Chandler. In spite of his notional objectivity, Chandler
himself recognised his conscious modelling of language for effect; his
aim was 'the creation of emotion through dialogue and description'.
He remarked that American language was basically foreign to him;
Ross MacDonald, his conscious follower, himself Canadian in
origin, has expanded the issue, arguing that he and Chandler both
work the language self-consciously to achieve meaning. Fredric
Jameson, in one of the most perceptive articles written on Chandler,
has identified the 'alien stylist' at work—'language can never again
be unselfconscious for him, words can never again be unproblemati-
cal'. Camus also recognised the 'most arbitrary form of stylisation'
which the tough-guy writers used to establish their effect, but he
gave no more specific account of the language itself, moving on to a

further-reaching critique of the total effect of the text, to which I will return. The best description of the tonal impact of Chandler's style was given by J. B. Priestley—and perhaps it is not surprising that he, a professional story teller who also used objectivity as a disguise for feeling and was himself alien to Chandler's milieu and language, was so sensitive to the effect. He saw it 'like a kind of private theatre, almost as artificial in its way as Restoration Comedy'. The remark is acute: privacy and a sense of theatrical performance are central to Marlowe's world-view. The analogy made is revealing; Restoration Comedy also validated the stance of a particular socio-intellectual group in the face of social and moral confusion. The force of Priestley's summary will become clearer in the course of this chapter.

Although the opening gambit of objective narration slides into a subjective control of the action by the narrator, this authority does not reveal itself in the narrator's dialogue. Where Lord Peter Wimsey or Nero Wolfe, in third person narrative, reveal their superiority to the world by speech as well as action, Marlowe makes it a secret between him and the reader. To other characters he speaks demotically, as if he were in fact on their level. Marlowe's acceptance of a language that seems unnatural to him, a sort of linguistic camouflage, links with the passivity of his methods and with the overall quietism of Chandler's view of the world, topics to be brought out later.

In the dialogue of the opening sequence, which sets the tone for the whole book, there is an intriguing key to the persona's feelings towards others. He says little to Moose Malloy, this massive, disrupting force, but tends to act as a passive chorus: 'It's that kind of a place . . . what did you expect'; 'Go on up and see for yourself.' But when he does speak substantively he employs a strikingly different tone and imagery: ' "All right," I yelled. "I'll go with you. Just lay off carrying me. Let me walk. I'm fine. I'm all grown up. I go to the bathroom alone and everything. Just don't carry me." ' Self-revelation lies in the childish petulance of the voice as the persona is forced to engage with the problem that will stretch before him. The superior intelligence that controls private narration is not projected into actual encounters—at best the voice in dialogue imitates what is judged to be the public voice. When the persona is infringed he speaks in various unsocial, non-adult ways; here he is explicitly childish, at other times sarcastically aggressive (to police) or negatively defensive (to Anne Riordan). The persona's public and private voices express the unease he feels in contact with external reality and the comfortable control he commands when mediating events in private reverie to his silent and invisible audience. The patterns of inner-directed, intellectualising self-defence, compensating for social fear and inadequacy, are realised in the style itself.

Chandler's presentation of his material is entirely consistent with the essentially subjective aspects of his style. The tangible location of the observing eye is a necessary preliminary; each new scene begins with a careful pinpointing on the map of the Los Angeles area. Time is not as important here as it was in Christie; the physical encounter of the persona with his environment and the people in it is primary, and the ticking clock that chronicles interrelations is now irrelevant because others are an undifferentiated threat to the physically located hero. The sense-available details of each scene are laid out in what Jameson has aptly called an 'inventory' style. The metaphor neatly implies the object-dominated consciousness of the narration and further suggests that the epistemology, for all its stress on romantic personalised feeling, actually relies on the reified, commodity-based knowledge characteristic of bourgeois thought.

The opening of the second sequence in the novel is a good example; Marlowe arrives at Mrs Florian's house:

> 1644 West 54th Place was a dried-out brown house with a dried-out brown lawn in front of it. There was a large bare patch around a tough-looking palm tree. On the porch stood one lonely rocker, and the afternoon breeze made the unpruned shoots of last year's poinsettias tap-tap against the cracked stucco wall. A line of stiff yellowish half-washed clothes jittered on a rusty wire in the side yard.

Chandler's 'writing' gives the aridity of the scene affective force—'dried-out brown' is repeated for monotony and the vocabulary in 'cracked stucco', 'poinsettias tap-tap' and 'jittered' creates in sound the nervy distaste the persona feels for the slovenly setting. Apparently neutral description and even, unanalytic syntax are imbued with the perceptions and the feelings of the describer who watches, feels, judges. Tangible objects are known and assessed through his sensitivity; they do not have full significance in themselves, merely as they are mediated through his view of the world. The palm tree is 'tough-looking', the rocker is 'lonely': his

feeling is the vanishing point on which the presentation of the
objects converges.

Chandler habitually uses the physical surroundings to foreground his hero's feelings. Here they register the shabby inadequacy
he finds in a low-income environment. He rejects as readily what he
sees as the artificial prisons of the rich; the Grayle mansion is one of
the many examples in his novels:

> It was close to the ocean and you could feel the ocean in the air
> but you couldn't see water from the front of the place. Aster Drive
> had a long smooth curve there and the houses on the inland side
> were just nice houses, but on the canyon side they were great
> silent estates, with twelve foot walls and wrought iron gates and
> ornamental hedges; and inside, if you could get inside, a special
> brand of sunshine, very quiet, put up in noise proof containers,
> just for the upper classes.

Privilege does not liberate, it seems Marlowe only feels free when
alone with nature. As he goes to meet Lindsay Marriott he senses
beauty and isolation together:

> I got down to Montemar Vista as the light began to fade, but
> there was still a fine sparkle on the water and the surf was
> breaking far out in long smooth curves . . . A lonely yacht was
> taking in toward the yacht harbour at Bay City. Beyond it the
> huge emptiness of the Pacific was purple-grey.

Marlowe consciously cuts himself off from urban society like the
person he now sees, who shares his viewpoint literally and
metaphorically:

> Beyond the arch the sidewalk cafe my client had spoken of was
> bright and cheerful inside, but the iron-legged, tile-topped tables
> outside were empty save for a single dark woman in slacks who
> smoked and stared moodily out to sea with a bottle of beer in
> front of her.

But to live he has to have a 'client', to engage unwillingly with
others and this setting provides for Marlowe a rather self-pitying
image of himself as he climbs the steps to his next encounter:

They were drifted over with windblown sand and the handrail was as cold and wet as a toad's belly.

When I reached the top the sparkle had gone from the water and a seagull with a broken trailing leg was twisting against the offsea breeze.

From Marlowe's viewpoint the city itself, stocked with hostile others, becomes threatening—'the slimy dirt of cities' oppresses the clear-spirited hero; he feels that Los Angeles degrades and reifies spring to be 'like a paper bag blowing along the concrete sidewalk'. Marlowe, like so many urban aliens, feels he can escape into unthreatening nature, as when Amthor's driver takes him past the 'Hollywood flesh-peddlers' into the 'still dark foothills', but even there human traps can be sprung. Jameson has shrewdly remarked that part of Chandler's success is to have imaginatively realised the sense of urban blight that has been so widely felt in recent years—his Los Angeles was and still is a leader in the field, and anomie-ridden readers have responded strongly when he rejects the city in a symbolic defeat of all its oppressive inhabitants.

If Chandler's fine writing imbues the physical environment with the hero's controlling and isolative feelings, it is hardly surprising that his treatment of the characters the persona meets is just as solipsistic. The hero who knows himself as the avatar of a gloomy, mannish woman or a wounded seagull has nothing to learn from or share with other people; his lonely quality is enough to inspect, judge and dismiss them.

It is inevitable that a first person narrator should to some extent present other characters externally; but Conrad, for example, shows that other characters can be given full development as autonomous figures even within this narrative pattern. In Chandler external-isation is taken to its limits; the other characters are constantly controlled by Marlowe's personalised presentation of crucial actions, dialogue and settings. They even talk in uniform ways, in short, unrevealing sentences and in the combative tone that Marlowe uses to them, however fluent and sensitive his address to the reader may be. Selection of detail is important. In each scene a character only acts towards Marlowe; Marriott's mannerisms, Mrs Grayle's leg-crossing, the threatening behaviour of the police all feed directly into his consciousness, attack him personally. There are no mass scenes in Chandler, and no scenes where other characters react to each other without paying attention to Marlowe.

This is curious. The basic passivity of his stance, the insistence on watching and listening to the world does not in fact make Marlowe a true observer of others. His passivity is strangely intrusive; as he watches he also controls a scene. Chandler said 'a crowded canvas just bewilders me' and the careful limitation of the scene itself orders experience and suppresses disturbing material. The narrative only gives us detail that feeds into Marlowe's consciousness of his own position vis-à-vis the world, through the plot-device of the particular problem he is working on and thinking about: the way the plot spins in towards Marlowe will be discussed below.

It has been noted by some critics who are not completely enthralled by Chandler's ideology that apart from Marlowe the characters are stereotypical, and act in a way that readily reveals both their type and an implied reaction to it. In this novel we have Mrs Florian the grubby drunk; Marriott the vain, effeminate semi-crook; Mrs Grayle the confident seductress; Ann Riordan the faithful and plucky sister-type; and a grim range of police figures, the sour failure of Nulty, the crudely corrupt Chief Wax, the smoother and sharper Randall. Less important figures are no more than caricatures—Mr Grayle the aging cuckold, the worldly-wise negro desk-clerk, Mrs Florian's nosy neighbour, the bizarre—even wooden—Indian who serves Amthor.

There is no doubt that many people in reality seem like stereotypes, because conventional patterns do exist and do offer a structure of response to life, but this is not what Chandler has in mind. He is content to offer simple, two-dimensional characters as the reality that Marlowe faces and judges so firmly. Neither Marlowe nor Chandler investigate why and how characters might have become stereotypical, nor does the narrative imagination go so far as to discover that each person in fact moulds a different conjuncture of patterns and pressures. The one case in the novel where a character does appear to speak for himself outside a stereotype is Galbraith, the half-bad policeman who explains his situation to Marlowe. But here what appears to be an exposition of a character's real tensions steadily turns into a thinly veiled sermon by the author on corruption, one that increasingly moves away from any social, interactive view of urban problems and develops into praise of Moral Rearmament:—a programme that typifies the personalised, holier-than-thou reaction to the world embodied in Marlowe himself and his own uninterested, uninvolved attitude to others.

The formulaic treatment of character that satisfies Chandler and permits Marlowe to be so superior is, of course, in itself a way of containing the disturbing knowledge that all other people are themselves individuals and face the world just as the writer does— Chandler never confronts that realisation, which Christie found so stunning. The pressure most clearly felt behind the stereotyping is a self-seeking individualist one, an anxious personal defensiveness. The treatment of women and homosexuals is clearly a way of neutralising their disturbing force as will be discussed later, but in general the hero knows and protects himself by rejecting others, and their flat, unappealing creation makes this process seem valid.

Marlowe studies nervously the people he meets. He lays much emphasis on eyes; their expression always bears an emotively described response to him, either steely hostility, grey caution or, occasionally, warm receptiveness. And watchfulness is his main function. In his scenes with others the persona is curiously indecisive and uncommitted—Anne Riordan brings this to a sexual head. His confidence and competence is outside the action, in his knowing narration to the reader. This feature, clear enough in the text, is more strongly confirmed by comparing scenes in *Farewell, My Lovely* with the original versions in the short stories from which the novel was largely assembled. Chandler has consistently cut out moments where the detective in the stories explains something to a character or passes clear judgement within a scene. A remark like 'Instantly I knew', or a judgement like 'usual' is omitted. In 'Mandarin's Jade' Dalmas says 'I just didn't like the man', but Marlowe generalises away from a specific evaluation of Marriott—'I just didn't like it'. Equally, Chandler amplifies the evaluative feeling and decisiveness conveyed by implicit means to the reader outside the action: the 'ecstatic fixity' of Moose Malloy's expression was merely 'rapt' on Steve Skalla in 'Try the Girl'. The harsh account of theatrical people intoned silently over Mrs Florian's photographs is a new expansion, and so are the sentimental sequences of natural observation that frame the scenes of interaction. Human contact for Marlowe is a sterile process where his arid preconceptions about others are constantly reinforced, and Chandler's shaping of dialogue, action and description allows no other knowledge of people to intervene. Nothing surprises Marlowe because he projects only self-interested mechanical actions onto others.

The banal and arid nature of Marlowe's contact with humanity has been read by critics like Albert Camus, William Ruehlmann

and Alain Lacombe as part of the fragmented, reified world-view of
the modern period; existential theory has been used to underpin and
locate the attitude. But the objective elements, the sterility of
response is not, in Chandler, allowed to develop into the bleak
reality of the existential novel. In *The Rebel* Camus said he found this
in tough-guy writing:

> Its technique consists in describing men by their outside ap-
> pearances, in their most casual actions, of reproducing, without
> comment, everything they say down to their repetitions, and
> finally by acting as if men were entirely defined by their daily
> automatisms . . . This type of novel, purged of interior life, in
> which men seem to be observed behind a pane of glass, logically
> ends, with its emphasis on the pathological, by giving itself as its
> unique subject the supposedly average man.

This is to an extent true of Hammett's writing, and may also be
applied to Chandler's early stories, where Hammett's influence was
strong. But in the novels, Chandler embeds the external treatment
of human beings in Marlowe's own inner life; he provides the
unique subject, dismissing and scorning the 'supposedly average
man'. Chandler has moved from Hammett's hard and partly
existential world (which nevertheless had evaluative underpinning
in a radical and proto-Marxist view of society) back into the
romantic certainties present in his early poems. He rejects the shape
of what Roland Barthes calls a 'readerly' novel, one that opens itself
to the reader's own interpretation and cooperation, and settles, like
so many authors before him, for a 'writerly' text, controlled by the
author to offer only one valid interpretation and viewpoint. The
'écriture' or narrative and stylistic control here means that people
and things are only valuable in so far as they stimulate the painful
sense of the suffering self. The mixture of an apparently open and
modernist technique and an actually authoritarian romantic core in
the style and presentation of the novel is a powerful and successful
illusion, appealing directly to an audience for whom the pull of
romanticism was great but for whom its characteristic nineteenth-
century formulation was no longer a viable medium of response. R.
W. Flint, reviewing *The Lady in the Lake* in *Partisan Review*, said
sharply that Marlowe was 'as much of the existentialist hero as
modern American has stomach for' and specified the audience
which enjoyed and was helped by Chandler's ideology as the

'upper-middlebrow market'. In *Waiting for the End* Leslie Fiedler sees Chandler's basic constituency in the same light, calling it a 'righteous middlebrow audience'.

This mixture of apparent modernism and actual romantic individualism is found in the larger structure of the novel. Chandler admitted several times that he was a poor plotter, that he valued 'writing' more than meticulous organisation of the story. He said of *The Little Sister* 'the writing is of incomparable brilliance but something has went wrong with the story', but for all the neat—and stylistically conveyed—self-mockery of the statement, he did not feel the need to make the plot less arbitrary. In the 1950 introduction to his short stories he clarified this (the collection was first called *The Simple Art of Murder*, then *Pearls are a Nuisance*; its introduction is different from the longer essay called 'The Simple Art of Murder'). Discussing the pattern of the *Black Mask* stories, he said: 'the scene outranked the plot, in the sense that a good plot was one which made good scenes. The ideal mystery was one you would read if the end was missing.' He realised he could press this tendency too far: 'as a constructionist I have a dreadful fault; I let characters run away with the scenes and then refuse to discard the scenes that don't fit'. Here, as in most cases, Chandler's comments see the pattern but do not correctly attribute its cause. The scenes are controlled by Marlowe's scrutiny of the characters, not by the characters themselves, and his need to react in full negative detail against others is what runs away with the scenes. Chandler was not willing to curtail this development for the sake of a shapely plot, because it was central to his meaning: he was writing personalised emotional adventures for a hero, not plots which created a sharply focused problem or a pattern of social reality.

In all the novels it is clear enough that the scene dominates the structure, rather than fitting into a worked out sequence of events, as Christie offered, working back from her ending. Chandler's own habit of working on half-sheets of paper was intended to sharpen his small-scale focus, making overall connections less evident and enabling him to concentrate his rewriting on detailed matters rather than plot-revision. Chandler remarked, only half in fun, that when he was in doubt he had a man come through the door with a gun in his hand, and particularly in the early novels a series of melodramatic scenes, strongly felt and communicated by the persona, are the key occurrences; both *The Big Sleep* and *The Lady in the Lake* have many fine examples. The relative lack of these in the later novels is part of their weaker emotive effect, and causes their increasing emphasis on mere statement of the persona's feelings. Herbert Ruhm observes but does not explain this change when he describes Marlowe's development 'from catalyst to character'.

In *Farewell, My Lovely* a whole series of such set-pieces, derived from three different short stories, are woven together to shape the core of the novel. The plotted links between them are sometimes frail. Anne Riordan merely chances to be driving past Purissima Canyon and to be extremely, and bravely, inquisitive, and so she creates the tense scene as Marlowe wakes from unconsciousness; Red Norgaard happens to see Marlowe returning in defeat from the Montecito and so the successful and vivid boarding party can occur; the link between the two similar imprisonments of the hero by Amthor and Sonderberg is sketchy at best. The relationship between Mrs Florian, Lindsay Marriott and Mrs Grayle, which ties together the set-pieces at Mrs Florian's and the canyon is tenuously explained, with some shuffling late in the novel when we are told that the photograph was not of Mrs Grayle at all. This is necessary to explain why Marlowe did not recognise her—two short stories as well as two set-pieces are being rather roughly jointed here. The presence of Amthor's card in the cigarettes Marriott carried, leading Marlowe into captivity, is similarly justified in a round-about and casual manner—it was much simpler in 'Mandarin's Jade'. The scene where Mrs Grayle shoots Malloy is full of unexplained details. We never know what message Marlowe sent Malloy, where he was, why Marlowe invited Mrs Grayle at that time, or why he wore pyjamas to meet her. The emotive melodrama of the scene is its essential quality and justification.

Chandler's plots may be sketchy, even unconvincing, but they do not actually break down. There is a misleading, but often repeated, story that when *The Big Sleep* was being filmed Howard Hawks, William Faulkner and Chandler himself did not know just how Owen Taylor, chauffeur to the Sternwoods and Carmen's former lover, died. Chandler may well have forgotten and the others may not have read the novel carefully enough, but the explanation is there. He committed suicide; the lump on his head was given him previously by Joe Brody. The essential feature of Chandler's plots is not that they are bad, but that plot-linkage was of secondary importance to him. Plot does not have the foreground importance it has in other crime writers: the central mechanism is the affective meaning of the scene as it dramatises Marlowe's position and shows him moving, by his virtues rather than any specific detection, towards comprehension of the problem and resolution of the threat that it causes to him personally.

There is an ongoing narrative, but just as the time factor is underplayed, so the development of the story is not a smooth one, proceeding discovery by discovery, nor is it even made consistently obscure by misapprehensions or false leads, as the clue-puzzle novel was—a movement which is a deliberate and conscious reversing of an onward development, by which a detective and attentive reader will not be deceived for long. There is a static, almost meditational quality to a Chandler plot as the hero moves back and forward across his closely charted city and its environs; the affective force of the structure is to retain the action and its interpretation in the hero's consciousness and to make it eventually come clear to him without his cumulative effort but through the actions of characters and his own catalytic presence: his personal value, not his active detection, is the structural focus, the method of detection and the value finally perceived.

When Chandler concentrates on scenes and what he called 'writing' to the relative disregard of close plotted development he discards both the plot-pattern and the central meaning of the 'organic' novel, which crime writers like Doyle and Christie had used to make criminal events resolvable by a skilful, persevering agent. The meaning implicit in the organic structure has been discussed in earlier chapters; it responds to bourgeois ideas of personal effort through diachronic time towards the improvement of one's moral and physical position. Chandler is less interested in reform than this, creating something much more like a gloomy meditation on disorder and a personal retreat into held values.

An episodic structural pattern, foregrounding the central virtues of the hero and involving him only negatively with his casual social encounters, is found in other genres: high medieval romance, the picaresque novel, the basically non-narrative romantic form of *Don Juan* or *Idylls of the King* come to mind. What has been called a 'vertical' structure operates, resolving the formal units not so much in terms of progress through time and events, but in terms of an ideally conceived absolute embodied in the central figure. This value enables him to defeat and correct errors in others, and so offers itself as an implied programme for superior living, whether the tone is moral or satirical. The essential idealism of the form, its disengagement with the difficult compromises of reality, the virtuous carapace the hero bears, all these features make this an attractive and meaningful form for Chandler.

Even though he rediscovers this type of form, or carries it over from early poems and essays, it is still true to say that in this rejection of the mechanistic rational plotting of the organic novel Chandler is in line with twentieth-century feelings that such a plot-myth distorted reality, a feeling which modernist writing has fulfilled in a variety of inorganic literary forms. He apparently refers to this in the 1950 introduction, when he says 'The mystery story grew hard and cynical about motive and character'. Yet in making the centrality of the single character's intelligence the dynamic of the plot, Chandler turns away from the crucially important modernist rejection of the individual as a sufficient authority. Here, as in his presentation, he has a certain gloss of modernism overlaying a conservative and fully bourgeois romantic structure, offering rhetorical attraction and actual consolation for those who feel the inadequacy of earlier forms but are not at ease with the full development of modernist perceptions.

The patterns of style, presentation and structure all show unease and distaste towards the authentic artistic realisation of bourgeois culture in the nineteenth-century novel. But in response Chandler withdraws into the myth of the individual artistic consciousness— which that culture itself generated from its fragmenting and privatising forces. This is imaginatively realised when he symbolises the vanishing point of his form in the portrait that dominates Marlowe's sparse office-hermitage. It is Rembrandt, master spirit of bourgeois oil painting, with all its reified and personalised resonances. In the portrait Marlowe reads his own position, seeing a sensitive realist who is enmeshed in the bourgeois process but consoles himself with a negative, disgusted vigour:

> His other hand held a brush poised in the air, as if he might be going to do a little work after a while, if somebody made a down payment. His face was ageing, saggy, full of the disgust of life and the thickening effects of liquor. But it had a hard cheerfulness I liked, and the eyes were as bright as drops of dew.

The patterns of content in the novel fill out the inward-looking formal dynamic, reveal how an apparent concern with the external world closes in to deal with and protect the personal anxieties of the alienated individual. Characterisation has already been discussed because it is here so intimately controlled by the I-dominated presentation that diverts inwards the novel's gestures towards objectivity. The plot that slowly and errantly works itself out through the persona-centred scenes in itself confirms all the implications of the form. In this, as in Chandler's other major novels, we have a double plot. An outer, socially attuned story concerns itself with gangsters and tough customers of various sorts, presents civic corruption and criminal violence as the possible cause of the disturbance that Marlowe is inspecting and, in his desultory way, investigating. But this outer story turns out to be no more than a mock puzzle. The real explanation of events lies in the inner plot, where Mrs Grayle is the cause of all the trouble. She is the 'Little Velma' Malloy is seeking; she originally betrayed him to the police; she killed Marriott and knocked Marlowe out; she finally shoots Malloy and tries to shoot Marlowe. The outer plot elements of police corruption, gangster influence, hospital imprisonments fall away as lesser and irrelevant issues against the desperate threat that a malicious but resourceful and seductive woman can pose. In the early stages of the novel the outer plot is frequently offered as the key to events. The notion that Marriott has been involved with a jewel gang who then killed him is dominant for some time; Marlowe's encounters with police corruption and gangster control in Bay City seem to develop from this possibility. Lieutenant Randall in particular is an agent of this outer plot, discussing jewel thieves and corruption with Marlowe on several occasions. But this material is finally rejected for a personalised, asocial explanation of events and view of the world.

In Chandler's short stories, as in Hammett's and in his novels *Red Harvest* and *The Glass Key* at least, gangster-based corruption was a genuine force of disturbance. Much of Chandler's reputation as a realist depends on the idea that he perceived the socio-political sickness in American society. He claimed as much himself in the 1950 introduction to his stories: 'Their characters lived in a world gone wrong, a world in which, long before the atom bomb, civilization had created the machinery for its own destruction, and was learning to use it with all the moronic delight of a gangster trying out his first machine gun. The law was something to be manipulated for profit and power. The streets were dark with something more than night.'

The general tone reflects what Jacques Barzun has, with some disdain, called 'the Marxist coloring of its birth years' in the background of the *Black Mask* tradition, which largely derived from Hammett. But Chandler's final sentence shifts from a generalised perception of urban decay into a sense-based personal feeling of threat, and this shift is evident in Chandler's novels—it is even present to some extent in a work as ostensibly political as *Red Harvest*. Socio-political perceptions about contemporary disorder come to act as only the background to the genuinely felt personal threats, where the gangster plot was valid to the end in 'Mandarin's Jade' and 'The Man Who Liked Dogs'.

The various titles of the novel show the transition in process. When he was first working on it Chandler had in mind 'Law is where you buy it', which derives from 'The Man Who Liked Dogs'. He shed this overtly political title (though the sentence remains in the text) and attached it to what became *The Lady in the Lake*, which has a corrupt policeman closer to the centre of the inner plot. He then intended to call the Mrs Grayle story 'The Second Murderer'; the reference to Richard III draws attention to Marriott, the hinge between the outer criminal plot and the actual threat to Marlowe himself. When Knopf rejected this title Chandler abandoned the distancing mediation of a literary reference and released personalised feeling: *Farewell, My Lovely* ironically disposes of Mrs Grayle and her sexual threat, leaving Marlowe free, and as the wording shows, witty and theatrically self-aware.

The plot structure indicates a similar movement as Brunette finally changes from the bogey of the outer plot to a helpful agent of the inner plot. His personalised man-to-man trust for Marlowe leads him to contact Malloy and set up the final melodramatic and emotively rich encounter between Marlowe, Malloy and Mrs Grayle. This slide from outer to inner is also evident in the affective force of scenes which start on the public, outer level, so fully steeped is the novel in types of withdrawal. In Chapter 29 Randall visits Marlowe at home—the setting itself is important to the effect. They discuss the jewel gang theory and corrupt constraints on police investigations, but as the scene goes on both Marlowe and Randall become steadily involved with Marlowe's personal routines. He makes coffee, tells Randall his culinary secrets, cooks and eats eggs, shaves and dresses. This domestic detail is a frequent motif in Chandler, and it has important effects. Marlowe's home affairs are emotively central. The outer material is considered, but its essential irrelevance is suggested by the way the whole scene spirals in on domestic, personal concerns, stripping external events of validity, even of a way being known in themselves. Internal knowledge and private situation provide the firm viewpoint from which Marlowe operates.

Even in its own terms the socio-political material in the outer plot is weak and invalid, shot through with attitudes and motifs that reveal the actual individualism of the analytic stance, the failure to engage at a genuinely objective and social level with disorder. The stereotypical presentation of negroes and lower-class people is one instance of this; Marlowe never sees them in autonomous terms as people struggling with their own problems, let alone in simple social terms as a class faced with repressive forces of various sorts, economic and ideological. The pressures which make negroes seem servile and lower-class people seem dirty are nowhere considered. Similarly Mrs Grayle's secret is never seen as a shameful lower-class background. The absence of such analysis is as ideologically forceful as the socio-political silences of Doyle and Christie, and especially notable because such pressures are recognised in Hammett's early work. But Chandler, like his friend Gardner, turns aside from these matters.

The perceived corruption is limited in range, personalised in the 'local power structure', as Jameson observes, not seen as a national phenomenon generated by the socio-economic system. And even the realities of such domestic crime and corruption are avoided or blurred. The criminals who are alleged to have stolen the jewels, killed Marriott and beaten Marlowe make no appearance in the plot—they are completely imaginary. The others who do appear are treated in an unrealistically simple way, some admired, some caricatured. The kingpin of Bay City, Laird Brunette, has a personality suiting the lordly, attractive resonances of his name (curiously feminine resonances, to an extent). He is a pleasant, business-like man, who is willing to trust Marlowe: an individual relationship is forged with the source of all corruption. The police who operate as Brunette's agents are presented as grotesques— Chief Wax is a suitably allegorical name for their head and he behaves accordingly being both slippery and malleable. The familiar distrust of society's own authoritative agents justifies the author's easy hostility; their controller, a free entrepeneur of corruption, is admirable.

An unexplained clean-up in Bay City does remove the corrupt caricatures, but this social reform is unstressed in the novel, and clearly incomplete. Nor does Marlowe purposely and consciously cause it: he tells Galbraith he will not pass on his information if it would interfere with his 'private job', and apparently does not do so. Yet even the hostility implicit in the presentation of the corrupt police is muted: their malignity is explained away by Galbraith as being at one with the business spirit of America. This analysis, supported late in the novel by the considerable authority of the good cop Red Norgaard, is not taken to mean that all business is crime: the mere link seems enough to satisfy the discontent the persona feels. Crime is thought natural to the system; certain immoral men do act greedily but by sleight of hand the hero's knowledge of their evil will make them innocuous.

The same personalised pattern is found in the perception of professional corruption. The imprisonment scenes that recur in these, as in all adventure stories, are partly caused by bad police, but their treatment is never as deeply felt as that handed out by crooked doctors. Chandler never realises corruption in the legal or political professions, whose interests are so firmly bound up with the reproduction of state authority. Marlowe's freedom is constricted by police, the agents of the law with whom the individual has real contact, but his major imprisonment is at the hands of doctors, the professionals who come closest to the treasured health and life of the individual consciousness. Chandler's imagination consistently traces a private path, even in his reworking of the socially aware material, the corruption plots he derived basically from Hammett. Thinly analysed as it is, personally directed throughout, this outer plot, this vision of a corrupt and manipulative society is only a blurred background to the damaged feelings and personal dangers of the hero.

The threats that are really basic are found to be private ones, felt by Marlowe as much as anyone, threats that grow on domestic ground. They come from intimate associates, former lovers—from women, above all. The villain is a woman Marlowe finds attractive, who has made vigorous and alarming sexual overtures to him. First she makes butterfly kisses on his face, but the pretty animal turns savage: he then feels burning lips and a snake-like tongue. Her victims are doubles for, extensions of Marlowe. They are men he feels close to: he has been alone with Marriott in his house and car, found homo-erotic fascination and repulsion in him that is the reflex of the child-like feelings he has for Malloy. Both men die in a clearly sexual setting that involves Marlowe. Malloy's death in Marlowe's bedroom while Marlowe is in night-wear is plain enough.

Marriott's death symbolises the same meaning. Purissima Canyon sounds like a dreamlike and notionally hygienic orifice that turns malign; the detail of the scene confirms this tenuous implication. Marriott's car is forced through a thorny, narrow gap and he is left dead inside; Marlowe is battered but escapes from this emblematic *vagina dentada*. The same victim-double pattern is visible in characters like Rusty Reagan in *The Big Sleep*, Roger Wade, Terry Lennox in *The Long Goodbye*—and indeed in Miles Archer in *The Maltese Falcon*. Derace Kingsley in *The Lady in the Lake* and Orrin Quest in *The Little Sister* are slightly different versions of this figure.

Chandler's ultimate villains are always women, and usually sexy ones as well. The one exception is *The High Window* where the grotesquely mannish mother, Mrs Murdock, has committed the central crime. No real victim-double appears here either, though Leslie Murdock and Vannier offer themselves as two parts of one. Chandler felt this novel had little vitality, and perhaps these two unusual absences explain why it lacked emotive validity for him. Elsewhere the constant patterns are the sexual link Marlowe has with the villainess and his closeness to the central victim. The motives, methods and settings of the central crimes are freely variable, though the repeated motif of falling or sinking into death and unconsciousness suggests a common understanding of death as a loss of control and erectness, with all its sexual and self-conscious connotations. Even *Playback* embodies some of these features, though they are reversed; the apparent villainess is pitiable, the possible double has himself become a worthless enemy of the woman, and can fall to death unmourned. *The Blue Dahlia*, another film-script, shows the basic features in a more familiar form.

The ultimate discovery of the villain in a Chandler plot does not reveal who threatened a client, as in Doyle, or a class, as in Christie, but who brought intimate danger to the hero himself and destroyed his double. Chandler, sensitive but vague as usual about his own patterns, said that he wrote a 'type of story in which the search is not for a specific criminal, but for a raison d'être, a meaning in character and relationship': he did not specify that his hero was always one term of the relationship.

The threatening nature of his contact with the sexy, manipulative woman has two major effects. Women with a reduced sex-drive are liked and trusted. Anne Riordan is the best example (though she briefly becomes 'sly' when she invites him to stay); Merle Davis in *The High Window* and Adrienne Fromsett in *The Lady in the Lake* are variants. Orfamy Quest in *The Little Sister* offers herself as such a figure but turns out to be the other sort of woman. She may be influenced by Bridget O'Shaughnessy in *The Maltese Falcon*: her reversal of type is the opposite of Betty Mayfield's in *Playback*, and the constant exchange of money links the two characters in an uncertain relationship with Marlowe, sometimes threatening client, sometimes trusted friend.

The other result of the sexual anxiety Chandler reveals is that clearly effeminate men are described in absorbing detail but firmly rejected by the persona—too firmly perhaps for conviction. Like Lindsay Marriott they are killed cruelly and disfiguringly. Lavery in *The Lady in the Lake*, Geiger in *The Big Sleep* and, to some extent, Vannier in *The High Window* also fit this pattern. Some critics have pressed the homo-erotic element in Chandler; Michael Mason has recently argued the case in some detail. The evidence is there, of course, but I feel to classify Marlowe—and so Chandler—as a latent homosexual is to give too definite, even too positive a description of the negative, self-defensive feelings the persona shows towards others. He fears interference with the exercise of his untrammelled freedom whether it comes from women, homosexuals, doctors or police.

This fear is not only resident in the plotting and characterisation; some striking pieces of writing show how fully Chandler could realise his immanent themes. At a moment of crisis Marlowe feels that he loses control over his limbs and senses; they begin to operate autonomously, out of his all-important conscious control. When he wakes after being knocked out in Purissima Canyon he hears a voice talking. It is his own voice working things out, struggling to reunite his consciousness, but the text conceals this for a while – the reader shares the confusion as Marlowe feels himself fragmenting. When Anne Riordan turns up, this new threat arouses the same process of reification: 'The flash in my hand went out. A gun slid into my hand all by itself.' This is not a motif showing Marlowe's instinctive heroic action; it meshes with the fact that when he is physically attacked his fall into unconsciousness dominates the description. This is developed with almost obsessive care when he wakes at Dr Sonderborg's. If the hero loses control he will become like the objectified people and settings that he finds so disgusting, so unlike his own inner-directed mastery.

The self-conscious authority of the subject is central to bourgeois thought, whether crudely expressed as in the politics of self-help or

subtly forceful as the transformation of Freud's dethroning of the
conscious mind into the subjective obsessions of bourgeois psy-
chiatry. Chandler has the imaginative power to dramatise the fears
of the individual consciousness in a plot and a set of images that
perceive the possible interference with personal liberty. But
Marlowe is not just a figure of the alienated individual, crouched in
the slit-trench of self-consciousness—he has much in common with
the archetypal spokesman of that figure, the lonely writer. He
watches the world, registers fluently his feelings of distaste and
superiority, is supervised by Rembrandt; though he is tired, he feels
'not as sick as if I had a salaried job'; he responds most to Anne
Riordan, freelance writer. As Russell Davies remarks in a recent
essay, he is 'a complete metaphor for the writer's life'. He realises the
consciousness that is most contented and best adjusted in reading—
and in writing—stories of the romantic individualist life.

Chandler expressed quite clearly his purely romantic views of
writing and the writer: 'It has to do with magic and emotion and
vision, with the free flow of images, thoughts, and ideas, with
discipline that comes from within and is not imposed from without.'
He wrote this in 'A Qualified Farewell' to Hollywood, where the
collective working systems dismayed him: true to the bourgeois idea
of property even in ideas and art, he felt his work could not be
'mine'. In these ways Chandler's personalised stance closed to him
any possibility of a real social and interactive analysis of the
pressures he embodies in his hero. Yet this ideological closure has
not, to Chandler's credit, been coupled with romantic optimism
about the solitary self. Marlowe's defensive course remains a painful
one, though in the pain he does find an element of self-pity that,
with his sense of intellectual superiority and moral rectitude, does
seem to give the emotional comfort and direction that cannot come
through a sense of fulfilled engagement with others.

The hero's alienation is realised approvingly in many ways.
Detective technique has been a central feature of the meaning of the
texts studied in previous chapters, but here there is little technical or
rational activity. There are one or two pieces of analysis of a simple
or random nature. Marlowe knows the smear on his business card
connects Marriott with Mrs Florian, and he is arbitrarily curious
enough to slit open the cigarette tips to find Amthor's own card.
These details reveal the shadow of the Gardner-like business
community that tracks the determinedly unbusiness-like Marlowe.
But these are isolated incidents and hardly form a 'deductive' chain

of reasoning. Nor does Marlowe indulge in the less rational and exotic aspects of detective work: he does not follow people, watch their apartments, tap their phones. His method is to receive data that characters lay before him; the archetypal Marlowe scene is to find him alone in his gloomy office: a client or an enemy will telephone or appear to engage his attention.

Even the non-detective Marlowe does act at times; he is not catatonic. But it is made clear that this is random activity, not carefully directed to discover something. A vague instinct leads Marlowe to the gambling boats to find Malloy, confirmed but not suggested by Galbraith; and he has no reason at all to choose the Montecito except its loneliness. In the original story there was a specific clue, an interpretation of a man's dying word 'Monty'. As he waits to go out to the Montecito he lies on a bed (once more) and dreams of the hostile corrupt world. The he gets up. 'After a little while I felt a little better, but very little. I needed a drink, I needed a lot of life insurance, I needed a vacation, I needed a home in the country. What I had was a coat, a hat and a gun. I put them on and went out of the room.' Separated by choice from the prizes of normal bourgeois life, he finds no significance in his own activity, but perseveres in it, alienated from external meaning as well as integration.

Isolation is embodied in his profession. Not only is he a self-employed specialist without help; his title makes overt the nature of the alienated individual: he is a private eye. His privacy even extends to interest and involvement in a case before he is actually employed on it or, as in most of the novels, before the real case emerges from the shadow of another commission. It is as much his interest as his employer's. A curious quasi-commission by Nulty (a bet in the original story) explains Marlowe's continued interest in Malloy. As a result of this interest Mrs Grayle employs Marlowe; it is not really a job, but a way of restricting his activity, actually infringing his privacy. This personalising of the case and the threat is a recurring motif in private eye stories. It prevents the hero acting as a mere agent, a tool whose labour is divided from his own interests, and so this pattern rejects the normal relations between employer and employed to realise both a notionally self-controlled personality and also the threats he feels in an alienating world. The privacy of Marlowe's own eye as a viewpoint has already been discussed, and the neat pun on 'private I' is ready support to the central ideology. The alternative title, 'private dick', it seems reasonable to think, suggests a disinclination to share his sexuality, and links with Chandler's sense that the mystery story was appropriate to the times because it was 'incapable of love', like the hero himself.

The character's name, class position, and education all make him clearly a marginal figure, disavowing allegiance to any socio-economic group. Barzun has insisted on the implications of 'Englishness, Elegance and Establishment' in his name 'from the first name to the final *e*'. Some critics, happy to remain in the world of literature for meaning, have felt a resonance of Conrad's disengaged narrator in the surname, others have deduced traces of poetic heroism to match Christopher Marlowe—though *his* connection with Alleyn, founder of Chandler's school has so far remained an undiscovered piece of academic trivia. The line from the clearly indicative name Mallory through to Marlowe is probably the real one; the resonances of the name are certainly artistic, undemotic and unAmerican, and this nuance is supported by names resonant with medieval allegoric romance such as Grayle, Quest, Sternwood, Steelgrave.

Marlowe's class is deliberately obscured, like his familial origins. He has equal distaste for the grubby poor and the artificial rich. The few characters he shows sympathy with are hardworking literary people like Anne Riordan or the bookshop attendant in *The Big Sleep*. Like them Marlowe is a marginal bourgeois, below the professional classes, educated above the workers, but insisting on a freelance position to replicate his alienated attitude. He appears to have had a college education, but to be guarded about it; education is not allowed to become a way of life, but merely validates the hero's superiority. The alienated persona is also shown in, and protected by, the deliberately unostentatious life-style, the neutral, potentially hostile public manners and the secret domestic pleasures like chess and coffee making: all these features confirm Marlowe's position as an archetype of the educated urban alien.

One of Marlowe's consistent habits is a wry irony towards himself. He says, when badgering Mrs Florian, 'I was a swell guy. I enjoyed being me . . . I was beginning to be a little sick at my stomach.' Similarly he comments on Anne Riordan's obvious approval of him: 'Pipe smokers were solid men. She was going to be disappointed in me.' He recognises not only his nervousness in the presence of tough men like Malloy and the police, but his own failures to connect with Anne Riordan, his indulgence with Mrs

Grayle. When he sympathises with the little pink bug in police headquarters the tone is deliberately self-ridiculing. These moments do not express dissatisfaction with the self so much as an awareness of the isolated frailty of the persona, likely to be embroiled by others' demands and expectations.

This irony is not projected against the sentimental feelings and self-pity so fully developed in the descriptive passages, especially in the extraordinarily indulgent scene as Marlowe rides out to the Montecito, dominated by heavy emotive gesturing. There are 'a few bitter stars' above and he experiences 'the rise and fall of alien waves' in 'wet air as cold as the ashes of love'. The brief ironies, like the wise-cracking, pseudo-tough character and the quasi-objective style and presentation are a rhetorical shell to protect this soft core. Outside the novel it was the tough stuff Chandler felt he had to defend, not the sentimentality. He insisted several times there was 'a strong element of burlesque in my kind of writing' to dismiss the charges of cruelty and sadism that reviewers brought against his work. An alternative defence was that he wrote of death 'in a certain spirit of detachment'.

He never suggests the sentimentality in his work is invalid; when he wrote in a letter 'all of us tough guys are hopeless sentimentalists at heart' he was justifying his own mood after his wife's death: there is a certain apology for his feelings, but no withdrawal of them. This guarded but retained sentimentality is evident in the title *Farewell, My Lovely*; it is never clear who might say those words, but Marlowe seems a likelier candidate than Malloy. The less overtly sentimental phrases 'The Long Goodbye' and 'The Big Sleep' are clearly attributed to the narrator. In the same way at the very end of the novel Marlowe's sentimentality is recognised, but protected; after his explanation of Mrs Grayle's final thoughtfulness in killing herself, 'Randall said sharply: "That's just sentimental."' Marlowe, passive as ever in a social situation, hurries to agree—'Sure. It sounded like that when I said it.' Chandler here can realise the charges to be laid against his hero; but he is able to avoid any sense of strain, any feeling that Randall's view may be right and the hero foolish or fallible. Marlowe falls back on his own totem for sensitive individuality, and physically withdraws at the same time: 'So long. Did my pink bug ever get back up there?' The ideological closure is complete and, in its own terms, effective. Marlowe, like many intellectuals, uses a certain self-mockery and physical isolation to sustain his position. A softly-drawn figure like Red Norgaard may support the persona's view, but he is finally alone, with his own conscious defences.

In this respect as in all the implications of his form and content Chandler shows that his ideology is different from, in some ways an advance upon, the aspects of bourgeois ideology examined so far in this study. Poe made isolated intellectualism stand as a sufficent weapon against crime; Doyle set it in a particular social and scientific conjuncture; Christie drew the techniques of rational detection back into an archetype of bourgeois collective knowledge. But Chandler has realised a thorough theory and practice of the alienated individual defending himself against the threats of the external world, betrayal and death being the ultimate actions against his free consciousness. His individualism is informed and self-defending, not fearful and hero-demanding like Doyle's and Poe's, nor class-coherent like Christie's. The man who feels his internal organisation is rewarding and sufficient can read Chandler as a validation of his own fear and hostility towards others and the environment. The nervous masculinity woven deeply into the persona's feelings makes the text less attractive to women readers, and Chandler's audience has been predominantly male. The élitism of the position proclaims itself; it basically resides in intellectual and emotional superiority, but the blank uninterest in poor and black citizens and the distrust of the rich indicate a strong underlying political attitude, that of the educated middle-class. A cerebral aristocracy is appointed, superior in mind and in manners to those above, below and less clever than the hero. Anne Riordan's phrase 'a hard-boiled gentleman' is rich with suggestion: Chandler said he disliked the 'affectation of gentility' in the British detectives, but he created another version of an élite hero.

A striking theoretical corollary of this position is in the work of David Riesman, who like Chandler was writing in the late forties. Two commentators, with the remarkably hard-boiled names Gutman and Wrong, describe Riesman's basic position as 'a view of society as the enemy both of individuality and of basic drive gratifications'. Riesman's distinction between the inner-directed individual and the other-directed mass man is plainly imbued with praise of the former, placing him in the honoured tradition of bourgeois culture and liberty as well as of Freudian self-fulfilment; 'other-direction' is denigrated as a modern deformation of what was once the shame-oriented value-system. Riesman sees the valued persona remaining true to his 'psychological gyroscope' (a tellingly scientistic metaphor) and so withstanding 'the buffetings of his external environment'. Chandler dramatises this viewpoint consistently, and the attitude presented is a powerful one. It validates and places in a defended position what Erich Fromm more objectively saw as the modern world's creation of 'the isolated individual, powerless and insecure'. John Cawelti has linked tough-guy writing with Riesman, but feels that the hostility to women and the rich rises from an other-directed projection of inadequacy. In this conclusion Cawelti fails to see the ideological self-justifications at work: the very concept of 'other-directed' rests, for its description and evaluation, on the individualist anxiety common to Riesman and Chandler, and those who fêted them.

The moral value of the individual is, of course, a powerful totem in contemporary thought, being the premise of movements as apparently separate as *laissez faire* economics, Moral Rearmament and Leavisite literary criticism. It is this sense of the private value of the choosing moral being that is the ultimate positive for Chandler and Marlowe. The hero's professional ethics are much more morally controlled than Hammett's heroes with their neutral, economist motives, as George Grella has observed in an interesting article. This is the feature that carries, for Chandler, 'the quality of redemption' he found lacking in Hammett; it is embodied in Red Norgaard, even in Galbraith and Randall as well as Marlowe. *The Big Sleep* finally located such feeling only in Marlowe but it is found at the end of *Farewell, My Lovely*—with high improbability—in Mrs Grayle's suicide.

Only in such personal acts that show private morality is positive value found; the collective world is innately oppressive as Marlowe's nightmare shows before he rides out, guided by his and Norgaard's inner virtue, to the Montecito. Such values are held tenderly against the wilderness of the city and its hostile human army: they are also tenuously held against the extinguishing threat of death. It is no accident that so many of Chandler's titles dwell on death in an indirect way—'The Big Sleep', 'The Lady in the Lake', 'The Long Goodbye' show the pattern as clearly as 'Farewell, My Lovely'. Even 'The High Window' refers to the scene of death, while 'Playback' refers to Betty Mayfield's fear of execution in error. Only 'The Little Sister' is an exception, referring to a different sort of betrayal.

The titles consider and mediate through the persona's euphemising indirection the death so much feared in the modern crime novel, so richly pondered and so skilfully screened by the detective's ability to identify those who cause it. Death is not a general, intangibly oppressive phenomenon: it too has become personalised, the effect of a single person's will. Jameson has written well about 'the reality of death itself' in the grim ending of *The Big Sleep*, a final reverie on the disappearance of Rusty Reagan, betrayed by wife and sister-in-law, a vigorous witty alien, who plainly doubles for Marlowe. In *Farewell, My Lovely* Marlowe twice cheats death at Mrs Grayle's hands; once because of his semi-legal authority, he explains rather thinly, once simply because her bullets run out. So by the skin of his teeth, in unmotivated but perfectly plain reward for his virtues, the sensitive, judging hero lives on. Just as he carried the little pink bug out of police headquarters, so he himself has survived the crushing forces of society—because the novel has personalised them in Mrs Grayle. Such encounters are a recurrent condition of living, though; Marlowe knows and defines himself by continual rejections of the world of others he fears and dislikes. He asks Randall if the bug ever returned. Randall, typifying what the novel's ideology sees as an insensitive, social colossus, 'didn't know what I was talking about'.

But many readers did. Not a huge audience, not the mass who identified with the furious physical hostility of Spillane's re-formation of the alienated hero, but a sizeable audience of college graduates and literary people like those who lionised the ageing Chandler in London—true to his lonely colours, he found them irritating and was often rude and rejecting. The fact that he always sold better in England may derive partly from the greater force there of cultured sensitivity as an ideological weapon, partly from the naive gratification English readers found in novels that rejected an environment genuinely alien to them. It took a long time for a Chandler novel to sell a million copies, but he did receive reasonable wealth from his writing. More importantly, the socio-intellectual group who valued his work were able to give him great prestige, a special position among writers of crime fiction and the accolade of being a 'real' writer. Chandler is always returning to this issue in his letters; it was of great importance to him to rise out of what he saw as the rut of simple popular culture and hack writing. He identified writers without 'emotional quality' as being 'suitable to an age which is incapable of poetry': terms very like those of the early aestheticist and idealist essay 'Realism and Fairyland', where he called these writers 'the machine minders of literature' and sought a place among the high culture pantheon.

He has gained it, and though the attempt and the achievement are shot through with disreputable ideological attitudes, in a sense the authenticity of his artistic creation would justify his standing in a less divisive and partial evaluation of writers. He did create the anxieties and the necessary defences of alienated intellectuals in a world that increasingly devalued their skills because of their separation from the interactive processes of living. It was personal spiritual survival, not the desire for property that excited Chandler and his readers. Crime in their world and his novels was merely a symbol for threats to the conscious control of personal life, and the means of detecting and controlling it were no more than sensitive vigilance—to be on watch against hostile forces, to be fully dependent on one's own resources was a sufficient defence of life and mental stability.

This personalised and quietist position hardly involves a credible treatment of the realities of urban crime, for all the initial gloss of realism and objective treatment. As Priestley shrewdly observed, a private theatre with coded values has been in operation; the threats have been perceived and channelled by the form and the content selection in ways that can only lead to their defeat. The whole formation has been very influential; variants of the private eye still flourish, and the figure has mutated into a special agent of espionage for international fantasies of security. But a newer genre of crime fiction has become popular, with a more realistic base for its optimistic resolutions and ideological patterns. This is the police story.

REFERENCES

Text
Farewell, My Lovely, Penguin, London, reprint 1949.

Criticism
Chandler's comments on his work are in the following sources:

'The Simple Art of Murder', reprinted in *The Simple Art of Murder*, Houghton Mifflin, Boston, 1950 and in *Pearls are a Nuisance*, Penguin, London, 1964.
'Introduction' to *The Simple Art of Murder* and to *Pearls are a Nuisance*.
Raymond Chandler Speaking, Dorothy Gardner and Katherine Sorley Walker (eds), Hamilton, London, 1962.
The Notebooks of Raymond Chandler, Frank McShane (ed.), Weidenfeld & Nicholson, London, 1977.

Jacques Barzun, 'The Illusion of the Real', Miriam Gross (ed.), *The World of Raymond Chandler*, Weidenfeld & Nicholson, London, 1977.

Albert Camus, *The Rebel*, Vintage, New York, 1953.

John G. Cawelti, *Adventure, Mystery and Romance*, University of Chicago Press, Chicago, 1976.

Russell Davies, 'Omnes Me Impune Lacessunt', in *The World of Raymond Chandler*, op. cit.

Philip Durham, *Down These Mean Streets A Man Must Go: Raymond Chandler's Knight*, University of North Carolina Press, Durham, 1963.

Leslie Fiedler, *Love and Death in the American Novel*, Criterion, New York, 1960.

R. W. Flint, 'A Cato of the Cruelties', *Partisan Review*, 14 (1947), 328–30.

Walter Gibson, *Tough, Sweet and Stuffy*, Indiana University Press, Bloomington, 1976.

George Grella, 'Murder and the Mean Streets: The Hard-Boiled Detective Novel', Dick Allen and David Chacko (eds), *Detective Fiction: Crime and Compromise*, Harcourt Brace Jovanovich, New York, 1974.

R. Gutman and D. Wrong, 'David Riesman's Typology of Character', S. Lipset and L. Lowenthal (eds), *Culture and Social Character: The Works of David Riesman Reviewed*, Free Press, Glencoe, 1961.

Fredric Jameson, 'On Raymond Chandler', *Southern Review*, 6 (1970), 624–50.

Alain Lacombe, *Le roman noir américain*, 1018, Union Générale d'Editions, Paris, 1975.

Ross MacDonald, 'Introduction' to *Archer in Hollywood*, Knopf, New York, 1967.

Frank McShane, *The Life of Raymond Chandler*, Cape, London, 1976.

Michael Mason, 'Marlowe, Men and Women,' in *The World of Raymond Chandler*, op. cit.

J. B. Priestley, 'Close-up of Chandler', *New Statesman*, 16 March 1962.

David Riesman, *The Lonely Crowd*, Yale University Press, New Haven, 1950.

William Ruehlmann, *Saint with a Gun—The Unlawful American Private Eye*, New York University Press, New York, 1974.

Herbert Ruhm, 'Raymond Chandler—From Bloomsbury to the Jungle and Beyond', David Madden (ed.), *Tough Guy Writers of the Thirties*, Southern Illinois University Press, Carbondale, 1968.

Edmund Wilson, 'Who Cares Who Killed Roger Ackroyd', reprinted in *Classics and Commercials*, Allen, London, 1951.

6 '. . . a deceptive coolness'— Ed McBain's Police Novels

Since the Second World War a new pattern has emerged in crime fiction, indicating by its wide success and many versions that it ratifies new attitudes to crime-control. The detective has become a policeman, acting with institutional support, conducting more or less accurately reported police business. Earlier police heroes merely professionalised the romantic pattern of a surpassing individual, and even relatively realistic writers like Crofts and Simenon gave special qualities of patience and insight to individualistic heroes. A democratic and factual pattern did exist in the thirties, but British novelists like Maurice Procter and 'Henry Wade' hardly claimed a large audience and the relative realism of Hammett and the Hollywood police films of the late thirties are still highly melo-dramatic and hero-centred. The 'police story' only emerged as a specific element in a new 'structure of feeling' after the war, when successful professional authors exploited the pattern and especially when it was given authoritative shape in radio and television.

The popular post-war British radio series 'PC 49' and Lawrence Treat's American novels showed the appeal of down-to-earth police heroes. The crimes treated were various, even minor. An emphasis on murder and the documentary attraction of the new form were authoritatively fixed in the early American television series 'Dragnet'—itself originally a radio series—where a hero with the workaday name of Sergeant Joe Friday operated successfully against urban crime with the help of other police and, in particular, their systems and technology. The visual realism of the new medium gave authenticity to the verisimilitude of the presentation, and especially validated the gadgetry newly marshalled against crime: Joe Friday's crisply mechanical salutation 'ten-four' became a catch-phrase to express technologically aware alertness in the television-equipped Anglophone world.

The protective romance of technology was greatly influenced by the much-publicised machines used in the war. But effects of the war in both Britain and the USA go further than this in determining the new form and its plausibility. Total war involved both general experience and widespread acceptance of bureaucratic organis-ation, and communicated a notion that security could come from organised, technically skilled collective effort. In Britain in par-ticular this involved the apparent levelling of long-standing class boundaries, as Angus Calder shows in *The People's War*. Whatever the surviving social realities in Britain and the rapid disenchant-ment with Labour rule, and whatever the continuing concealed class and race divisions in the USA, a new notion of how to preserve security was produced, and found its way into the fiction of personal security. The change is more notable in Britain, simply because most of its detectives had been so élitist, but the change in the USA from the private enterprise of lone agents to the collective activity of state employees is clearly marked and part of the same pattern.

Other factors are discernible in the success of this new form. Growing leisure and education led to a better informed public. Much fuller coverage of events in print journalism and the realistic pressure of news and documentary programmes in radio and, especially, television helped to created an audience which rejected the naive illusions of past crime fiction as improbable. Film, theatre, poetry and the novel all show this pressure for greater verisimili-tude. The new media were crucial in shaping this new form of crime fiction; it was not till the mid-fifties that authoritative and widely successful versions of it were produced in prose. Although television and, to a degree, cinema, have remained prominent forces in the police story, here I will look in detail at one particular successful novelist in the form. The sheer difficulties of film analysis, my own lack of expertise in the area and the overall literary direction of this book all make such a choice inevitable; but it is clear that a full grasp of the meaning and influence of this most recent version of crime fiction would require a formal and ideological understanding of the intervention of the visual media in public consciousness.

Two successful professional novelists, one British and one American, naturalised the new form in prose fiction. John Creasey had already produced a staggering number and range of crime novels; he had created a classic 'gentleman amateur', named with old world naivety 'The Toff', and a classic hero-policeman, Inspector West, as well as numbers of spy stories and clue-puzzles. Taking the name of J. J. Marric, a suitably austere, unromantic pseudonym, he produced in 1955 Commander George Gideon, a senior Scotland Yard Officer. The name is ideologically rich, combining military rank, a common (but also royal) Christian name, and a biblical heroic surname—its resonance may have been suggested (as the general pattern of the stories certainly was) by the television series 'Fabian of the Yard'. 'Marric' showed Gideon leading, largely from his office, a team of police against crime; the novels retained a hero, but made him a coordinator and delegator. The settings were in readily identifiable London, and the crimes dealt with were grave threats to order; even murders were shown to threaten the public at large, not just one family or individual. Creasey put more work into these novels than into his normal potboilers, trying, as he said in a preface, to create 'a sense of urgency, of dedication, of danger, of excitement, of second-by-second vigilance'. He felt he was writing something important and valid about security and the community. The novels assert the power of moral, skilled, managerial authority to protect the citizen from threats perceived to come from aberrant individuals and a hardened criminal class. Creasey is not without some awareness of the social origins of crime; though the closure of each novel recreates the *status quo*, there is some reformist pressure in his work. The novels align with the technocratic and managerial reformism that Harold Wilson invoked as a new value in the sixties. The authoritative form of this ideological notion of security has been in the set of television series that began with 'Z Cars'; Barlow and Watt are detective leaders in Gideon's mould. Because the novels have been less than dominant as a form, I have here chosen to concentrate on an American writer who worked in much the same way as Creasey, whose novels have been very widely successful and have themselves been authoritative, giving rise to a television series and to a range of imitations and variants in prose and film form.

Evan Hunter was, in 1956, a newly established writer of popular serious novels. *The Blackboard Jungle* was very successful; it realised the disorderly state of American public schools, but finally presented a hope based on the bourgeois liberal idea of finding the conformist good naturally present in the leader of disruly adolescents. There is no sense of any class-aligned patterns in curricula and pedagogical systems, of any need for structural changes to schools and society. A certain amount of research, a drive for 'realism' rather than romantic optimism—such elements create a self-consciously 'unsentimental' approach which conceals static liberal humanism. These attitudes naturally enough led Hunter to the police story, which offered verisimilitude as a mode and optimistic problem-solving as a content; in this form he could create pragmatic liberal humanist fables about crime, the police and the city.

He took the pseudonym 'Ed McBain', itself suggesting a link with the demotic American-Irish New York police tradition. The novels were successful at once and he produced them quickly. Three appeared in 1956 and there were a dozen in print in the USA by the end of 1960. He has continued to write under his own name, and has published a few titles under other pseudonyms, but the flow of 87th Precinct stories has continued to the present. Here I will concentrate on the first four novels to establish the ideological impact of his form and content, but will also note ways in which later novels continue the patterns and even absorb newly recognised problems into the controlling and consoling meaning of the series.

The form is the first area to examine. Unlike Agatha Christie's novels, from the beginning Ed McBain stories have a positive and overt formal force. They offer a mixture of styles and mimetic techniques that directly creates the central illusion of the texts, a quasi-objective mode which is actually controlled by specifically moral and humanist subjective modal patterns. McBain does recognise to a degree the pressure of modernism, the impact of alienation and reification on the modern consciousness (as he sees and recreates the disordered schools in *The Blackboard Jungle*). But having raised this mode and its innate feeling, he contains it by subjective evaluations. The conflict of modes is plain, realising a fissure between them, and locating there the central tension of the novels. The same opposition and the same subjective, optimistic resolution is intrinsic to the content patterns of the novels, and the details of this closure will be examined later after establishing the nature of the formal tension.

The very first novel, *Cop Hater*, has a typical McBain opening; the voice is authoritative, capable of reliable and sensitive judgements:

From the river bounding the city on the north, you saw only the magnificent skyline. You stared up at it in something like awe, and sometimes you caught your breath because the view was one of majestic splendour. The clear silhouettes of the buildings slashed at the sky, devouring the blue; flat planes and long planes, rough rectangles and needle-sharp spires, minarets and peaks, pattern upon pattern laid in geometric unity against the wash of blue and white which was the sky.

The subject of the verbs is the audience, those 'you' who inhabit or visit an easily identifiable Manhattan. That 'you' sounds plural; but it can also denote singularity. The past tense implies the scene is habitual: it has always been there for 'you' to see, if you are subjectively skilful enough. The speaker interprets for the citizen evaluatively—'magnificent', 'majestic'; and analytically—'planes', 'rectangles' in 'geometric unity'; and with metaphoric wisdom— 'minarets and peaks', 'slashed', 'devouring', 'wash'. The narrator offers a shared sensitivity stating in vocabulary and rhetorically self-conscious syntax his authority to do so. Passages of this sort are frequent in the novels, arousing the personalised romance of city-living. But McBain also engages with urban anxiety, and he realises this in a mode which at first appears to reject the opening presentation for a tough-minded objective view:

> The buildings were a stage-set.
>   They faced the river and they glowed with man-made brilliance, and you stared at them with awe, and you caught your breath.
> Behind the buildings, behind the lights, were the streets.
>   There was garbage in the streets.

Urban decay and threat are realised without stagy language, in the plain empirical statement 'There was garbage in the streets'—a tone reminiscent of Sergeant Joe Friday's stern monosyllabic voice-over introduction to 'Dragnet'. In the opening action of *Cop Hater* we watch a character plunge into this hard world:

> At eleven forty-one, when Mike Reardon was three blocks away from his place of business, two bullets entered the back of his skull and ripped away half his face when they left his body.

This is extremely objective; nothing but the event is detailed, even the bullets have no cause or origin. But such a harsh, existential view is not the dominant mode in this sequence, more an occasional, emotionally disturbing way of emphasising the depersonalising death. We have already been told Reardon's thoughts by an invisible, omniscient narrator, and now that commentator exerts an ultimate power:

He felt only impact and sudden unbearable pain, and then vaguely heard the shots, and then everything inside him went dark, and he crumpled to the pavement.

He was dead before he struck the ground.

The grim tone and drummingly repetitive syntax are one side of a rhetorical duality: the prose realises a hard, cruel world as the narrator's subjective omniscience creates the pain, tells us the tragedy. This emotive humane feeling, conflicting with a clipped style is a constant feature of death scenes in McBain. In *The Pusher*:

His eyes were wide and his mouth was open, and there seemed to be life coiled deep within his body, ready to unspring and catapult him into the room. Only the colour of his face and the position of his arms betrayed the fact that he was dead.

Here the narrator interprets a possibility of life, only to find it absent; the same conflict is found through colour and the sense of touch in *The Mugger*:

The girl had blonde hair, but the bright yellow was stained with blood where something hard and unyielding had repeatedly smashed at her skull.

In each case the prose offers to face the reality of death with tough-minded clear sight, but our human feelings are invoked as well. In the context of brutal death this is no doubt a proper human reaction; the point here is to show how McBain's ostensibly empirical style is value-laden. It shows a deceptive coolness. This phrase is taken for the title of this chapter from a description of the morning air in the heat-laden city; a later discussion of the hostile function of weather in McBain's novel will show that to use this to characterise his style is no rhetorical trick, but a valid connection of his formal and thematic creation of meaning. As I will argue, the contradiction between a mechanical, value-free view of and treatment of events and a humanly valued, subjective world-view is central to the impact of the novels.

In the presentation of the opening chapters it appears that this objective descriptive style is a way of containing subjective pain, and potentially a way of resolving it. Chapter 1 ends with Reardon's death, and then follows a lengthy sequence of police procedures as the body is examined *in situ*. The sequence leads up to another moment of painful feeling, when Carella and Bush identify Reardon as a fellow detective. The next chapter immediately sets out in dry detail the nature of the 87th Precinct and its station house. Information, facts, objective description surround the awful reality of brutal murder. This material offers authority to the novel, appearing factual and useful in a world-view that values positive information. It also implies, through the police-oriented nature of this objectivity, that a cool technique can draw the sting of fearful events, move towards their cause and provide a fictional protection against them. Pragmatism and professionalism, even when a colleague is killed, are embodied in Lieutenant Byrnes's instructions to his men: 'Handle it however you want it, you know your jobs.' The narrator's comments clearly suggest that police numbers are needed to control crime:

> There were sixteen detectives assigned to the 87th Precinct, and David Foster was one of them. The precinct, in all truth, could have used a hundred and sixteen detectives and even then been understaffed.

Numerical perceptions, a staffing analysis, these seem, 'in all truth', the ways to think of crime control. The bureaucratic police organisation appears to stand as the means to control crime. Even when the narrator intervenes, with heavy-footed irony, to defend the police against press slurs he sees them at bureaucratic tasks, not in heroic action:

> In the graft-loaded Squad Room on the corrupt 87th Precinct, two detectives named Steve Carella and Hank Bush stood behind a filth-ridden desk and pored over several cards their equally corrupt fellow officers had dug from the Convictions file.

The most striking realisation of this objective, bureaucratic approach to crime is the series of documentary inserts which McBain reproduces in the text of his novels. In *Cop Hater* a pistol licence, a ballistic report, a prisoner's record card are reprinted in typescript facsimile and, with only a little less marked effect, McBain sets out in documentary form an autopsy report, a technical formula, a hair growth chart, a legal definition, a blood group analysis. This feature of presentation, in the context of the weightily objective accounts of police work, strongly implies value in such technical, procedural approaches to crime. We seem in the presence of an ideology where technological achievements have joined the fight against crime.

The plot contradicts this impression. Unlike the little maps in a Christie novel or the technical sketches Austin Freeman actually made himself, McBain's facsimiles and reports do not provide clues to the murderer. They often initiate a false trail (the gun licence and the prison record), confirm a fact we already know (the bullets are from the same gun), or provide information that does not bring about an arrest (the killer's physical description). Sequences of objective description function in this negative way, as when Carella and Bush visit a line-up and are led on to a false trail after a long documentary account. These passages are often placed immediately after moments of high feeling, scenes of death or danger, or emotive reportage in the narrator's subjective mode—which may at times be located in the mind of a detective, usually Carella or Kling. Such a context makes objective sequences function as a means of cooling the anxiety. They provide an empirical illusion of control; but it remains an illusion because anxious feeling will return, and its authentic subjective mode will, as I shall argue, be ultimately privileged through the contentual means of detecting the crime. The objective mode will have been used for rhetorical purposes only, not authenticated by the plot, not accepted as a fully operative world view. The reasons for this will be considered in the light of the content details themselves.

One other formal element has a large presence in these novels. There are long sequences of uninterrupted dialogue presenting police interrogations of a suspect, long conversations between detectives themselves, extended question and answer sessions with members of the public, witnesses and people under general suspicion. These dialogue passages often stand without any narrative mediation, and can provide over half a chapter—almost the whole of Chapter 18 in *Cop Hater* and Chapter 15 in *The Pusher*. In these sequences, as in the documentary inserts and the objective passages (among which these could really be classified), the striking feature is their irrelevance to the plot. Little is discovered that actively leads to the criminal, and only rarely is something revealed that the reader does not already know. The passages do show the perseverance of the police and the stubbornness of suspects, whether guilty or not, but apart from this rather marginal characterisation, the principal impact is one of verisimilitude, of the slow and awkward procedures of 'real life' detection. The sequences have the same intricacy and formal impact as the documentary passages and objective descriptions, and like them play little part in the unravelling of crime.

The curious lack of authority found in the objective mode can only be understood if the ontological force of the objective epistemology is grasped: a mechanistic view of people and their behaviour is created, but the overall ideology must reject it. A mechanical reading of man is basic to the documentary sequences, created in the objective reporting and imposed upon the dialogue sequences. Documents are just inhuman things, the reporting is made objective, but the dialogue is objectified by a specific piece of illusion. As in Chandler, everyone talks in the same way. There is one exception, in *The Mugger*, where Fats Donner uses a marked 'hip' style, but this is quite atypical for McBain—and for Donner as well, because elsewhere he merges into the background of the shared wisecracking, controlled and defensive speech style. McBain, like Chandler, has used a stereotype of tough defensiveness as his model for dialogue, and also uses the fall-back position of the narrator's sensitive, 'poetic' style to show how arid and unfeeling this non-individual, mechanical response to urban life must be.

In general, if the patterns of style are seen in the context of the representation the novels make of reality, it is clear that the authentically modern and urban mode of an objective, empirical view of reality has never been allowed to get far on its own. Left to itself, McBain's objective and documentary mode, charting in authentically fragmented form the mysterious and threatening nature of urban life, would develop a pattern of existential, even nihilistic writing. It would lay out in uncontrolled form events and sensations in the manner characteristic of modernist fiction, that mode that Barthes called 'white writing', a presentation stripped of a knowing and manipulative authorial subjective control or 'écriture'. Such a mode of creation mediates the contemporary experience of a world, apparently without control by human agency, where commodity values dominate and so, as Marx described and predicted, people behave like commodities and commodities behave like people. Such a perception is caught in an objectified style where the sentence itself behaves like a quasi-human commodity, as Fredric Jameson observes in *Marxism and Form*. McBain does to some extent realise this type of writing, and so partly creates the experience of the urban dweller, the fearful alienated individual living in a mysterious reified world. The use of documentary inserts is in itself an authentic artistic mediation of this experience; as Jean Duvignaud has argued in *The Sociology of Art*, the technique of collage directly responds to and invokes the reified and fragmented knowledge modern man has of the world.

But as I have shown in the preceding argument, McBain closes down the tendencies of this objective mode, and controls it through subjective moralism. The very dominance of the objectified urban world-view, which demands a presence in the fiction for it to be convincing, is so disturbingly oppressive that the fiction cannot give it privileged force and make it the master-mode. The fiction must recognise the power of objectification, but must also falsify it out of a controlling force, because the bourgeois capitalism that has produced a world of commodities has also produced the image of humane individualism, its diametric and dialectic opposite. The marked duality of form, the fissure in the text, points directly to the valid modernity of part of the form and also the illusionary way in which liberal humanism seeks to master the contradictory realities of its world by ideology.

The overall structure of the novels shows the same dual pattern in a simpler and more lucid way. It emerges later in the series than the characteristic stylistic, modal mixture. The essential structure of a McBain novel is not fully formed until the fourth novel *The Con Man*, though strong aspects of it are present in the earlier books. This presents more than one narrative line, and different police investigate several cases simultaneously. A multiple, even a fragmented structure and a plurality of heroes is created. This is most fully seen in later novels like *Fuzz* and *Hail, Hail, the Gang's All Here* which in form and titles show their awareness of the methodical police procedural novel, like Robert Pike's *Police Blotter* and *Mute Witness* (filmed and later reissued as *Bullitt*). But even in these most fragmented of McBain's novels, an emphasis is thrown on to particular cases and others are made marginal; certain detectives have more authority than others, Carella in particular, and they and their cases, effectively centred in a subjective position for all the illusion of objective fragmentation, bear the weight of the equally subjective liberal humanism the stories advocate as a final response to events and threats.

In this way the structure recreates the offer of, and withdrawal of, a literature which replicates a world without a hero-centred, organically united, individualistically controlled form. After clarifying McBain's patterns of content I will discuss the specific politics of the ideological position he adopts, and look at its contemporary manifestations, but it is relevant in the context of form to note that a quasi-objective empirical treatment of the world which is actually heavily laden with values and premises is no surprising formal pattern from this period. The social sciences, especially in America, were in the grip of allegedly value-free empiricism. Writers like D. and J. Willer have revealed the value-laden, premise-based nature of work which claims to be fully empirical, to be without any preconceived attitudes, to face reality in a stark pragmatic way. If most of the scholarly sub-class across the Western world was satisfied with empiricism and its specific evaluative premises, it is hardly surprising that a popular writer like McBain should offer it as a new way of looking at crime in fiction. Nor, if allegedly scholarly and objective accounts were riddled with unseen premises, manipulated conclusions and loose optimisms for the future, is it surprising that, when we look at the content details of McBain's novels, we find them similarly filled with naive moralism, conservative social attitudes, and frail acts of faith in human ability to counteract the threats of crime against the urban individual.

The urban setting and a constant awareness of the city are dominant features of McBain's novels. It is, then, surprising that New York has been fictionalised and its rivers, suburbs, parks and streets are carefully given new names. To a degree this might be a professional precaution against errors and libel cases, but few other crime writers have felt the need to obscure the setting of their 'realism'. The detail shows a clear conflict, and the name McBain gives the city, Isola, shows that even so collective a reality as New York and its police operations is ultimately subdued, fictionalised and even named in terms of the isolated individual mind. In a later novel McBain does say the name came from an immigrant term for 'island', but this internal explaining away has little force against the plain implication of the name.

The name is not the only unreal and asocial treatment of the city. A strong feature of the texts is the way in which urban physical phenomena are seen as forces in themselves. The present condition of the city, especially its darker aspects, is somehow resident in, even created by the buildings themselves:

The lot had once owned an apartment house and the house had been a good one with high rent. It had not been unusual, in the old days, to see an occasional mink coat drifting from the marbled doorway of the apartment house. But the crawling tendril of the slum had reached out for the brick, clutching it with tenacious fingers, pulling it into the ever-widening circle it called its own. (*Cop Hater*)

This striking passage disavows any knowledge of human causes, even of human effects. People do not own buildings, collect rents, even wear mink coats. An automatic process of pauperisation has taken place, only caused and felt by the buildings. Even the possibility of improvement is depersonalised: 'A City housing project, it was rumoured, was going up in the lot.' The objective style creates an objectified content: human intelligence conceals itself in the language to deny any connection with the events that materially affect the world. Anxiety about city living, itself a product of a commodity-based culture, is felt in and through objects. Commodity thinking obscures the real causes of pauperisation, is generalised and naturalised into a vague sense of institutional, unalterable distress.

In *The Pusher* the city itself has degraded the Puerto Rican immigrants. At home they were poor but dignified; here they drift into crime and drug addiction. The city is seen as an inevitable force, irresistibly overpowering the simple morality of the parents. No sense enters the text of the class position of immigrants, their degrading role as cheap and disposable labour, or their specific exploitation by capitalists of vice. Vague moralism that can feel pity but offer no cause-finding critique and no plan of action is the response; the passivity of the reaction, fixed in the fetishised idea of objects that act badly, quite obscures the real patterns of greed and exploitation in which buildings are merely instruments.

The city is also the only means offered of perceiving race and class in any general way: here too buildings objectify issues and prevent genuine analysis. The sections of the city occupied by negroes and Puerto Ricans are described, and the white suburbs are themselves classified by income. Changes in these patterns are located in the suburbs, the buildings themselves. Race and class units and conflicts are not categorised in any other way, though as I will show they may be perceived and mystified in purely individual terms within the experience of specific characters. This localised notion of disorder can provide escapes; characters are often described as moving away from the 'bad' areas of the city to find security—if they can afford it.

The process reveals one of the major political aspects of empiricism: it deals only with detailed events and can only offer pragmatic, isolated cures. Theoretical interconnections and causes are not considered, and the empirical data is seen as the only reality. This is not how Newton discovered gravity —in spite of the seductive empirical fable of the apple.

A major source of perceived distress in the novels is the city's weather. Again a physical phenomenon is felt to be hostile, operating against the characters by heat, cold and rain. As in Doyle the threats of city life are euphemised into a dehumanised force. In *Cop Hater* a pervasive heat affects the detectives; the cool mornings only remind them that the hot day is coming, and no technological devices, light clothing, diet, medication are offered against this force. A passive distress is the only response, until, just when the crime is resolved the weather itself breaks: a quite unmotivated relief descends, just like the narrator's subjective delight in the city which relieves the anxious gloom often felt about the urban setting. New York weather is certainly trying; the point here is that it carries a crucial part of the novel's unanalysed and passively self-pitying distress. These forces impinge on the individual, and can only be suffered, with hope that the worst will not be long, that, as with the environmental dangers, good luck or shrewd personal decisions may mitigate the distress.

A similar phenomenal force, of lesser impact, is found in the news media. In the early novels this is confined to newsprint, but later on television reporting and entertainment is seen as part of the threat. In the first novel a reporter, simplistically named Savage, is made an individual focus for an untheorised hostility to the media's treatment of police work. A carefully contrived piece of plotting, based on the coincidence that he and Kling look and dress alike, shows Savage to be a damaging nuisance. The use of the media as a demonological scapegoat is common enough on the left and the right in politics. The way in which the media embody the practices and values of the dominant socio-economic system is less often explored: it is easier to have conspiracies than structural analysis. McBain treats the press as just one of the general hostile forces that make life harder for the police heroes; and like the weather and the hostile city, the press threat has to be made specific, identifiable and emotively available. It is not analysed as part of a pervasive social pattern of conflict among people, and between people and the environment. But these forces do not press despair on the novel, though they cause discomfort. The single reporter is humiliated, the weather finally breaks, the city can be exciting and fictionally freed of gloom by the plot resolution. By faith, chance, natural processes and plot-manipulation threats are contained. This unprogrammatic approach, like the lack of a theoretical structural analysis of society, is itself a model of pragmatism, of day-to-day phenomenological concern grounded on optimism. Such an attitude bears in towards the fragmentary world of the individual's own experience and private concerns, private resolutions and hopes, and away from collective social thought and action. Such a direction is very clear in the crucial core of the novels' content, the nature, cause and detection of the crimes that are committed.

The emphasis is, as in most modern crime fiction, on murder. The selection of murder among all the other crimes of the city is explained:

You can really get involved in the investigation of a homicide case because it is the rare occurrence in the everyday life of a precinct. It is the most exotic crime because it deals with the theft of something universal—a man's life.
Unfortunately there are other less interesting and more mundane matters to deal with in a precinct too. And in a precinct like the 87th, these mundane matters can consume a lot of time. (*Cop Hater*)

The notion that a particular man's life is 'universal' is a fine key to the pervasive individualism of all murder-based crime fiction, and on such a basis the writer feels justified in dismissing the 'mundane' and unexotic crimes that 'unfortunately' detain the police—and that in fact are the basic criminal reality in society. Although McBain does present minor crime it is always marginal to the plot; but so is professional crime, even professional murder such as gang killings or murder in the furtherance of theft. The investigated murder is caused by a rift in a private relationship. This is, of course, true of the majority of murders, and McBain dramatises the fact when the early novels first offer and then reject organised crime or general madness as the causes. In *Cop Hater* the murderous wife and her lover deliberately suggest that an anti-police maniac is at work; in *The Mugger* the treacherous brother-in-law tries to confirm the police theory that Jeannie Page is a victim of a notorious mugger. *The Pusher* makes the murder and the consequent implication of

Byrnes's son appear to be normal activities by a dope ring, but they turn out to be a specific, and rather poorly explained, attempt to put pressure on Byrnes, involving a betrayal by, and then of, the murdered boy's sister. In *The Con Man* a professional criminal is at work, but his crime is to betray women who think he loves them. This is highly personalised through the detailed presentation of his last intended victim, and his final attack is on Carella's wife.

The audience is offered the notion that breaking a natural bond is the crime most worth detecting. Normal criminal activity is either a potential mask for it or, as in *The Con Man*, a commentary on its immorality: there the minor con men act out at a trivial level the same patterns of infidelity. This view of professional crime as unimportant is not merely an inevitable result of concentrating on murder; it was actually a public attitude in the very period when urban anxiety was rising, paradoxical though this may seem. Daniel Bell, the pragmatic social scientist whose 'end of ideology' stance is like McBain's, ignored political conflicts and theoretical critiques of society together, and also questioned the extent of crime in society. In two essays written in the fifties (reprinted in *The End of Ideology*) he doubted the existence of the Mafia and organised crime in America, and belittled statistics indicating a general increase in crime. McBain's view is not an aberrant, personal blindness; in itself it belongs to a structure, rooted in the individualistic interest in personal betrayals and conditioned by the myopic and essentially optimistic pragmatism of contemporary liberal humanism.

For all the emphasis on police method, the rhetorical impact of objective, documentary style and the frequent encounters of police method and minor professional criminals, the real direction of the novels is to bring a convincingly bureaucratic, well-equipped police force to bear on the disorders in private relationships, and not on the organised criminal world it was actually developed to counter. But just as the objective style was subjectively controlled, just as the generalised threats of city, weather and the press were felt individually, so the apparent technological and methodical skills of the police have very little part in catching the central criminal.

In *Cop Hater* the gunman is traced because Hank Bush, the last and essential victim of the killings his wife has planned, manages to shoot his killer, and a doctor reports the wounded man. The doctor reads about the case in the papers, not through any methodical police notification. Even then the murderer eludes the police until the final melodramatic scene when—also because of Savage's newspaper report —he has gone to trap Carella and his fiancée, Teddy. Effectively there is no detection at all here: the murderer is revealed by the action, for all the mirage of police work.

This also happens in *The Pusher*; a chance encounter with drug addicts eventually leads to the man. The elaborate identification of a feather at the scene of Maria Hernandez's murder connects with the fact that the killer keeps pigeons, but the link is never made by the police. *The Con Man* also uses an accidental connection and a final shoot-out scene; this time a tattooist is visited once more by the villain who has the unlikely habit of tattooing his prospective victims.

Only in *The Mugger* is there any effective detection, and this as well is quite unmethodical and even unprofessional. Kling is at this stage a patrolman, so an amateur outside the detective machine, who is specifically warned off the case by the Chief of Detectives. Eventually he puts side by side, by accident, two pieces of paper which bear the same handwriting. This reveals to him the significance of the text's hidden clue, that the station where Jeannie Page regularly left the train had a cab-stand: the cab-driving brother-in-law is revealed as the murderer. In later novels similar trivia and accidental discoveries unlock the whole mystery.

In *80 Million Eyes* Meyer's rambling conversation about his cold unveils the secret of slow-release capsules; in *Lady, Lady, I Did It* the victim's wife accidentally makes Carella realise that in their heavy Jewish accent her husband's dying word was not 'carpenter' but the immediately incriminating word 'car-painter'. In *Like Love* Hawes realises, through personal experience, that a woman takes off her suspender belt after her briefs, and a notional suicide is revealed as murder.

Detection, where it occurs, is slender, chance-derived and banal—a single thing heard or seen is enough. This technique suggests the importance of specific objects, but lacks the systematic reasoning of Holmes, the thorough domestic logic of Poirot or Miss Marple. Among the fragments of experience there lie fortuitously found keys to security, it seems. Police work, with its detail and method, does often enable the detectives to rule people out, or catch the minor professional offenders in the plot, but it cannot close in on the human betrayers who pose the central threats—and when it seems to have done so, as in *Shotgun* or *Give the Boys a Great Big Hand*, the police assumptions have been quite wrong, secret betrayals have gone unnoticed.

Like the central meaning of Chandler's structure, the moment of discovery comes as reward for the persistence and moral excellence of the inquirers. The resemblances to the Catholic dogma of salvation by divine grace rather than by human works is striking, and is presumably produced by a similar sense of human incompetence to master a threatening world. There is a basic uncertainty about the efficacy of a police bureaucracy, linked with the need to control subjectively the implications of the objective style. Not all police story writers have shared this view: Hilary Waugh and Robert Pike in America, Creasey and Alan Hunter in Britain and some television writers in both countries have been able to conceive of watching, waiting, careful tracking and methodical inquiry as viable ways of finding a murderer. But in McBain and in many of the successful American television police series, it is clear that the ideology does not accept police method as a self-protection system, but prefers to rely on the vague force of good morality and fortune to fabricate a defence against feared betrayers of the self.

The detectives who are the instruments of this faith-based dream of security are almost completely admirable; they embody the virtues of patience, duty and tough-mindedness, defensive and unromantic responses to urban tension, and so appear to earn the fortuitous gift of resolving crimes. There are traces of contemporary realism in their characterisation, but such verisimilitude is never taken so far as to be negative or to move outside a stereotype: they remain heroes. Carella, the most nearly central of the detectives is an Italian, yet this urban realism is blurred. He does not look Italian; he is clearly not an American white Anglo-Saxon Protestant, but his foreignness is strangely distanced and so defused. His eyes look Oriental, and he is tall, hard, elegant in an unostentatious way. According to James McClure, McBain has admitted basing Carella on himself, but essentially he is a hero who, like his television successors Banacek, Kojak and, in a different way, Columbo, makes reference to the cosmopolitan nature of modern America but retains the strong, resourceful qualities of the older Western and private eye heroes. Other detectives represent physical and racial types and specific associated stereotypical virtues. Kling is young, tall, handsome and persevering, though often uncertain; Hawes is big, tough, brave and confident; Meyer shrewd, patient and, like Carella, distinctly unlike the physical stereotype his name implies; Willis is small, skilled at Judo and cunning; Hernandez honourable, sensitive and courageous; Brown is very big, black and ironic. None of these has a malign element, though Hawes is initially hasty and bad-tempered. There are police with dubious characteristics: Haviland in the early novels is over-physical and crude in his methods but this is explained away by his bad experiences: he was cruelly beaten when a normal kind, sensitive policeman. In any case he is shot fairly early, in *Killer's Choice*. Andy Parker is a later, less brutal version of this figure. Genero, for long a mere patrolman, promoted by luck, is distinctly stupid—and, a racist touch, much more Italian than Carella. Byrnes, their leader, is little characterised after his fatherly anxieties in *The Pusher*; the problems of leadership may well introduce too systematic and structural a perspective for McBain's essential pattern of individual responses to threats.

Each of the characters represents a sparely depicted type and in the sub-plotting one or more of them will face personal problems as well as the natural hazards of police work. In each case the detectives are brave, resourceful and personally triumphant, imply-ing personal threats can be defused by individual action. In the early novels the police are themselves the targets of violence, personally or through their families. This pattern changes, and members of the public suffer these personal threats in later novels (with occasional threats to police, especially to Kling). The detectives still face crises, particularly the prospect of failure and racial tensions, but patient dutiful application brings them through their work difficulties; a similar private endurance is shown to be a protection against racial difficulties. Meyer's consistent character-isation tells how he was baited as a Jew when young. This moment of racial conflict is doubly insulated from reality; first it is at least partly based on his father's cruel humour in naming him Meyer Meyer—family betrayal enters even this quasi-social discussion. And secondly Meyer copes through patience and wisdom; the only cost is baldness, a neatly reified and trivialising token of this token encounter with anti-Semitism. Brown, especially in later novels, is able to confront and defeat racism—his enormous size and self-control are a help in this, and in *Cop Hater* Foster is an early version, soon to be murdered, of this successful black type. Hernandez's qualities are a sufficient answer to the hostility directed against Puerto Ricans. In each of these cases the racial problems are contained by an individual possessing the stereotypical assets of the race. The treatment of this basic American conflict is in itself racial as well as being trivialised and individualised into an undisturbing resolution.

Other detectives face problems which do not even have large-scale social elements. Willis compensates for his small size by Judo and shrewdness, and big women find him very attractive. Carella is more often wounded than others, but never dies even when, as in *The Pusher*, he is expected to or, as in *Doll*, when he is thought to have done so. Sheer courage and a sense of duty justify his good luck; and more than any other character he is the one whose thoughts reveal the problems of adapting routine police work to the disturbingly private aberrance of the crimes investigated, and accordingly he is the detective who most often makes the final fortuitous discovery that resolves the problem. His purity even seems to extend to his informer. Danny Gimp is not only handicapped, sensitive, helpful and loyal; he was not even guilty of the crime that sent him to jail and so qualified him to be an informer. Kling appears, in spite of his name, to have no racial problems—because of his WASP background, presumably. But he does face uncertainty with women, and the subplots often chart his problematic sex life. One girl friend is killed accidentally in the 'car-painter' shooting, another deserts him for a doctor (*Sadie When She Died*), and even his new wife, a suitably stereotypical magazine model beauty, is abducted on their wedding day (*So Long as You Both Shall Live*). Self-control and police discipline keep Kling on course in spite of his distress, and inevitably lead to the possession of the beautiful, loving woman that is, for the central characters, the private reward for their excellence.

There are many women in the stories, but they essentially support the masculine narcissism of the detective's world as victims, villains, witnesses and police comforts. The one women detective, Eileen Burke, comes from another squad and is only used in a sexist content, as bait for the mugger, and as part of a plant, necking with Willis, in *Fuzz*. Though she is tough she is feminine in the most male-oriented sense. Teddy Carella is, of course, the grossest example of McBain's sexism; literally a beautiful dumb (and deaf) woman. She is highly sexed, always available, silent and servile to Carella. She does at times suggest ideas to him, and she shows great courage in pursuing and facing criminals in the early novels. But she does so entirely in response to Carella's stimuli and as an extension of him: her curious masculine name indicates a lack of separate feminine identity. The same pattern emerges when Kling marries

Augusta, known to him as Gus. This seems to indicate that his role as conveyor of male sexual anxiety is over in the novels, perhaps caused by a sense of his increasing age, though her abduction at the wedding reception recreates briefly the tensions caused for Carella in the early novels when his possession of Teddy was threatened. Hawes represents a different type of sexism; he is a successful lecher, who never lets his encounters with mysteriously unattached, model type beauties, interfere with his work. This Playboy pattern is particularly strong in the early novels, where sexism can surface in especially rank forms, such as Meyer's running joke about 'instant pussy' in *The Mugger* and the extraordinary description of Byrnes in *Cop Hater* as 'a man trapped in the labial folds of a society structure'—a comment which revealingly combines masculine neurosis and urgent individualism.

The purity of the police, their admired masculine morality is the basis for their casual, barely explained success in most cases. The pattern is like that used by Chandler, except that here the urban setting is not seen as inevitably hostile and the idea of a group activity is presented as viable: however much fear of the city there is, however much the actual mechanics of the story and meaning are individualist, there is none of the self-conscious alienation of Marlowe. The anxiety is that of the urban dweller without an élitist sense of authority, unlike the basic Chandler audience. And the detectives, unlike Marlowe, are in general social beings; they do internalise their morality to a degree, particularly in Carella's case, but it is a shared sense of duty, not personally constructed rules to set against a corrupt world, as Chandler creates in his hero. And apart from the early novels, the threats are not directly felt by the detectives; that pattern, perhaps borrowed from Chandler (like the plot of *The Mugger*, where Kling is brought in because he is thought too foolish to solve the case), gives way to a structure where the victims and those disturbed by murder are ordinary citizens.

They are not readily identifiable members of a class, as they are in Doyle or Christie. The clearest definition is that the characters and victims live in the city; class position, income, employment are not central to the material, but act as a vague background to the personal betrayals. The characteristic setting is violence in a city flat, and the world implied is a fragmented city community, of people living separate and vulnerable lives, able to call on their paid officials for dutiful and good-fortuned help in a crisis. At one point the narrator realises this atomistic, barely civilised view of the city:'. . . the cave-dwellers have thrown up a myriad number of dwellings which they call middle-class apartment houses.' (*The Mugger*)

This perception of a 'concrete jungle', a world where material sophistication has not brought real ease is a common view of modern urban living. It is based on a false metaphor, of course, because savage 'jungle' society excluded alienation from its many anxieties. Its problems were to solve the physical problems of maintaining life; the urban society is replete with material goods and comforts, but fills out its quantum of misery by a sense of alienated fearfulness, looking for the enemy within the family, the one close by who will betray a crucial fidelity. As a study of McBain's form showed, an objectified consciousness was realised, but controlled, and the view of the city shows the same commodity and consumerist conscious- ness at work. As the detectives visit a new apartment or tenement block, it is defined in terms of the objects observed, just as a comprehending of a single object, or isolated word will often be the clue to the crucial detection. McBain often used specific objects as titles when he fully established his form—*Axe*, *Shotgun*, *Doll*, even the neatly reified slang word for money, *Bread*.

The actual consumerist orientation of police stories is documen- ted. The massive shift from Westerns to urban crime stories on the American television networks in the sixties occurred because an older, largely rural audience liked Westerns, while younger urban viewers preferred the police stories. The numbers were much the same: the crucial factor was that city people had and spent more money on the goods that the advertisers, who controlled the decision, wanted to sell.

The formal pattern of the novels does, as has already been argued, realise a consumerist objectification only to control it subjectively. But consumer society does not only have its own epistemology; it has its authentic ontological anxieties. As Marx first explained in *Capital*, when commodities do behave like people, having and conveying values, people may behave like commodities, that is be morally neutral, devoid of expected values and respond to physical stimuli only. This is just what McBain's murderers do. A wife betrays her husband like Alice Bush—and she alone of all the characters does not suffer humanly from the heat that pervades *Cop Hater*. Peter Ball seduces his sister-in-law and beats her with the 'unyielding' tyre iron, so reducing to dead flesh what he has merely treated as seductive flesh: he also betrays his friendship with Kling, treating him like a puppet. The villains in *The Pusher* manipulate the drug-addicted plasticity of Byrnes's son and so neutralise Byrnes as a force for morality. The central con man in that novel uses a facsimile of love to gain tangible profit from women, and then he discards them like waste products of an industrial process.

The whole idea of empiricism, the pragmatic, objective approach to the world that is so rhetorically important in McBain is itself a way of thinking based on a commodity-dominated world, as his treatment of buildings, the weather, the press indicates. C. Wright Mills has spoken forcefully about Daniel Bell's work having its basis in 'the fetishism of empiricism'. Bell's pragmatic, facts before all, facts being all approach was seen to be so innocent of theory and structural analysis that it was itself a fully consumerist and objectified view of the world. Bell offers consumerism as his description of contemporary society, but because his own method is fully in line with such a world-view, he finds rest, an end of ideology, a passive contentment in such a conclusion. He even, most strikingly, defends alienation as a position from which to know the world without bias, as a valid system for independent academic inquiry. The notion of the value-free can hardly go further and the actual basis of the position in the anxieties of individualism is quite clear—Arthur Brittan's recent book *The Privatised World* expounds the matter.

For Wright Mills and others, on the right as well as the left, the answer for this was to retheorise, to identify the structures in society that caused the conflicts Bell regarded as minimal. Such a view is very far from McBain's; he espouses just the end of ideology viewpoint that Bell was developing in the fifties. As I have argued, racial problems, urban decay are moralised and naturalised away from a conflictive presentation, and so no politics, no need for ideological tension is perceived. Bell had said that in the contemporary world, politics mean international politics, that theoretical dissensions have no place at home. McBain realises that view; and he dismisses the international as well—Kling, in *The Mugger*, has no further thoughts about why the girls he saw in Korea were so skinny and unhealthy in comparison with the fine fleshy American girls he admires so much. The show of empiricism, of police method and objective treatment is offered as a calming force in the novels, as it is in Bell's work and journals like *Encounter*, which claim to be clear-headed, real and unbiased accounts of the world. Yet just as these versions of empiricism are value-laden with defensive, liberal self-confidence, so the empirical and objective material in McBain's novels is not and does not do what it offers to be and do. The objective mode of writing is subjectively controlled, the methodical detection finds no murderers.

This central contradiction in the novels is the fissure along which their full ideological meaning presents itself. The empirical approach for Bell and his colleagues is a credible contemporary cover for their liberal humanism: but for a writer like McBain, who can tap contemporary anxiety as well as assuage it, the empirical approach, revealing in itself objectification and a consumerist world, is itself the medium of a central fear: the novels walk a nervous line, and the narrator's plotting and constant humane, even romantic, interventions reassure the audience that police method and objectivity are not Frankenstein's monsters being created to dehumanise and destroy them, but are under humane control. The citizen both shelters under and shelters from the bureaucratic professionalism typified by the urban, modern police force. Degraded as it is to a rhetorical bromide, methodical and technical police work does not mechanise the policemen, does not control the plot, and so does not in fact function to resolve fictionally the central fears of dehumanised, mechanistic betrayal by those who are humanly closest to the anxious individual. The contradiction basic to capitalist society, the distress it has caused as it has, in Marxist terms, in Eli Zaretsky's words, 'mass produced specific forms of personal life' is resolved through a sham of mechanism and a flimsy web of human, individualist action and accidents. The gap between objective and subjective styles, between police method and casual resolutions of the central mystery reveals what the novel cannot speak, but must say: that the objectified consciousness of the modern world is deeply hostile to the bourgeois ideal of individual consciousness.

In essence the novels expose both the consumerist source and liberal individualist basis of empiricism; bereft of a historical and structural social analysis, it cannot explain or rectify the conflicts intrinsic to the society whose epistemology and ontology it reproduces. Bell's rejection of ideology is, plainly, a deeply ideological act. But empiricism is today still a dominant mode of thought, and essential features of McBain's pattern are readily seen in novels and, especially, in television series today. The effectiveness of pragmatic empiricism as a force for stasis is seen not only in its sheer power to survive in polarised societies, but also in McBain's own ability in his more recent novels, to recognise, partly realise and also defuse issues which have come into public consciousness since he started writing.

He has paid more attention to the negro problem, to the threat of street gangs, and recognised the Vietnam war as a source of disturbance. Each issue, however, is diluted, diverted into controllable, resolvable forms. Brown typifies an individualist solution of the black problem in *Jigsaw*, where he uses a white southern girl's fear of negroes to scare a confession from her: it is an easy and clearly meretricious victory (it may be an unconscious sign of McBain's continuing racism that the title, differently justified by the plot, contains 'jig', a derisory term for a negro.) Hernandez gives his life in *See Them Die* to defeat a Puerto Rican gangster who was being imitated by youths; with a single heroic act he defuses the threat of racial and youth violence. In *Hail to the Chief* the gang topic is taken up again, and such disturbances are found to be caused by a deluded leader. Similar individualist and sterilising techniques deal with the Vietnam war in *Long Time No See*. A negro blinded in Vietnam is murdered, by a war criminal, Major Tagliacci. But the victim is a blackmailer, not an opponent of the war, and Tagliacci's crime was not murdering Vietnamese, like Lieutenant Calley. He killed an American fellow soldier. So the international politics of that war vanish, and it becomes a background for Tagliacci's double betrayal of his brothers in arms, themselves filled with patriotism and acquisitiveness.

There are signs in the later novels that McBain sees as central at least some crimes which are not mere betrayals. In *Hail to the Chief* and *He Who Hesitates* the criminals are mentally disordered, not amoral. This is in itself consistent with a pervasive individualism, and these novels tend to put formal emphasis on the criminal's mind, using a good deal of stream of consciousness material to move away from the quasi-objective elements of the main pattern. The non-police novel *Guns* confirms this development, giving criminal disorder a clearer cause than normal, but in no way taking it outside an individualistic world, or seeing social and environmental impact in the production of an individual personality.

Another sign of development in the criminal motivation occurs in the three 'Deaf Man' novels, *The Heckler*, *Fuzz* and *Lets Hear it for the Deaf Man*. They present a master professional criminal, whose aim is money and who may commit murder to get it. Yet here too McBain defuses reality; the 'Deaf Man' is a true individualist, always hiring a new gang for each crime. Humiliating the police is as important to him as making money, and his efforts are frustrated by improbable coincidences and child-like accidents. These novels belittle the threat of professional crime much like Donald Westlake's knock-about comedies of criminal failure.

Although it is easy to see a consistent and self-defensive ideology at work in the later novels, absorbing and naturalising new notions at times, it is also clear that the novels become less serious, aimed at entertaining buyers. Sexy scenes become more frequent after the first half-dozen novels, and a joky aestheticism often enters the titles after *Give the Boys a Great Big Hand* (1960). In the same way the illustrations become more often sheer diversions, and not the original pieces of police documentation, illusory and rhetorical though they were. In these ways the trivialising nature of a consumerist world affects the novels as they become increasingly well-known, as bigger markets are sought. A certain playfulness is not, of course, absent from the early novels, where the narrator's wry wisecracks both tonally linked him to, and structurally set him apart from, the tough-minded world of the detectives and the citizens they dealt with. In that detail, as in so much in the novels, the mixture of tones and modes in the form, the curious juxtaposition of method and sheer chance in the content, both refer directly to the puzzled and contradictory feelings of the citizens of capitalism's greatest city, whose attitudes are shared by those other urban dwellers who make up McBain's considerable audience. They are all isolates of the modern city; in the dual, self-contradictory patterns of his novels, McBain creates an illusion of security, enabling his readers to feel that a human protective quality is still present among the oppressive modern reality of the mechanical world of commodities.

REFERENCES

Texts
Cop Hater, Penguin, London, 1963
The Mugger, Penguin, London, 1963
The Pusher, Penguin, London, 1963
The Con Man, Penguin, London, 1963

Criticism
John Creasey's comment is in the introduction to *Gideon's Week*, Hodder &

Stoughton, London, 1956, the second novel in the series.

Daniel Bell, *The End of Ideology*, 2nd rev. edn., Collier, New York, 1962.

Arthur Brittan, *The Privatised World*, Routledge and Kegan Paul, London, 1978.

Angus Calder, *The People's War*, Cape, London, 1969.

Jean Duvignaud, *The Sociology of Art*, Granada, London, 1972.

Fredric Jameson, *Marxism and Form*, Princeton University Press, Princeton, 1971.

James McClure, 'Carella of the 87th', in *Murder Ink: The Mystery Reader's Companion*, Workman, New York, 1977.

Karl Marx, *Capital*, Progress Publishers, Moscow, 1957.

C. Wright Mills, 'The New Left', *New Left Review*, 5, 1960, reprinted in *Power, Politics and People*, Oxford University Press, New York, 1963.

D. and J. Willer, *Systematic Empiricism: Critique of a Pseudo-Science*, Prentice-Hall, Englewood Cliffs, 1973.

Eli Zaretsky, *Capitalism, the Family, and Personal Life*, Pluto Press, London, 1976.

Index

The normal function of an index is to help readers retrieve useful information from the text, and accordingly listed here are the authors, works, critics and subjects discussed. This index is also intended to provide a synoptic analysis of the book's argument, to systematise what has necessarily been a discursive treatment in the text. Subjects have been entered generously cross-referenced where relevant, and they are often analyses of the text, not just evident key-words. Subject-entries have been sorted under the different authors in order to make contrasting ideologies readily accessible, even visibly different in the index itself.